DICKENS IMAGINING HIMSELF

Six Novel Encounters with a Changing World

Morris Golden

UNIVERSITY
PRESS OF
AMERICA

Lanham • New York • London

Copyright © 1992 by
University Press of America®, Inc.
4720 Boston Way
Lanham, Maryland 20706

3 Henrietta Street
London WC2E 8LU England

Library of Congress Cataloging-in-Publication Data

Golden, Morris.
Dickens imagining himself : six novel encounters with a changing
world / by Morris Golden.
p.   cm.
Includes bibliographical references and index.
1. Dickens, Charles, 1812–1870—Criticism and interpretation.
2. Self in literature.   3. Narration (Rhetoric)   I. Title.
PR4592.S38G65   1992   823'.8—dc20   92–15650 CIP

ISBN 0–8191–8739–9 (cloth : alk. paper)
ISBN 0–8191–8740–2 (pbk. : alk. paper)

 ^{TM} The paper used in this publication meets the minimum requirements of
American National Standard for Information Sciences—Permanence
of Paper for Printed Library Materials, ANSI Z39.48–1984.

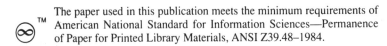

To

Hilda, Olivia, Dan, Kathy

Contents

I. What Sort of Consanguinity 1

II. *Barnaby Rudge:* Two Cheers for Maturity 21

III. Martin Chuzzlewit: Ambiguously Whittington 53

IV. *David Copperfield:*
Memory and the Flow of Time 87

V. *Bleak House:* Passing the Bog 125

VI. *Great Expectations:* Defining Estella 163

VII. *Our Mutual Friend:* Reborn with Galatea 195

VIII. Eclectic Affinities 231

Notes 253

Index 261

Acknowledgments

It is gratifying to have this opportunity to thank the librarians of the University of Massachusetts (particularly Melinda McIntosh of Microforms) and of Amherst College, Smith College, and the University of Arizona for the usual courtesies; my friends and colleagues, Meredith Raymond, Robert Keefe, and David Paroissien for their valuable comments at various stages of this work; Tamas Aczel, who left immersion in his own richly imagined worlds to read it all, some of it twice, for his wise responsiveness; Doris Holden, for helping prepare the manuscript; and my wife, for all of the above and more.

I. What Sort of Consanguinity?

Like Tristram Shandy's Uncle Toby and the Vulgar, who felt that despite legal decisions to the contrary "there must certainly . . . have been some sort of consanguinity betwixt the duchess of *Suffolk* and her son," I can't help sensing a family tie between Dickens and his novels. Neither could Dickens. Refusing an invitation on January 17, 1844, he characteristically gave as his reason "my next number unborn and unbegotten,"(*P* IV,23)[1], and everyone remembers his conclusion to the preface of the Charles Dickens Edition (1867) of *David Copperfield*: "It will be easily believed that I am a fond parent to every child of my fancy, and that no one can ever love that family as dearly as I love them. But, like many fond parents, I have in my heart of hearts a favourite child. And his name is DAVID COPPERFIELD"(p.752). If we trace the signs of consanguinity, we may understand the child better, know more clearly how its moods and tendencies and general character please and fulfill us. Hence the old critical retailers of gossip that found a lover for every love child, from Shakespeare's sonnets to Arnold's Marguerite poems, and hence the renewed discoverers of primal scenes and Oedipus complexes in whole authorial broods.

Everyone acknowledges the mutual influence of mind and body, even if we assume that the direct influence of parental mood on physical birth is superstition. No one past childhood takes seriously Dickens's mark of John Rudge's bloodshed on

Baby Barnaby, as we see at once that Dryden was joking when he attributed the Duke of Monmouth's good looks and manners to his father's being "inspir'd with some diviner lust" when he begot him. But with literary children we can confidently remark connections, for the work of art lies wholly before us as the human being—happily—does not. We can examine it at leisure. We need not murder books to dissect them; if explaining them explains away their life, we can be sure they never had any.

In the living bodies of Dickens's novels, then, we can legitimately seek the extent of his presence: in what characters, in what turns of plot or developments of theme, in what meaning their relations convey. For defining that presence in specific works, moreover, we know a great deal, perhaps more than we can assimilate, about Dickens's changing circumstances, actions, and even thoughts. He recorded them in a mass of surviving letters, and those who knew him left their records too. Although we can never be quite sure of how far he was conscious of his involvement in the characters and events—how much of the past or of the present intensities he was aware of and what proportions he could guide—we have enough information for at least plausible estimates even there. I can therefore hope, if as a Vulgar common reader I can sensibly infer what was intensely on his mind when he conceived a work, to understand better his ties to that work and—any critic's proper goal—perhaps to understand it better.

To trace the effect on Dickens's novels of authorial consanguinity, I shall build on three simple hypotheses, hoping that the reader will always think of them as hypotheses, not revealed truth: 1) that in conceiving the world of his art the artist's imagination (like anyone else's) reflects fantasies centering on himself; 2) that it conceives others as projections, aspects of himself elaborated into social and psychological actors; 3) that in enduring art its idiosyncratic conception of these actors moving about forms a metaphorical world that will satisfy the fantasies of enough readers over time and space to qualify as universal. How far these hypotheses can lead us to know Dickens's worlds the following chapters will try to show.

Since this study is of Dickens's novels only, I need not distinguish them from creations that fail to achieve universality, but one difference would be in the variety of impulses in the author's self-perception that the imagination can fuse. The comic-book Superman touches worldwide fantasies, but after childhood we smile at its insufficiency. After adolescence, we reject the easy fantasies of Robinson Crusoe and Dick Whittington (favorite foils for Dickens), of Frankenstein and Mr. Hyde, even of Jane Eyre and Peregrine Pickle, for the richer imaginative room of an Emma Woodhouse or a Leopold Bloom. These too begin with simple archetypes (Lady Bountiful, Poor Little Rich Girl, Queen of the May, Hero Home from the Wars, Wandering Jew, Complaisant Cuckold) but go on into fuller life.

Third-person narrators, presumed to be detached from the plot and directing their narration and judgments to readers only (not to characters), tacitly acknowledged on all sides to stand for the author, are his most immediate offspring: for example, Boz the creator of *Sketches* or the figure George Orwell liked to imagine as Dickens behind his novels,[2] the angry ironist who shares the narration of *Bleak House* with Esther Summerson. Next in order of conscious creation come the first-person narrators, roles an author assumes at one remove—Moll Flanders, Tristram Shandy, Jane Eyre, Huckleberry Finn, Jake Barnes, Augie March. These are not simply their authors' selves, as witness the thriving "Is Swift

Gulliver?" industry. But they certainly differ from each other, stamped by their authors' individual natures, unimaginable as anyone else's offspring, surely consanguineous with him. For Dickens, such figures appear from *Pickwick Papers* through *Our Mutual Friend* in inserted autobiographies; as speakers in magazine and Christmas tales and personae Dickens used— old Master Humphrey and his collaborators—and considered ("The Cricket," "a Shadow") for magazines; and of course David Copperfield, Esther Summerson, and Pip Pirrip.

At a further remove from the umbilicus are single heroes whose minds the author occasionally enters as he follows their fortunes, like Jane Austen's Elizabeth Bennet or Kafka's K; but after Oliver Twist and Nicholas Nickleby, such figures recur in Dickens only in short pieces and the autobiographical narrations. Instead, he distributes his own impulses, leanings, and imagined situations among a number of characters. Even in *Oliver Twist* we spend intense passages in the minds of Bill Sikes and Fagin as well as Oliver, and in the first of the variedly focused works, *The Old Curiosity Shop*, we feel with at least Little Nell, Dick Swiveller, and Kit Nubbles; and as critics have noticed we also share Quilp's nasty thoughts.

I would go even further than Alexander Welsh, who has recently argued for Dickens's tendency toward multiple projection,[3] and say that from the beginning Dickens develops sides of himself in all the major figures in his moral and social spectrum, male and female, young and old. In some confessional figures and situations, I believe this projection is unconscious, though with so self-observant and sensitive a mind as Dickens's that can never be certain. At any rate, though he uses models from the great range of his reportorial observation, he shapes them toward sides of himself acting as he imagines he would in the world he has created. And even if his range of selves was extraordinarily wide, it was finite; those projected by his early and late contemporaries Balzac and Dostoievski, also extraordinarily wide-ranging, are for that reason not like his or each other's.

1

Dickens was intensely and immensely self-conscious, aware of how he looked before others, asserting a year before he died that he was "accustomed to observe myself as curiously as if I were another man."[4] From the vast number of his surviving letters, we can see that he was his own most persistent subject of observation, familiar with himself in a variety of roles, and therefore inescapably his best model. He seems to have used this quality deliberately in his fiction. A passage familiar to Dickensians, a recollection by Dickens's daughter Mamie, shows us how earnestly he tried to project himself into literary offspring who at first seem unlike him. Convalescing from an illness on a sofa in his study, she saw him busily writing, "when he suddenly jumped from his chair and rushed to a mirror which hung near, and in which I could see the reflection of some extraordinary facial contortions which he was making. He returned rapidly to his desk, wrote furiously for a few moments, and then went again to the mirror. The facial pantomime was resumed, and then turning toward, but evidently not seeing, me, he began talking rapidly in a low voice. [Years later] I knew that with his natural intensity he had thrown himself completely into the character that he was creating, and that for the time being he had not only lost sight of his surroundings, but had actually become in action, as in imagination, the creature of his pen."[5] To make a character live before his imagination, he was shaping it into his own features.

Moreover, how Dickens appeared to other people con-tinuously fascinated him and no doubt shared in the process by which he imagined characters and situations. Sometimes the connection seems obvious. His public separation from his wife and his new dramatic readings before large audiences, for example, surely contributed to Charles Darnay's crowded trial scenes in *A Tale of Two Cities*. But figures singled out before bitter mobs, famously Sikes and Fagin, arrested his and his readers' emotional attention from the beginning. We could profitably examine the differences in the scenes—Sikes and Fagin are guilty, and so are the similarly situated riot leaders in *Barnaby Rudge*, whereas Darnay is not—but that would not affect the larger issues, that Dickens had long found the role congenial, and that his imagination recurrently projected it.

He habitually saw himself acting before his mental eye, if not more than other prolific narrators, more on record than any English writer of comparable eminence but Boswell. A memorable expression of the oddity he thereby described was his picture of himself on the miserable Atlantic crossing in January 1842, lording it in the Ladies' Cabin as a makeshift doctor for his seasick wife and her maid. When he tried to cheer them with brandy and water during a storm, they kept rolling away from him, shifting helplessly every time he staggered to catch up: "And in all the misery of the time, I had a keen sense of the absurdity of my position which I cannot, even now, surpass" (*P*, III, 228). At his arrival in Halifax, he lightened a pleasing scene with a deprecating self-reference as "the inimitable" (an epithet bestowed by an old teacher, according to Dickens's friend and biographer John Forster): "I wish you could have seen judges, law-officers, bishops, and law-makers welcoming the inimitable" (*P*, III, 15).

Throughout his career, his letters are full of invented metaphoric, usually comic, self-references, momentary fictions centering on himself. Here is a small sample, merely an illustrative snack, of his self-creations. While working on *Nicholas Nickleby*, he writes that he must "buckle to again and endeavour to get the Steam up," for he may yet " 'bust' the boiler" (*P*, I, 527). A few weeks later, on April 7, 1839, "I am doing the Snail at present—not the Railroad" (*P*, I, 540). From America, on March 22, 1842, he asks a friend to "Imagine Kate and I—a kind of Queen and Albert—holding a Levee every day (proclaimed and placarded in newspapers) and receiving all who choose to come" (*P*, III, 154). At Niagara Falls, May 1, 1842, "believing the statements I heard, I began putting my ear to the ground, like a Savage or a Bandit in a ballet, thirty miles off, when we were coming here from Buffalo!" (*P*, III, 229). Bitter at American booksellers' and newspapers' mistreatment of authors, "I seem to grow twenty feet high" in avenging wrath (*P*, III, 230). Nearing a deadline on a *Martin Chuzzlewit* installment on April 12, 1843, he plans to hide and write now, "But on Sunday *Week* . . . I shall be visible here, between two o'Clock and half past. I contemplate making a longer stay than the Comet did; for after that time, I have no idea of being out of my sphere (supposing this place to be my proper orbit) for some months" (*P*, III, 472).

After the strain of simultaneously finishing *Martin Chuzzlewit* and writing *A Christmas Carol*, he informed his American friend Felton on January 2, 1844, that "I broke out like a Madman. And if you could have seen me at a children's party at Macreadys the other night, going down a Country dance something longer than the Library at Cambridge with Mrs. M. you would have thought I was a country Gentleman of independent property, residing on a tip-top farm, with the wind blowing straight in my face every day" (*P*, IV, 3). Thinking of a new book, March 2, 1846, he was wandering, "seeking rest, and finding none," which as the editor of the *Letters* notes (*P*, IV, 510), is the phrasing for the "unclean spirit" in Matthew. When he came out of those doldrums he assumed another part, writing his actor friend Macready on

October 24, 1846, that he would not invite him to the
dangerous Alps but instead, "Onward! To Paris! [Cue for
Band. Dickens points off with truncheon 1st Entrance. P. S.
Page delivers gauntlets, on one knee. Dickens puts 'em on,
and gradually falls into a fit of musing. Mrs. Dickens lays her
hand upon his shoulder. Business. Procession. Curtain]" (*P*,
IV, 646). At work on *Dombey*, "I am taming a spider or two in
my solitude, and weaving a small web of my own—with a
very long beard, and talons in place of nails—and shaking my
grizzled locks refuse to be comforted or to come out" (*P*, V,
96). On June 12, 1848, he "would have come to you at
Whitefriars today, but between the Scotch correspondence, the
Birmingham, . . . the Leamington . . . and Shepherd's Bush, I
am like an over-driven Bull" (*P*, V, 333). Reviewing notes for
a magazine biographer on June 6, 1856, "I feel like a wild
beast in a caravan describing himself in the keeper's
absence"(*MDGH,I,439*). Preparing for a meeting of the Royal
Literary Fund, he reports on March 19, 1857, "that I have my
war-paint on, that I have buried the pipe of peace, and am
whooping for committee scalps" (*MDGH*, II, 12).

He delighted in assuming personae, invented or implausibly
real. On June 11, 1839, for example, he sent the sculptor
William Behnes an advertisement for a lost dog named Boz,
saying he belonged to Behnes, had been traced to Surrey, and
should be restored by June 24, "up to which time he will be
perpetually engaged, it is supposed, in a monthly fit of
barking [the *Nickleby* installments] to which he is
unfortunately subject" (*P*, I, 555). On July 27, 1838, he wrote
a mock love-letter to Forster, from "Louisa" (*P*, I, 422), as he
signed a cockney letter to him of July 12, 1849, "Sloppy His
X mark" (*P*, V, 571) and on November 20, 1849, described a
house party through the persona of a foolish American travel
writer, signing the man's initials, "HC" (*P*, V, 661-63). A
dinner invitation to his friend Stanfield, January 30, 1843,

came as an order signed "Victoria," for "her trusty subjects John Forster and Charles Dickens" to arrest him and bring him to Dickens's house (*P*, III, 433). Accompanying half a crown he owed Macready, Dickens manufactured a legal notice to "Yourself v Dickens," signed "Pitchcock, Swabber, Trillington, and Dawberry" (*P*, IV, 529).

He enjoyed playing at self-deprecation through journalistic cliches, as when he announced the reception of the *Christmas Carol* to his American friend Felton through the persona of a resentful American reporter: "Its success is most prodigious. And by every post, all manner of strangers write all manner of letters to [the author] about their homes and hearths, and how this same Carol is read aloud there, and kept on a very little shelf by itself. Indeed it is the greatest success as I am told, that this Ruffian and Rascal has ever achieved" (*P*, IV, 2). In Birmingham, an evidently unfinished banner in a hall where he was to speak read "Welcome Dick," leading him at times to be Dick, as in a report by a favorable persona on February 28, 1844: "Dick with the heart of a lion dashed in bravely and made decidedly the best speech I ever heard him achieve. Sir, he was jocular, pathetic, eloquent, conversational, illustrative, and wise—always wise" (*P*, IV, 55). January 17, 1844, accepting an invitation by Forster and others, he addressed his "FELLOW COUNTRYMEN," proud "to respond to such a requisition. I had withdrawn from Public Life—I fondly thought for ever—to pass the evening of my days in hydropathical pursuits, and the contemplation of virtue. For which latter purpose, I had bought a looking-glass.—But, my friends, private feeling must ever yield to a stern sense of public duty. The Man is lost in the Invited Guest, and I comply" (*P*, IV, 21). Though he thought that public burlesques of other writers were bad for the dignity of literature, he could slip into the mode privately, as in his plan to come as "a stately form" to a friend's birthday celebration: "A practised eye will be able to discern two humble figures in attendance, which from their flowing crinolines may, without exposing the prophet to the imputation of rashness, be predicted to be women. Though certes their importance, absorbed and as it were swallowed up in the illustrious bearing and determined purpose of the maturer stranger, will not enthrall the gaze that wanders over the forest of San Giovanni as the night gathers in. Ever affectionately, G.P.R. James" (*MDGH*, II, 195).

Such comic self-perception, always trembling on the edge of the grotesque, can easily fall over and join both fantasy and fiction. Congratulating a new father on May 10, 1843, he suddenly inhabits his own family in a crazy future: "I am grey, and Kate is bald. Charles (you remember him a little boy?) was married some years ago to a fascinating girl (with no prospects) and is just appointed the Government Inspector of Egyptian Balloons, which is a very good post. Mary's second husband is not quite equal to her first, poor fellow! —but in his capacity of chief clerk to the chief magistrate of Bow Street, which office I have filled, as you know, for nearly ten years, he is always near me, which is a great comfort, I find, in the decline of life" (*P*, III, 487).

2

In addition to the effects of current pressures, critics have long recognized that powerful infusions of feelings from the whole range of Dickens's past melt into the present moment to supply the coming amalgam of art. His recollections surfaced, presumably involuntarily, at the deaths of family members and in his early fiction; from *David Copperfield* on (if not before), he summoned them lightly for magazine pieces and in depth for novels. Twice he recorded extensive and powerful immersions in memory: in a deliberate attempt at private autobiography around the critical age of thirty-five, and in an unexpected correspondence at forty-three with the woman he had passionately loved in youth.

Though the fragment of a Memoir (according to Forster, whose biography is its only source, written in spring or summer 1847) has long sedated Dickens scholars, it is so important for understanding one set of impressions on his imagination of life that I must cite some passages for everyone else. When in 1824 Dickens's father, John Dickens, was arrested and jailed in the Marshalsea for debt, James Lamert, a relative who was the manager of Warren's Blacking factory, offered to employ the twelve-year-old Charles at six or seven shillings a week. The parents agreed. Whatever the actual motives and conditions at the time, Dickens's memories—still on his mind in his last years, as his son Henry recalled—in maturity were bitter. "It is wonderful to me how I could have been so easily cast away at such an age," he wrote; "even after my descent into the poor little drudge I had been since we came to London, no one had compassion enough on me—a child of singular abilities, quick, eager, delicate, and soon hurt, bodily or mentally—to suggest that something might have been spared . . . to place me at any common school."[6]

We cannot know how the twelve-year-old boy had felt. But the author at thirty-five infused his childish consciousness with terrors and bitter resentments of an alien, degrading, hopeless condition. "No words can express the secret agony of my soul as I sunk into this companionship; compared these everyday associates with those of my happier childhood; and felt my early hopes of growing up to be a learned and distinguished man, crushed in my breast. The deep remembrance of the sense I had of being utterly neglected and hopeless; of the shame I felt in my position; of the misery it was to my young heart to believe that, day by day, what I had learned, and thought, and delighted in, and raised my fancy and my emulation up by, was passing away from me, never to be brought back any more; cannot be written. My whole nature was so penetrated with the grief and humiliation of such considerations, that even now, famous and caressed and happy, I often forget in my dreams that I have a dear wife and children; even that I am a man; and wander desolately back to that time of my life" (Forster, p. 26).

Shunted off to lodge alone at an old woman's house, he had "No advice, no counsel, no encouragement, no consolation, no support, from anyone that I can call to mind, so help me God. . . . I know that, but for the mercy of God, I might easily have been, for any care that was taken of me, a little robber or a little vagabond" (Forster, pp. 27-28). After his father was released and the family reunited, "My father said I should go back no more, and should go to school . . . I never afterwards forgot, I never shall forget, I never can forget, that my mother was warm for my being sent back" (Forster, p. 35)—to work, not school. Many years after his death, his daughter Katey is cited as believing that Dickens "always seems to have had a 'down' on his mother since the early days when she was 'warm' for his being sent back to the boot-blacking warehouse, which incident he could never forget." If recent scholarly estimates that he was mired there, hopelessly and needlessly, for five months to a year are right, his resentment is not strange at all.[7]

Commenting on the Memoir, Forster said that the many pitiful adults and children in Dickens's works "were not his clients . . . but in some sort his very self" (Forster, p. 39). And since his day, critics have found the fragment to record concisely a number of recurring elements in Dickens's imagination besides those associated with abandonment: attitudes to his father and mother, to family relations, to social class, to education, to politics, to his prospects in life, to those who helped him and those who might have but did not, to a world that must be faced on one's own.

As to the equally well known involvement with Maria Beadnell, which forms the heart of the Dora sequence in *David Copperfield* and the Clennam-Flora plot in *Little Dorrit* and probably contributes to Pip's feelings about Estella in *Great Expectations* and to those of the male lovers in *Our Mutual Friend* for the two heroines, Dickens's letters record its power. Although he had had several minor contacts with Maria's father, and perhaps with her, in the intervening decades, when he found a letter from her in his mail early in 1855, he responded with an overwhelming rush of memories to her appeal for renewed familiarity: "Three or four and twenty years vanished like a dream, and I opened it with the touch of my young friend David Copperfield when he was in love" (*N*,II,625-26).

Writing of the affair to Forster in December 1855 (months after he had found her a duller Flora Finching), Dickens said he was quite serious about the passion of those recollections. He reminded him to "think what the desperate intensity of my nature is, and that this began when I was Charlie's [his son's] age; that it excluded every other idea from my mind for four years, at a time of life when four years are equal to four times four; and that I went at it with a determination to overcome all the difficulties, which fairly lifted me up into that newspaper life, and floated me away over a hundred men's heads. . . . And so I suffered, and so worked, and so beat and hammered away at the maddest romances that ever got into any boy's head and stayed there, that to see the mere cause of it all, now, loosens my hold upon myself. . . . No one can imagine in the most distant degree what pain the recollection gave me in Copperfield. And, just as I can never open that book as I open any other book, I cannot see the face (even at four-and-forty), or hear the voice, without going wandering away over

the ashes of all that youth and hope in the wildest manner"
(*N*, II, 716).

Besides these two episodes, other habits, conditions, and
specific events also retained their place in Dickens's memory
from before his novel-writing days: the insignificance of
childhood Rochester, reinvented as Mudfog and Dullborough;
his dreary schooldays at the Wellington House Academy,
recalled derisively in *David Copperfield*'s Salem House and
elsewhere; his stretch as a beginning law clerk, which
spawned so many youths in his fictional law firms; his
residence as a very young man in chambers, elaborated in
David's experiences and an Uncommercial Traveller piece,
"Chambers" (*AYR*, August 18, 1860), that includes an
anecdote combining Traddles's games with his sisters-in-law
(*David Copperfield*) and the suicide of an old friend of
Tulkinghorn's (*Bleak House*); joining with his sister Fanny to
hide a one-legged tramp in their cellar when they were
children, available for division into Magwitch (*Great
Expectations*) and Wegg (*Our Mutual Friend*);[8] and most
poignantly, wandering in the Strand as a small boy, with all
"the child's unreasoning terror of being lost," including Jo the
crossing sweeper's incomprehension of the cross atop St.
Paul's, in "Gone Astray" of the August 13, 1853, *Household
Words*. For larger effects, no doubt—as has been suggested by
Dickens biographers—his usual childhood companion before
she left to study voice on a scholarship, his sister Fanny,
remained also as a nurturing friend in his memory and
fantasies.

3

Though Dickens from the first conceived aspects of himself
inhabiting a variety of ages and both sexes, his obvious
projections in the rush of the early novels were into his
contemporaries. The current moment, always modified by the

past and fantasies of the future, is always a time of excitement, of change, for the charged imagination. In that moment, Dickens's characters of his own age become obvious analogues of himself, models, reflective commentaries, foils, monitory fools or villains, other selves he can be or reject, as he rejects all the subjects of the *Sketches of Young Gentlemen* in favor of the cool, judging persona, young Boz. Even where the imagination's focus is intently on a version of the past self like Oliver (among Oliver's contemporaries little Dick, the Artful Dodger, and Charley Bates), and Oliver's situation at the end glows with the just-arriving Dickens's own happy prospects, he tests life through others his own age in Bill Sikes, Noah Claypool, Monks, and Harry Maylie. In projecting current possibilities, he not only elaborates old self-evaluations and fantasies of having his beloved dead return, of achieving genteel prosperity despite guilt, envy, and slander, of escaping confinements like marriage, of flouting repressive convention, and of finding love or childhood ideality, but also admonishes himself about dangerous tendencies, to rush headlong like Nicholas Nickleby or Martin Chuzzlewit, trust too much like Newman Noggs, waste life like the early Dick Swiveller, or submit to social constrictions like Kit Nubbles.

In the first novels the aging men, notably Fagin and Brownlow in *Oliver Twist*, suggest older possible selves or older figures of authority who affected Dickens (his uncles, his publisher Bentley, even in the larger world political dignitaries like the Duke of Wellington), modified in personality by aspects of himself.[9] Though in some conditions their age is irrelevant—Fagin on the eve of execution, Ralph Nickleby about to hang himself—their significance usually lies in their effect on the young projections. In *Nicholas Nickleby*, the Cheerybles, Tim Linkinwater, old Ralph Nickleby and older Arthur Gride willingly or resentfully prepare the world for the young. There, Dickens imagines a variety of young men around the touchy, widely talented, industrious, responsible central projection: besides the thin cliches Sir Mulberry Hawk, Lord Verisopht, and John Browdie, the more richly idiosyncratic Smike (the Oliver Twist or blacking-factory self), Kenwigs (the harried young paterfamilias), and Mantalini, whose comic impudence like Jingle's (*Pickwick Papers*) and Fagin's scores off conventional society for Dickens. In addition to their youth, these and other figures share his real or imagined private condition. Miss Snivellici successfully scouting for a husband, Miss Petowker digesting Lillyvick, John and Matilda courting and marrying, the ever-fruitful Kenwigses and fruitless Wittiterlys, the Mantalinis and the absurdly theatrical Lenvilles all reflect, and reflect on, not only Nicholas's progress to marriage and success but also Dickens's burgeoning domestic life, while the Crummleses offer a burlesque vision of the future. Dickens's letters through this period laugh at his own intermittent failures managing his household—rather like the German baron's in the inserted tale on the coach ride—and coping with its increases.

In *The Old Curiosity Shop*, the novel just before those I discuss at length, critics have recently noted how much the chief figures Little Nell, Dick Swiveller, and Daniel Quilp project conspicuous sides of Dickens as he behaved and as he imagined himself. To them, I think, we can add the other vivid characters. Kit Nubbles, as an upwardly mobile lower-class boy, develops a rare favorable fantasy about what might have become of Dickens if his parents had returned him to the blacking warehouse, as the vicious Sam and Sally Brass suggest a comic outcome of his legal training. In the interaction of character and event imagined for this novel's world, Nell's death is the end of youth for Dickens as for us— as if Oliver Twist had died from his wound, as if Nicholas and Kate had let Ralph Nickleby destroy them young—not the preparation for adulthood but a memory and an ideal, a state without sin never to be regained. Quilp's death complements it, as the death of childhood's egoistic anarchy, so that Dick Swiveller and the Marchioness—like Nell a resolute self of blacking-warehouse age when we meet her—and Kit Nubbles and his Barbara offer the author and reader the promise of an ordinary, cheerful future.

The elegiac old people gathering at the end of the novel now confirm the passing of the vision, as Nell's grandfather's life and death signal the inevitable dissipation of great expectations; in the remaining young, Dickens both jokes about his own prospects and awaits chastened joys. Imagining himself in this complex variety of figures, he shares with us a coherent, resolved world. Wishing to escape after fulfilling in the next few months his old commitment to write *Barnaby Rudge*, disappointed in a *Master Humphrey's Clock* that would not go without his novels, he affects us most powerfully here with Wordsworthian intimations of immortality in loss. The shades of Earth's prison house, an early haze in *Oliver Twist*, vaguely noticeable in Nicholas Nickleby's move to a lifetime of bourgeois complacency, bring us and the young people of *The Old Curiosity Shop* to a sunny, but far from radiant, common day.

Since age significantly affects Dickens's sense of his situation as he projects it in his novels, I have chosen to examine novels written at points in life to which most of us pay special attention. For Dickens, always observing his own character, achievements, and psychological condition in a world filled with others, always comparing his current self with what he might have been or might still be, the usual chronological milestones seem even more than usually arresting: turning thirty, when he made his escape from unremitting industry, demanding relatives and children, and the crowding consequences of fame to seek new meaning in

America; facing forty, when after experiments, expedients, and escapes to the continent he recreated his own growth in *David Copperfield*; a decade later, when he did it again after exploding his family life. Assuming his self-analysis, always sensitive, to have been heightened at these times, I select them for study of its consequences in his imagined worlds: in *Barnaby Rudge* and *Martin Chuzzlewit* before and after thirty, *David Copperfield* and *Bleak House* around forty, *Great Expectations* and *Our Mutual Friend* around fifty.

Though I regretfully omit extended analysis of the other eight novels out of consideration for the reader's patience, that is not because they lack relevant material. Each of them shows Dickens similarly imagining his current selves projected through his imagined world. In *Hard Times*, to pick not quite at random a work usually admired for *not* dealing with private matters, the heroine Louisa Gradgrind is almost destroyed because of her father's misguided guardianship; that father, well meaning, fails to cope with two daughters the age of Dickens's; his wife is the silly and self-pitying mother in the Dickens pattern of revenge on his own mother begun with Mrs. Nickleby; Bounderby, the chief villain, brags of exactly Dickens's miserable experience in a blacking warehouse and nurses his social deprivations; Stephen Blackpool, the noblest figure, intensely suffers from a bad marriage just when Dickens's bitterness about his own was becoming acute, as Stephen also suffers the regular Dickensian subjection to mob hatred; and Sissy Jupe brings the only light to the Gradgrind household as Dickens felt that Georgina Hogarth had brought it to his at the same age.[10] As Dickens was complaining of lonely dissatisfaction at the time, so the novel ends with no good prospects for the industrially riven society, death for Stephen, frustration for Gradgrind, and barrenness for Louisa and Rebecca. In these and other respects, wherever the book lives humanly and not just ideologically it projects Dickens's sense of his personal world.

In these brief paragraphs, as in the chapters that follow, I have tried to look freshly at the characters and the structure of the novels, and I believe that my overall sense of them is new. But as to individual aspects of them, some or most have been noted somewhere, perhaps even often, in the Dickens criticism, before whose limitless flow I stand awed and abashed, like Dickens at Niagara: "the first effect, and the enduring one—instant and lasting—of the tremendous spectacle, was Peace. Peace of Mind, tranquillity, calm recollections of the Dead, great thoughts of Eternal Rest and Happiness; nothing of gloom or terror" (*AN*, xiv, 200). I can only hope to thread my own way along my particular line of sight, thankful for the guidance I have found, and to ask forgiveness where I overlook a guidepost.

In what follows, I do not claim that the pressures of self-serving fantasy are the only stimuli to Dickens's imagined worlds. He is one of history's great gadflies on the passing procession, always stinging society with spears of conscience. He charged into political battles on Reform and the Poor Laws, on copyright, on conditions of labor, and generally on European oppression and American slavery; impartially attacked financial speculation, utilitarianism, laissez-faire capitalism, puritanical religion, abstract philanthropy, and militant teetotalism as heartless; demanded human dignity and decent living conditions for the poor, and better sanitation, usable education, and a functioning legal system for all; exposed a government stagnant through red tape and jobbery, fruits of the obsolete class system and rigid social convention. In short, he was unceasingly responsible and responsive toward events and conditions outside him.

But except in Christmas stories and magazine pieces, he spares us homiletic social allegories, using Poor Laws and Yorkshire schools, Chancery and financial bubbles as obstacles, failed machinery, motivators or discouragers, but

not as the heart of his novels. *Hard Times*, his nearest
approach to the didactic novel, has had such illustrious lovers
as Ruskin and Shaw, but they never claimed that it was
pleasurably full of life; whatever there is of that comes from
Dickens's projection into the characters, primarily Louisa,
Stephen, and Bounderby. When we enjoy rich Dickensian life,
I think our own imaginations respond to the intensity,
complexity, and sensitivity with which he imagines himself
into his imagined worlds. That at least is my assumption here,
which I invite the reader to judge in the following chapters.

Although I hope not to neglect influences from without, I
wish primarily to show what the constituents—career-long or
briefly flaring—of Dickens's current self-conceptions
contribute to sharing the nature and courses of the major
characters. To trace these shadows of his high romance, I shall
seek in all the major figures in each novel (not one or two, as
has been customary) aspects of his self-conception brought
into a coherent created world. My concern is primarily
critical, not biographical. Stepping an inch or two past Uncle
Toby and the Vulgar, I take the consanguinity as confirmed
and look for the sort in its effects: in that created world itself,
the dead author's child, the self fully imagined and always
alive, whom we embrace now.

II. *Barnaby Rudge:*
Two Cheers for Maturity

February 13-November 27, 1841

How else but in his novels could the Dickens of 1841 find time to think about his life? As he began serializing *Barnaby Rudge* in his weekly magazine *Master Humphrey's Clock* right after his twenty-ninth birthday, Dickens was tired, restless, eager for relief after five years of enormous labor amid growing family responsibilities and recurrent pressure from his feckless father. In that time, he had produced four volumes of *Sketches*, three farces, an edition of the *Memoirs of Joe Grimaldi*, and the massive fictions *Pickwick Papers*, *Oliver Twist*, and *Nicholas Nickleby*; planned the monthly *Bentley's Miscellany* and edited it for two years; and planned and edited *Master Humphrey's Clock*, which he soon had to fill with weekly installments of *The Old Curiosity Shop*. Now, to conclude the magazine, he labored over the new book that had long been on his mind. As early as August 17, 1836, he had described his contemplated historical novel—in a genre exalted by the recent predecessor he most admired, Walter Scott, and currently exploited by the prestigious Bulwer—as "a work on which I might build my fame" (*P*, I, 165). Occasionally dickering with publishers to improve a bad contract for *Barnaby Rudge*, he immersed himself in other work until early 1841, when he needed to fill the magazine.

By then, the idea had absorbed enough private and public influences for imaginative shaping as he looked forward to diversion—the American trip that had long been on his mind—nearing thirty.

While feeding on the past, as a living work by a writer alert to the world around him *Barnaby Rudge* drew contemporary breath. In a general way, Catholic equality—against which the book's Gordon Riots were rioting in 1780—was still a political issue, kept prominent in 1841 by the eloquent Irish parliamentary leader Daniel O'Connell and his supporters. Even a more immediate and powerful imaginative stimulus, as scholars agree, was the Chartist convention that lasted into the 1840s after bursting into violence at the end of 1839 and frightening liberal journals like the weekly *Examiner*, which was produced by friends of Dickens whose views—allowing for their magisterial rhetoric—were close to his. This paper regularly devoted large columns and even pages to the convention and its aftermath, usually deploring it (e.g., November 17, 1839, "The Chartist Riots at Newport," pp. 726-28), into early 1840 for the trials of Fergus O'Connor and other arrested leaders.[11] Moreover, new evidences of discontent among the poor were replacing or complementing the Chartist ferment. All over Britain, as regularly described in sections headed "The Demonstration" in the *Examiner*, crowds protested against the Corn Laws. Among other works responding to this national upheaval, Carlyle's *Chartism* memorably placed blame on the irresponsibility of the ruling classes. Harriet Martineau's novel *The Hour and the Man* (published two months before *Barnaby Rudge*'s first installment), like Dickens's on a different uprising under a different leader, Toussaint L'Ouverture, reflects the same prodding by the current English world; Ainsworth's *Old Saint Paul's*, on another public convulsion, the plague of 1665, was running weekly in the *Sunday Times* in 1841.

Although Dickens was courting the analogies to Scott—made specially current by Lockhart's grand biography, which had been appearing in the late 1830s, everywhere excerpted, reviewed, and commented on (as by Dickens in the *Examiner*, March 31, 1839,[12] and September 29, 1839)[12]—he had not nostalgic or picturesque old places and people in mind, but the world he currently saw transposed into an earlier setting. Moreover, though he worked hard to make the setting and the account of public events authentic, from his first reference to the title as "Gabriel Vardon, the Locksmith of London" he was clearly centering his imagination on a fictional individual man. Soon it was Barnaby Rudge, a man of about his own age. His political views were also uncongenial to Scott's genre. In the midst of writing *Barnaby Rudge*, he welcomed the Tories' return to office with "The Fine Old English Gentleman. New version. (To be said or sung at all Conservative Dinners)," *Examiner*, August 7, 1841, on the Tory past:

> The good old times for cutting throats that cried out in their need,

> The good old times for hunting men who held their father's creed. (p. 500)

Besides political ambivalence about a past that included both idealized villages and real oppression, and private ambivalence about coping with his own past once his imagination was engaged, he also had to face the historical romance's temptations of easy, stereotypical plotting and character drawing at a time when he was eager to leave on a recuperative trip. As he was to write his editorial colleague Wills on June 6, 1867, reassuring him about his capacity to weather a series of Readings in America, "When I went to America in '42, I was so much younger, but (I think) very

much weaker too. I had had a painful surgical operation
performed, shortly before going out, and had had the labours
from week to week of Master Humphrey's Clock" (*N*, III,
530). But if impatience permitted John Rudge, the Haredales,
Gashford, and Dennis to glide through their roles no more
distinctively than they might have for Monk Lewis or Mary
Shelley, he did become imaginatively involved in exploring
his own world through most of the other figures.

1

In developing the many characters for his epic intention,
Dickens spread his sense of himself most obviously among
the six young men, all of whom were about his current age in
the main two-thirds of the novel. Of the two adaptations of the
projected self within the stereotypical hero, Edward Chester
and Joe Willet (both, like Dickens, burdened by intolerable
fathers), the more individualized is the innkeeper's son Joe, at
the beginning a "strapping young fellow of twenty, whom it
pleased his father to consider a little boy, and to treat
accordingly." Physically rebelling like the projections Oliver
Twist and Nicholas Nickleby, he beat a tormenting crony of
his father's, "dropped from his window" at daybreak, and
went off into the world. Once in London Joe turns—for one
intense sequence, Chapter xxxi—from a comic boy to an
intensely imagined young man painfully in love with "the
most developed 'Maria type'" of coquette in Dickens's early
fiction.[13] Anticipating their meeting, he faces the immensity of
choosing his path in life, without anyone's advice or
sympathy, and wanders all day "with the desolate and solitary
feeling of one who had no home or shelter, and was alone
utterly in the world for the first time" (xxxi, 237). With the
helplessness of the child exiled to the blacking factory and
lonely lodgings, Dickens combines the misery of the youth
whose first response to Maria Beadnell's rejection—according

to his later recollections—was to consider the traditional lure of the king's shilling.

Such a desperate rush into an unknown world fits the romance pattern Dickens was borrowing—as well as the adventurous spirit of the nineteenth century and the plots of his old favorites Fielding and Smollett—but it so regularly recurs in his fiction that we can fairly see it reflecting a deeper personal quality. Recurrently, Dickens yearns to cut the tie that his extreme sense of responsibility imposed on him: in desperation at twelve, to abandon the blacking factory; to repudiate his exploitive parents and brothers; to quarrel with publishers over excessive commitments he himself initiated; to throw up any work tinged with the demeaning; in short, not to compromise. As he went through life after Maria's rejection had set off his transforming effort of will, Dickens made a point of daring himself in small ways and large, of introducing swerves in the rain of habit and pattern—leaving for America in 1842 and taking an unprecedented sabbatical to Italy in 1844, undertaking new forms of book publication as well as magazines and a newspaper, climbing up smoldering Vesuvius, managing and starring in ambitious theatricals, starting new organizations and reforming existing ones, finally separating from his wife in a burst of publicity, diving into a whirlpool of public readings, and in middle age courting scandal with a teen-age mistress.

Oddly disorienting the usual reader of historical ro- mances—say Catherine Morland of *Northanger Abbey*— Dickens gives much more sympathetic attention to the lower- class than the aristocratic hero, just as he centers the novel's symbolism in the mad poor Barnaby rather than the mad rich Lord George Gordon. An equal-opportunity adventure novelist, he departed from the traditional Quixote-Sancho or Tom-Partridge social distinctions so that Joe and Edward share the heroics to save Varden, Haredale, the vintner, and the young women. But where he vividly imagined himself into the painful flight into life and its ambiguous outcome—gaining lovable Dolly but losing an arm—of the lower-bourgeois figure, he left the aristocratic one pretty much where he found him in the genre. Aside from some heartfelt suffering from a father's improvidence, he has Edward Chester on his higher social level merely act out the stereotypes. Like Joe Willet he leaves home, like him he suffers the pains of suspended, uncertain love, and like him he has been maligned by an unsatisfactory father of whom his creator relieves him in the end.

More consistently arresting than the balanced juvenile leads is Edward's half-brother Hugh, the brutalized natural man, the self doomed (like Dickens's prototypical modern savage Bill Sikes) by a childhood without family or education. Like Oliver Twist the illegitimate son of a gentleman and a deserted mother of a lower class, Hugh draws energy from the resentful fantasies directed at both of Dickens's parents that would be suggested in the Memoir. But where Oliver's (like David Copperfield's) were versions of the pre-blacking gentle incompetents, Hugh's were the worst devils imaginable by the child fearing the factory hell for life. A huge and feral self aimed at respectable society, the savage man of the forest in the Maypole's cargo of folklore, Hugh yet responds to anyone who troubles to consider him, not only accepting the despicable Dennis and derisory Simon Tappertit as comrades and blindly obeying John Chester, but also protecting old John Willet—who thinks him an animal but has nothing against animals—in the heat of the riot. Always generous and encouraging to Barnaby—like Dickens to his brothers, particularly his favorite Frederick—joining his wild energy with Barnaby's irresponsible visionary character to form two essential aspects of the artist, he can be even more easily exploited by evil because he has a rebellious will: the side of

Dickens that Edmund Wilson magnified into sympathy with the rioters.

As Dickens showed in the coming summer's *American Notes*, he was currently fascinated by the possibilities of the human spirit that, like Hugh—and like his own childhood self at the factory—craved fulfillment. As the greatest horror that he found was "the darkness—not of skin, but of mind" forced on American slaves by laws forbidding their education, so his happiest discovery was a mind elevated from brutality. Having read Dr. Samuel Gridley Howe's *Education of Laura Bridgman* in 1840, he made a pilgrimage to the Perkins Institution for the Blind in Boston to see the teen-ager who magnificently achieved humanity despite an infantine illness that had left her blind, deaf, and almost bereft of smell and taste. Before Howe began working with the isolated child, Dickens writes, "the moral effects of her wretched state soon began to appear. Those who cannot be enlightened by reason, can only be controlled by force; and this, coupled with her great privations, must soon have reduced her to a worse condition than that of the beasts that perish, but for timely and unhoped-for aid" (iii,33-34). When she realized that she could make up her own words from letters Howe put in her hands, and thereby communicate to others what she thought " 'at once her countenance lighted up with a human expression [Dickens is quoting Howe's book]: it was an immortal spirit, eagerly seizing upon a new link of union with other spirits!' " (iii, 35).

Raised to this full humanity only at rare moments by Barnaby's innocent good will, Hugh otherwise wallows in brutality as John Chester's dog, "cowering before him" (xxiii, 179) or sleeping outside his door; exemplifying and animating the riot's drink, destruction, and self-consumption; and spending his defeated last days before hanging as torpidly as he can manage: " 'To eat, and drink, and go to sleep, as long as I stay here, is all I care for' " (lxxiv, 571). Like Pope's benighted Indian, insofar as Hugh is *natural* man he craves only his dog, his bottle, and his woman. But as a natural *man* he senses something beyond the brutal, on his way to the gallows attacking the chaplain's party for indifference to the imminent execution of Barnaby:"'I had faith enough to believe, and did believe as strongly as any of you gentlemen can believe anything, that this one life would be spared' " (lxxvii, 596). Through Barnaby's associations with Christ, Dickens hints at salvation for the Hugh self wasted by society and helplessly molded to rebellion.

In his bewilderment and social resentment but not his redeeming love, Hugh finds a congenial complement, again about Dickens's age, in his physical opposite Simon Tappertit. More directly than Hugh, Simon revives and embodies the class fears of Dickens's early years, burlesquing a self incapable of distinction but always living in Malvolio's dream (" 'patience! I will be famous yet. A voice within me keeps on whispering Greatness' " [viii, 67]), exposing the reality under the cliches about noble-spirited apprentices that Ainsworth was seriously retailing in *Old Saint Pauls*. Mocking Dickens's experiments with mesmerism, Simon thinks he can dominate women with his staring eye, and he delights in the masonic mumbo-jumbo of his 'Prentice Knights[14] like his creator in amateur theatricals. Whereas Dickens makes the other young men of consequence heroes, or extraordinary examples, he treats Simon with contemptuous savagery—deriding his lust for his master's daughter, then crushing his legs in the Riots and marrying him to a sadistic widow—as the self-aggrandizing fantasist in himself that he stood aside to watch.

As a historical figure with certain known qualities and a symbol more than an actor in the novel's drama, Lord George Gordon, also "not yet thirty" during the Riots, cannot be a wholly imagined projected Dickensian self. Still, Gordon takes some shape from that self. Performing before a grand audience the delusions that Simon plays at, he exercises the artist's demonic power as speaker, exhibiting in "the violence of his tone and gesture . . . something wild and ungovernable which broke through all restraint" (xxxv, 270). Combined with this madness, Lord George's high social class makes him a particularly powerful instrument, a tool like the other partial artists Barnaby and Hugh. At this time, perhaps not coincidentally, Dickens was playing in his mind with the danger of manipulation in which his own prominence placed him. Asked to stand for Parliament as a Liberal Whig, he excused himself for acceptable reasons, but also wrote a friend that he did not "choose to be bound hand and foot to the Reform Club" (*P*, II, 304). Moreover, the very emptiness of Lord George's character emphasizes the volatility of the mass of mankind, which will presumably go equally mad when other managers push forward other tools and which itself is thereby their tool. By choosing riots associated with this one deluded man, and centering the book on a sympathetic analogous figure, Dickens not only personalizes mass action but rejects political theories for moral psychology. The worst evil becomes the manipulation and corruption of imagination, defiling the distinctive mark of the human.

Barnaby, in whom Dickens vaguely symbolizes the nation at the time—and therefore humanity under those conditions— concentrates the self as imagination stimulated by powerful emotional signals, the artistic temperament without a principle of order, as some reviewers had been praising Dickens's freshly perceived details and lamenting their disconnectedness. Barnaby's poverty (caused like the boy Dickens's by his father's behavior) and his status as son of an upper servant in a manor house (Dickens's grandfather's position) are more than compensated for by his gift of imagination. When John

Chester, the worst of realists, tells Barnaby that the people he
has seen dancing, whispering, leaping, whirling, and plunging
are merely clothes on a line, Barnaby refutes the dullness of
common day for Dickens: " 'Ha, ha! Why, how much better to
be silly, than as wise as you! You don't see shadowy people
there, like those that live in sleep—not you! Nor eyes in the
knotted panes of glass, nor swift ghosts when it blows hard,
nor do you hear voices in the air, nor see men stalking in the
sky—not you! I lead a merrier life than you, with all your
cleverness. You're the dull men. We're the bright ones. Ha!
ha! I'll not change with you, clever as you are,—not I' " (x,
81-82).

But the gift is equivocal, as we can infer from the intensities of Dickens's violent figures from the beginning and
from Barnaby's frequent pain and fear. Born after his father's
crime, "upon the very day the deed was known, [bearing]
upon his wrist what seemed a smear of blood but half washed
out" (v, 41), Barnaby is an innocent memorial to that and a
foreboding of the riots before they occur. Although Dickens's
symbolic intentions are muddled by lumps of residual
gothicism, he implies, and his angelic spokeswoman Mary
Rudge says (lxxiii, 564) that Barnaby's madness flows from
his father's infraction of moral order through the unprovoked
murder of a just, kind master and an innocent fellow servant.
The essence of that madness is an unrestrained capacity to
imagine, which overpowers the murderer himself at crucial
points and dominates the innocent son. England's acting out
of Barnaby's "phantom-haunted dreams" (vii, 59) constitutes
the Gordon Riots, and turns the dreamer and victim of visions
into a prophet.

Having paid for his father's sin with his madness,
thoughtless as the spirit of sensitive, imaginative, destined,
innocent, troubled humanity, without a directing intellect " 'a

notable person, sir, to put to bad uses' " (xxvi, 198), Barnaby
is swept into the mob of more selfish rioters. Carrying a
banner in the vanguard, visible and marked by opponents, he
is no slight version of the public Dickens recently subjected to
vicious rumors—notably of madness.[15] After the seduction by
cheaply altruistic talk into the riotous, comradely whirl—
exploited but also promoted from seeing visions to acting—
Barnaby reflects the pain of that activity. Lacking a prudential
reason, he had no sense of guilt, "but he was full of cares now,
and regrets, and dismal recollections, and wishes (quite
unknown to him before) that this or that event had never
happened, and that the sorrow and suffering of so many
people had been spared" (lxix, 529).

By the end, if Dickens intends anything in the associations
with Christ—" 'He shall march, my lord, between me and
Dennis,' " says Hugh (xlviii, 369), and the hints thenceforth
increase—the early stain and bad dreams have been purged
away: not original sin but charity transcending it determines
this representative essence of mankind. Fulfilling for Mary
Rudge the meaning of his name in *Acts* 4: 36, "the son of
consolation," Barnaby can elicit humanity from those who
have its spark. His spiritual function follows on Little Nell's,
to draw Mary, probably Hugh, and perhaps even those who
pardoned him, to heaven. As innocent as Little Nell in will, by
the strange operation of imagination he personifies an
untainted participation in evil as she does not: a kind of self-
justification for the visionary artist, who acts in the morally
mixed world but can reject moral infection.

From this perspective as from others, Barnaby performs the
function that was to attract Dickens throughout his career as a
man of many roles and to provide the title of his last
completed novel, acting insofar as others will let him as
everyone's "mutual friend." Though he has an obvious double

in the novel—in Lord George, as Hugh and Edward are
doubles as half brothers and Joe and Simon as aspirants of the
same age for Dolly—he figures as an alternative to all the
other young men too, as the ally of Joe and Edward in their
private lives, of Hugh and Simon as rioter, of Joe, Hugh, and
Simon as physically or psychologically handicapped. Above
all, he shows everyone good will and elicits good will from
any who have it: the reader's guide to everyone's moral
condition in the world of the novel.

2

Besides offering elaborate and complementary aspects of
Dickens in other capacities, Joe, Hugh, Edward, and Barnaby,
even Simon and Lord George metaphorically, are all
alternatives to Dickens as son, family member, potentially
husband and father. Among these roles, as Stephen Marcus
showed at length,[16] the father-son relationships, implicit or
surrogate in the earlier novels, here overtly shape the
imagined world, initiating plot for Edward and Joe,
stimulating feeling in Hugh and Barnaby. All four sons are
morally superior to their fathers. Beset more than usually by
his own father's irresponsibility, obliged to disown that
father's debts through public advertisement on March 8, 1841,
in the midst of *Barnaby Rudge* (*P*, II, 225, n. 1), Dickens
richly appeases his filial conscience here. All the villains are
father-aged men, even the childless Gashford, Stagg, and
Dennis; and Chester manages to be two kinds of evil father to
his very different sons. Authority, claimed by the middle-aged
and older—both Varden and Chester are described as
somewhat past "the prime of life" and Rudge starts the book
at sixty—acts rightly by daughters, but only Varden treats
young men decently.

At the same time, Dickens by no means makes rebellion against fathers—and by extension all authority—in itself sympathetic, as Edmund Wilson and his psychoanalyzing heirs have it. Only Joe Willet and Edward Chester rebel unequivocally against their fathers, and both assert traditional order in the face of tyranny—order of nature in Joe's case, of common justice in Edward's—rather than defy it. Simon's anger against reality, ironically admonishing Dickens's own tendencies, makes him contemptible; Hugh, hating his life, lies at his father's feet; Barnaby embraces the murderous father who throws him off. Dickens's feelings about John Dickens bring the complexity of life, not formulas, to the relationship in the novel. Having John Willet remark that Hugh has all sorts of "faculties" left corked up inside him— " 'What would any of us have been, if our fathers hadn't drawed our faculties out of us?' " (xi, 86)—Dickens ironically reminds us of paternal deficiencies in the whole society, from the aloofness of the virtuous Haredale and the exploitive selfishness of Chester and Gashford to the Lord Mayor's cowardice. But he does not anticipate our current catchwords about riots as anti-patriarchal metaphor. Although the vividness of his riot reflects his violent resentments, he insistently shows it to be directed against victims, not bastions, of established power; exhibits the aristocratic double-father Chester and his school-fellow Gashford as its controllers and the aristocrat Lord George as its engineer; and praises those who put it down and (of all people!) George III and his Prince of Wales.

For the men of fatherly age, as for the sons, Dickens had seductive models in the book's genre, which welcomed a guilt-ridden murderer, an amoral aristocrat, a self-respecting craftsman, a lustful traitor, a sturdy yeoman, and so on. Roles in his national drama, as well as in the gothic romance, needed filling. But even these were sometimes susceptible to his imaginative impulses. Though Dickens's admirers on the *Examiner* and elsewhere chose Gabriel Varden as the most successful character in the novel, some evil ones seem psychologically more alive; on occasion, Dickens pours energy deeper into them than what supplies Varden's calm or perplexed cheerfulness. We may or may not believe that Rudge would see the ghost of his victim, or that Chester would be haunted by dreams of Hugh, but Dickens shared their mental states as intensely as he could in an effort to persuade us.

The murderer Rudge, the symbolic begetter of the national horrors, attempts to repeat his lonely crime when the book opens on its twenty-second anniversary, and he continues before us as a principle of envy and unfulfillment, an early self imagined as warped and aged in sin, roaming like so many Dickens projections "shelterless and alone in open country" (xviii, 138). Until Haredale catches him at the scene of the old crime, now the focus of the riots, instead of individual identity he inhabits the universal role of Cain. Then, however, not his stereotypical situation but his special child's isolation and terror affect us when he hears the Warren's alarm bell rung by a retributive universe (lv, 419). In Newgate, where the Dickens of Fagin and Ralph Nickleby imagines himself again into a condemned mind, Rudge (like Sikes and Fagin) comprehends in the mob's rush not freedom but a wish to tear him to pieces: "In all the crime and vice and moral gloom of the great pest-house of the capital, he stood alone, marked and singled out by his great guilt, a Lucifer among the devils" (lxv, 496). Guilt and fear, the purest infusion of Dickens's childhood emotions, memories of despairing isolation and fantasies of retribution fostered by ghost stories—with no admixture of adult appetites, of lust or greed or even luxuriousness (compare Raskolnikov's or

Svidrigaylov's dreams in *Crime and Punishment*)—define the mind and effect of this figure.

Another criminal of fatherly age, the blind Stagg, is cynical, atheistic, grimly comic like Fagin and Quilp, a spokesman for the chaos that he believes rules life. As the unobserved mingler who takes from the crowd what he wants, the unexpected and specially sensitive malicious registrar of behavior beneath the visible appearance, Stagg is a side of the young Dickens that could disturb conventional acquaintances. Eleanor E. Christian, for example, recalled meeting him in 1840, when she was a girl of nineteen or twenty, and finding him pretend to be so abstracted that people around him might say silly things "under the impression that he was miles away in a land of his own peopling, surrounded by characters of his own creation. Then suddenly up would go the curtain from his veiled vision, and he would break forth into most amusing but merciless criticism of all our conversation; such twisting and distorting of every thoughtless word and unfledged idea that we were covered with confusion, though convulsed with laughter." [17]

A villain who rationalizes his villainy as justice for the arbitrarily handicapped, Stagg animates one painful perception of the sources of envy. Condoling with Henry Burnett on the death of his crippled little boy soon after that of his wife (Dickens's beloved sister Fanny), Dickens was to write on January 31, 1849, "A child so afflicted, even with the inestimable blessing of a mother's care to support him, must, if he lived, be inevitably doomed to great mental anguish, to a weary struggle with the difficulties of life, to many years of secret comparisons in his own breast between himself and more healthy and more fortunate children" (*P*, V, 482). Surely Dickens's fears for his own psychologically affected child self lie in this perception of what happens to the socially insufficient, the guilty as well as the merely unfortunate, Fagin as much as Oliver, Stagg as much as Hugh. Guilt, it almost goes without saying, complements such an imagined self. A spider lurking in his " 'devil's cellar' " (viii, 62), where he encourages Simon Tappertit and the lesser apprentices in their mischievous fantasies, like those other projections of childhood guilts Sammy and Sally Brass of *The Old Curiosity Shop*, he creeps out to feed on people above ground. Always tempted toward self-pity like any artist who successfully undertakes pathos, Dickens imagines a Stagg or finally a wooden-legged Silas Wegg, as in an opposite way a magnificent Laura Bridgman, to goad himself out of its confines.

The hangman Dennis also vainly claims to be free of guilt, and like Hugh and Lord George he could plead madness in a modern court. Edmund Wilson saw him as an expression of Dickens's ambiguous response to authority, the one interesting figure in the novel because he both affirmed authority's death penalty and rebelled against its order. But Dennis's obsession with executions is an obsession only with his own importance, not in the slightest a respect for authority; he is crazed by long habituation to hanging people. Believing himself society's healer as the priest of death (xxxvi, 285), he has lost human brotherhood through a sense of aloof superiority, not rebelliousness. His justification, like Stagg's, mocks Dickens's fear for his own character, for as a dedicated artist putting an elegant close to life—his motto is " 'art improves natur' ' " (xxxix, 298)—Dennis joins the Gordon cause to recruit materials for that art among the young and gullible. Pretending bonhomie as he moves among the rioters, indifferent to political or other theories, madly loyal to his art and disloyal to all human needs, he is a fine straw man self for the work-weary artist Dickens to reject.

Three middle-aged characters, Chester, Gashford, and Haredale, to some extent represent aspects of the past, for Dickens stresses their shared schooldays and competitive courtships a generation ago. Of these, two are worse villains than Rudge, Stagg, and Dennis. One, Gashford, is a mere device for manipulating Lord George. But the double father John Chester, the book's evil genius, concentrates self-centeredness so rich that it includes the roots of Rudge's murderous impulses, Stagg's blind bitterness, Dennis's mad obsession with death, and the uncontrollable rage, lust, and greed of the rioters. Like Goethe's Mephistopheles ("'I fear I may be obliged to make great havoc among these worthy people,'" Chester smirks about the Vardens), he seeks no allies in his war with all mankind. Ironically congratulated on membership in Lord George's association, he says, "'I don't belong to the body; I have an immense respect for its members, but I don't belong to it'" (xliii, 327). The only association he accepts is with Parliament, for a reason suggested perhaps by thoughts of Dickens's father or perhaps by Disraeli's recent run for Parliament—membership, we learn, was "quite as good as an Insolvent Act" (xl, 302) to protect him from debtors' prison.

In the gothic plot, Chester is to interfere with his son Edward's pure love (mixing in the heavy father of eighteenth-century comedy and the loathsome qualities Dickens attributed to Lord Chesterfield), further brutalize his animalistic son Hugh and speed him to the gallows, and work his way, hint after hint, to the duel with his opposed equivalent, his twin or double Geoffrey Haredale. He thinks of himself and Haredale as Valentine and Orson (xv, 116), the princes in a medieval French tale, one raised as a knight and the other (by a bear) as a savage, who ended with Valentine taming Orson and taking him as a servant. But as Dickens indicated in the headings introduced into the Charles Dickens edition (xxiii, 175-81), he means Hugh, the natural man ironically related to the picture of Nature on Chester's wall, as the real Orson to Chester's corrupt Valentine. Taking their variously apportioned roles, Chester, Hugh, and Haredale suggest complexities in Dickens's relations with his father, as well as cautions to himself about the isolating dangers of manipulating others and of lacking a sense of society.

The virtuous Haredale also comes from the generic storehouse, featuring aloofness tinged with guilt and loss (Ravenswood sauce, from the recipe by Scott), haunted by incriminating rumors and even a sense of partial responsibility for the murders Rudge had committed. To the slight degree that he has individual qualities, they remind us of his author. Like Dickens, he suffers from multiple obligations and dependents, as guardian of Emma, landlord of the Maypole, and provider of pensions and homes to the Rudges, all out of a limited income. He blames his sullen detachment on a wrong response to " 'my share of sorrows' " (lxxix, 605), among which we know was the loss of his beloved to another man (Chester), as Dickens was to write Maria that her rejection had led him to an undesirable restraint on his feelings from then on. Accepting Emma's judgment that he has been a kind foster father to her, satisfied that he has fulfilled his obligations to Mary and Barnaby Rudge, unwillingly disposing of unfinished business by killing Chester in a duel, Haredale ends by going abroad to recuperate from the effort of maintaining sanity in the face of violence and disappointment: not quite Dickens eager to finish and go off to America, but close enough. So justified—and not only by the conventions of the genre—is Haredale's culminating duel that the guilt remains unexplained, diffused weltschmerz like Childe Harold's, except by its existence in the author.

Alone in cheerful virtue among the fatherly figures is Gabriel Varden, whose single deficiency, too much loving ale, merely grows out of his delight in socializing. An obvious projection of the hard-working craftsman Dickens who animated birthdays and addressed dinner parties, he also reflects in the comic, rueful dealings with his wife—a second love after rejection by the first, as with Dickens—the familial joking projected earlier through Kenwigses and Quilps. As Varden's craftsman's heartiness leads back to prototypes in Scott, his cheerful hammering (xli, 307) ties him to the rhythms of the primordial Maypole society. Refusing to serve the rioters under threat, like Haredale he faces a howling mob alone: a symbolic attitude Dickens uses not only for them but also for bit players, as shorthand for virtue. John Grueby, the sturdy yeoman who serves Lord George, plays the same scene along with Haredale; high on the social scale, the bluff old-style military, General Conway and Colonel Gordon, defy the mob and save Parliament (xlix, 376-77). This projected self-dramatization, notable as early as the *Sketches* and *Pickwick Papers*, surely contributed to Dickens's American pugnacious stand on international copyright. On February 24, 1847, when he wrote to the mayor of Boston describing the vicious attacks on him in American papers, he also wrote Forster of speaking out on the author's lot: "My blood so boiled as I thought of the monstrous injustice that I felt as if I were twelve feet high when I thrust it down their throats" (*P*, III, 83). Although simple to the reader, Varden becomes a complex projection for Dickens—a model half-ironically held up, a positive extreme to oppose the evil extreme Chester, a slanted mirror reminding himself to be spontaneous and unaffected in all his calculated decisions.

For a foil to Varden, Dickens imagines the equally bourgeois John Willet, as a tavern owner associated with an equally timeless vocation, as more drugged by the past than any romance-plot aristocrat. Spectacularly insensitive, a bad guardian who tries to stifle his son, he cannot absorb even such vital signs of change as the ruin of his bar, his son's maturing, and the world's renewal after the riots. In *American Notes* (ii, 13-14), Dickens said that while seasick he had been just in John Willet's condition of mindless consciousness after the Maypole fire, so that we can detect a trace of projection. But in his general complacent, popeyed stupefaction old John reflects not Dickens but a conventional response to any young man's rise to significance. Naturally, therefore, Dickens puts literary criticism in his mouth as he charges Hugh with the limitations attributed to Dickens by conventional reviewers like one in a *Quarterly Review* piece of October 1837, who thought he was only a brilliant reporter. Hugh, old Willet tells Chester, will " 'get out of a'most any winder in the house. There never was such a chap for flinging himself about and never hurting his bones. It's my opinion, sir, that it's pretty nearly all owing to his not having any imagination; and that if imagination could be (which it can't) knocked into him, he'd never be able to do it any more' " (xxix, 220).

The women are not so completely developed or so clearly animated by Dickens in this novel as in *The Old Curiosity Shop* or the novels beginning with *Dombey and Son*, though Mary Rudge shares some qualities with him and the Varden women pleasingly exaggerate their stereotypes. If her speeches assayed high enough in dialect or sentiment, any of them could move gracefully into a Scott tale, Mary Rudge and Emma Haredale as noble endurance and ladylike comportment within their stations, the Varden women as two clowns and a saucy lass. Aside from Miggs, Dickens individualizes them just enough to fill their traditional parts without dissatisfying the reader. Aside from Miggs also, they act as rewards or goals, what the world has to offer—the conventional role of women in men's novels—more than as projections. In a work where the men reflect Dickens as son and father, as aspirant and mature actor, the women are mothers or young lovers; and the mothers are recalled as possible lovers in youth.

Mary Rudge, named for the holy mother as Barnaby carries associations with the Son, must choose between love for the child and honesty in dealing with her evil husband, as Dickens may have recalled his own mother in the debt-ridden time before she betrayed him. Fleeing with her childish dependent to evade corruption, Mary Rudge follows the similarly burdened Little Nell in the dream escape that had arrested Dickens's imagination through all the novels so far and was coloring prospects of the trip to America. Finally, standing firm in a more difficult and less stereotypical situation than the heroic men's, she refuses to be blackmailed into evil by threats against her son, preferring to trust in heaven for him— a much nobler form of abandonment than Elizabeth Dickens's. At that stage, Dickens has moved the major events and passions of the novel elsewhere, so that he need not force himself or her through the intensity of Nancy's payment—also for saving a child—in *Oliver Twist.* The first significant Mary in Dickens's fiction since the death of Mary Hogarth (who was still much on his mind, *P*, III, 52, 56), she carries enough of his sense of loss to affect readers beyond her limited role.

As Mrs. Rudge undertakes tragic heroism for Dickens, Mrs. Varden, her parallel as Varden's (second) choice, plays the comic bourgeoise in a Dickensian line from Mrs. Weller of *Pickwick Papers*, who also anticipated her as a besotted evangelical, to Mrs. Wilfer of *Our Mutual Friend.* Balancing her as a Martha with a Mary, Dickens slyly points out her perversion of her biblical namesake's domestic and religious activities. And as "a lady of what is commonly called an uncertain temper" (vii, 54), when her excursion to Chigwell with husband and daughter turns into "quite a Progress rather than a ride" from inn to inn (xix, 150), she and Dolly pick up an amusing trifle of national context. For some years, Princess and then Queen Victoria had often progressed in stately form before the public, with her mother and lately with her husband, as Dickens amused himself by comparing his and Catherine's American traveling to a progress by Victoria and Albert (*P*, III, 154, 205). Moreover, the squabbling combination of the assertive Victoria and her equally assertive mother had long kept irreverent publications like *Figaro in London* in jokes, as in the women's speculation on a suitor in the issue of August 1, 1838, or on the mother's possible remarriage, January 28, 1839. Mrs. Varden's eventual restoration to a cooperative condition, like the country's, offers peaceful prospects for now. Both retain eruptive possibilities.

The ingenues are less developed than the mothers. Emma Haredale fills the standard romance obligation, and no more. A model of young aristocratic femininity, she need only be steadfast and courageous, treat Dolly democratically, love Edward Chester, and accompany him willingly to reap wealth in the colonies. Her complement Dolly Varden, the plump and rosy to Emma's fair and delicate, plays the coquette like a few of the rejected girls in earlier novels, but with a basically steady heart and sensible head, as befits Varden's daughter, that keep her focused on Joe. And as with Joe, she comes most nearly into personality as part of the Dickens-Maria memory, as the fantasied beloved who does—as Maria did not—beg for a renewal of love. Winning her surely recalls fantasies about Maria, as her marriage to Joe and her similarity to her mother also suggest the participation of Dickens's wife Catherine in her shaping.

As a female villain with the irreverent wit of Jingle, Fagin, or Quilp, a spokesman for lower-class resentments who won't cooperate with what is established, Miggs is a good deal more interesting than Emma or Dolly. Recognizing her social deprivation—which made the condition of English "female servants of all work in the families of those who keep lodging-houses, tradesmen, and other small housekeepers" "less enviable than that of Asiatic slaves" according to James Fenimore Cooper[18]—Dickens still uses her as an admonition against inveteracy. Like Simon, she resents not just social distinctions but a world created with differing qualities and abilities. Where Mary Rudge constitutes a model of how to respond to adversity and Hugh cannot help his violence, Miggs (like Simon and Stagg) morally yields to it. The Marchioness of *The Old Curiosity Shop*, much worse treated than Miggs, leaps to joyous humanity at the first opportunity; Guster, subject to fits as well as a nasty mistress in *Bleak House*, more than retains her humanity; Tattycoram, with Miggs's resentments, overcomes them through a wish to be loved in *Little Dorrit*. If such deficiencies as Simon's and Miggs's—fear of which affected Dickens's recollections of the blacking-warehouse period—are arbitrary, they raise questions not about society but about universal justice.

So do the novel's families. If they say anything about that crux of psychological talk about Dickens, the relations between authority and rebelliousness, it is that selfishness lurks in all conditions and always tends to subvert a desirable order. When the figure granted authority by society, the proper guardian, is infected—in Chester's or Willet's home, in London during the Riots—tyranny or chaos results. Even among the Rudges, who occupy a separate symbolic place vaguely related to the nation and mankind, it is clear that once Rudge selfishly rebelled the order was forever broken. Mary helps him through pity or fear, accepting not wifely subordination but religious union with him and their child. If the authority figure—Varden, Haredale, King George—holds firm, Dickens applauds him and helps him check rebellion and restore order. Varden's career in the novel reflects an ambiguity not about the need for authority but about its efficacy in trying circumstances. With the best of intentions, and none of Haredale's deficiencies, Varden still cannot either keep his wife from shrewish folly or control his malevolent servants. He influences his daughter to be good, recognizes Joe Willet's merits, and in general fills all his social and professional roles as he should. Even so, he cannot guarantee order or happiness in the house. What then of the nation under George III? or under Queen Victoria?

Despite his sympathy with its impulses, for Dickens not rebellion but its motives and circumstances call for our judgment. Joe Willet and Edward Chester have good reason, grounded in traditional conceptions of nature and order, to rebel against paternal tyranny. A victim of social injustice and perhaps also of inherited violence, Hugh raises larger questions about man's lot. But Simon, like the Miggs who lusts for him, rebels out of mere envy. Even if Dickens consciously or unconsciously intends us to sympathize with the rebellious Hugh, he surely means us to reject Simon and Miggs. He gives Sir John Chester and Gashford, the rebel devils, mad or helpless figures like Lord George, Hugh, Dennis, and Barnaby to seduce against order, pitiful misfits and not heroes like Adam, Faust, or Ahab. The Riot scenes are a vivid warning to the nation's complacency, but without a good deal of doubletalk we cannot read *Barnaby Rudge* as rebellious outburst.

3

Taking stock as he approached thirty, Dickens chose to aim for a long vacation in America, write a second novel to wind up his magazine, and make that the historical romance

Barnaby Rudge, to which he had years earlier committed himself. Despite occasional lectures about the need for civilizing the poor, the horror of public executions, and the incompetence of government, his motives for these choices were not theories about society or history, but rather impulses generated by a sense of his own present and immediate past.

Problems of class, prominent in Dickens's later evaluations of his situation, he routinely shrugs off in *Barnaby Rudge* by relegating them to the gothic plot. There, Chester is an evil aristocrat combining literary models and a caricature of Lord Chesterfield, and Haredale must disappear with his Warren. Where class division comes closer to Dickens, in Varden's household, he treats it as comedy. Those who survive cheerfully, the Willets, Vardens, Rudges, Edward Chesters, either are or become middle class. Those whom Dickens in later years might have conceived with legitimate class grievances—Miggs, Simon, and Simon's fellow apprentices— are instead gratuitously vicious, whereas the deprived Mary and Barnaby find decent possibilities for living once the pressures of corrupted family relationships and gothic violence have been eased. Even Hugh ends as the victim not mainly of social distinctions but of his father's idiosyncratic villainy. The Carlylean attitude, that abandoned aristocratic duty had left the mass to suffer, may be implied in Hugh's and the mob's aimless resentments, but Platonic feudalism was not Dickens's idea of a cure. Indeed he offers no cure for England except subsiding into a vacation like the one he hoped to take.

For the country (as now within himself), this historical novel desires what Dickens's earlier fiction had implied, not restoration of an idyllic past but evolution to a primordial bourgeois democracy sanctioned by the natural order. Considered merely as a stretch of time, as time played out rather than frozen, the past is no less chaotic than the present for Dickens, as he had vividly shown in *The Old Curiosity*

Shop. The merchandise in the shop itself, Mrs. Jarley's waxworks, and the effigies in the church at the end, all mean no more than the wild fires of Birmingham industry or the current junk in Quilp's warehouse. In *Barnaby Rudge*, as in its predecessors, the past takes on value only when it helps the mind conceive the possibility of harmony.

Different emblems of the long past take on differing significances, some supporting the changeless concerns of the folk or the species, others moving out of the living stream for good. We start in 1775, at the Maypole Inn, named to suggest not Merrie Englande but folk myths of social harmony preceding civilization and transcending time, and return to it to open the second, main section of the novel amid a terrible storm in 1780. After the more horrifying human storm, matured youth revives the Maypole, now freed of its balancing gothic associate the Warren. A symbol of feudal class, the Warren had long ago tempted the murders that culminated in the worst throes of the Riots. Despite some virtues, it is as irrelevant now as its noblest representative, Haredale, who approves of its passing. Unlike Scott and his American followers from Cooper to Faulkner, Dickens does not assign these virtues to an aristocratic code. John Grueby, Haredale, and General Conway have their honorable roots in that soil, but they are no more honorable than the time-free Joe Willet or Gabriel Varden; and that past, the Tory dream, has been rich manure for John Chester, Gashford, and their mad spiritual son Lord George.

One kind of past shines briefly in *Barnaby Rudge*, but only as a mirage, a film before the mind rather than a physical possibility. The small country town to which Mary and Barnaby flee shows us that eternal ideal past, an escape from the problems of life like its predecessors in *Oliver Twist*, *Nicholas Nickleby*, and especially *The Old Curiosity Shop*.

Still, its uneventful flow does nothing for Barnaby, whereas the passing five years absorb Joe and Edward, like Dickens or any other young man shocked into the active world, in work and suffering, in growth from youth to maturity. The virtue of the idyll, then, is its detachment from the changes that constitute life, its ability to enshrine memories of the dead, not its traditions or old habits. When reality intrudes on the innocent mother and son, it easily seduces Barnaby back to " 'the world, the merry world, . . . not solitary places like those you pass your time in, but . . . crowds, and where there's noise and rattle' " (xlvi, 350). However much the dreaming, damaged side of the self must be protected from that chaos, Dickens—as exhausted (or purged) as Barnaby after his resurrection, stored like Barnaby with visions—contains also active, fertile, order-making selves like the optimistic survivors Joe, Edward, and Varden, and the living echoes of Hugh's passion, to move the world along.

For the individual, looking back and around necessarily involved the relations between parents and children, one's private past and present. For Dickens, such observation had to be complicated by the intensity of his own memories of childhood, reflections on his family life in the recent past, current problems with his father, and even his recent battles with the father-aged publisher Bentley. In the world he imagined when he wrote *Oliver Twist*, the old had held power over the young, Mr. Brownlow and Fagin contending for rule; Dickens's contemporaries like Sikes, Nancy, and the Maylies struggled to assert themselves; and the child Oliver represented everyone's dreadful past and limitless future. In *Nicholas Nickleby*, the old Cheerybles and Ralph Nickleby still have great power, but the exploitive father Bray dissolves in death; Squeers, Gride, and Lilyvick, and the silly mother Nickleby are laughed out of the world; and the aspiring young push and shove to significance. In *The Old Curiosity Shop*, the

very old grandfather and very young Nell move into the
eternal ideal together, and after the elimination of villains (the
aging Quilp, the forty-ish Brasses), young couples remain to
live good, ordinary lives. In *Barnaby Rudge*, arbitrary rule and
betrayal, the deliberate misleading of the young by the old, are
(as they had been with Fagin, Ralph Nickleby, and Quilp) the
crimes of which Dickens accuses the fathers. Happily, though
with losses, the young are freed of the troublesome old, of
fathers, as he wanted to be.

Through frequent direct focus on son-father situations in
Barnaby Rudge, of a sort not before prominent in the novels,
Dickens seems deliberately to be courting the question of
heredity. As we might expect from a fantasist resenting
mediocre parents and a job lot of siblings, he was fascinated
by it throughout his career. On February 5, 1839, he had noted
in his diary that Wordsworth's son was "decidedly *lumpish*.
Copyrights need be hereditary, for genius isn't" (*P*, I, 639). To
the time of *Barnaby Rudge* at least, in his fantasy of the world
parents are badly chosen, and need to be replaced. Oliver
Twist is illegitimate. Instead of their own defective parents,
the young Nicklebys and Madeline Bray need the surrogate
paternalism of the Cheerybles, which has already nourished
their nephew Frank Cheeryble. Little Nell's parents are dead,
and her grandfather is a weak incompetent, while Dickens
plucks the jewel of a Marchioness from her dunghill parents
Sally Brass and Quilp.

In *Barnaby Rudge*, Dickens's competing attitudes to
heredity contribute to the superiority of data to theory. Only
Dolly suggests the conventional novelist's genetics, mixing
her mother's coquetry and variable moods with her father's
sturdy integrity. John Chester, the devious, cruel, debt-ridden,
extortionate father, shares nothing with his son Edward but
appearance and nothing with his son Hugh but a gothic
affinity in dreams. Both sons inherit their mothers' putative

characters—mothers dead and never portrayed; both decisively reject their father on Dickens's behalf. Barnaby, child of an angel mother and devil father, brings into the world not inheritances but moral symbols: the mark on his wrist, a chaotic mind, and a face (like his mother's) easily expressing terror, all eruptions of his father's violent act, as well as his mother's openness to love. The visionary capacity—without mind, a rich but uncreative imagination, a chaos needing to be shaped—ties him to both only as it ties him to everyone as bare forked man.

Facing thirty and looking behind and about him, Dickens could wonder at the world of activity in which he had immersed himself and now, matured, pause in awareness that he had his proper work to do. And that is what he projects into his imagined world of sixty years before as he had projected into *Oliver Twist* the sense of glorious arrival from obscurity, into *Nicholas Nickleby* adolescent stumbling through odd jobs and passion toward terminal respectability, and into *The Old Curiosity Shop* a farewell to innocence and welcome to a perplexing world. A similar acceptance ends *Barnaby Rudge* for one side of Dickens, the established paterfamilias and craftsman. With his reformed wife, his daughter Dolly, and his son-in-law Joe, Varden is at the pitch of earned happiness: "there sat the locksmith among all and every these delights, the sun that shone upon them all: the centre of the system: the source of the light, heat, life, and frank enjoyment in the bright household world" (lxxx, 612).

But the Dickens of 1841 is not merely equivalent to the busy locksmith. In *Barnaby Rudge*, Dickens effectively projects himself into both generations, having now achieved adult success among the adults important in the world as he was also undergoing, in his memory and in current life, the complexities of growing as a son. The most conspicuous aspect of the novel's structure, the five-year hiatus, precisely suggests the balancing of maturity. In the young men, all about Dickens's current age in the 1780 second part, he conceives the romance elements to act out or reject and personal decisions to determine a future. Within a kind of composite self, the mad passions, delusions, and resentments of struggling youth work outward and more or less dissipate. In the older men, he explores himself in the professional role primarily, as observer, judge, authority, responsible or irresponsible participant in the lives of others. The older men therefore carry professional implications—generally admonitory—and an internal dialogue on the uses of his gifts, while the younger ones project his progress through time, the pain of his early love, aspects of his character, and the nature of those gifts.

Deeper into the self, Dickens conceives Barnaby, the central imagining self, resurrected after the aching joys and dizzy raptures of fighting and comradeship, and after great human losses, as "more rational," retaining "his love of freedom and interest in all that moved or grew, or had its being in the elements" (lxxxii, 633), and tending a garden and domestic animals. Resurrected because of his innocence, without his wild complement Hugh he will lead no savior-seeking swarms, nor will he suffer the incomprehensible violence of gothic dreams. After the intensity of public display, sentence to death and reprieve, the visionary artist self inhabits the pasture of Chigwell, where Joe and Edward live out their roles as well. Purged by the years and the Riots, the trio of variously mature young men are now restful, their (and Dickens's) fires damped down while the world pauses.

Like Wordsworth looking at his wild-eyed young self in "Tintern Abbey" (also after five years), Dickens feels that the part of him that was Hugh has been paid to the world, perhaps in exchange for more sober, less destructive apprehensions of life. But if Dickens feared loss of creative impulses, at this point they would be of the tendencies toward heedless farce and horror, the raw materials of his sensational success *Pickwick Papers*: a loss here conceived as purging the imagination. With Hugh the riots in the self also carried away Rudge, Chester, Dennis, and Stagg and quenched Lord George, Miggs, and Simon. At least in the world imagined for this novel, these forms of bitter envy and corrosive delusion forever disappear as influences; even aloof Haredale and stupid John Willet no longer stand in the way of maturing youth. Much was to be made of the gentler, compensatory joys remaining in the Vardens, Joe and Dolly Willet, and Edward and Emma Chester as overlays on Mary Rudge and Barnaby, who is after all named for consolation.

In *Barnaby Rudge*, all the ambiguities of Dickens's recent novel-writing years, the exhausting work and great fame (and subjection both to envy and to condescending criticism), the wearing in of his heavy married life complicated by his father's irresponsible raids on his means and sense of decorum, even the rumors of debilitating madness when grief over his sister-in-law's death caused him to miss an installment deadline for No. XV of *Pickwick Papers*, mix with the national ambiguities of riots, demonstrations, and a Tory victory to shape his imagined prospects at thirty. He wrapped them all up in the Gordon Riots, and if he could not quite push that ball through the iron gates of life, he did wring from it meaning by way of the various elements he sensed in himself. Capping, destroying, purging, cleansing, expelling the extremes of his gothic fantasies and familial resentments in the book as the Riots expelled the worst of them personified, he left his surviving projections calmed and productive, his imaginative self chastened and more coherent—as it seemed, more grown up.

Like his own situation, *Barnaby Rudge* offered not clear meaning or order, but a world of promise. The Riots formed a core on which to build the action, but that action meant only that life brings violence, exhaustion, and recuperation. More intensely, the novel's movement records the shock of youth assuming maturity, of sons replacing fathers. Immediately after finishing the novel, Dickens expressed his expectations of new vigor and ambitious achievement. In an "Address Announcing the Termination of 'Master Humphrey's Clock'" dated September 1841, he said that following his trip to America "to satisfy a wish I have long entertained, and long hoped to gratify," he planned a new book "in monthly parts, under the old green cover, in the old size and form, and at the old price." [19] But at thirty he did not expect to sell the same old pleasures at the same old bar like Joe Willet. Matured and made whole, the visionary self would revive and leave the Chigwell garden to cultivate limitless vistas. Like a famous predecessor in the art of welcoming maturity (twitching a mantle blue, not green), he would move on to pastures new.

III. *Martin Chuzzlewit*: Ambiguously Whittington

31 December 1842 - 30 June 1844

After pausing some months in America at thirty and writing up his American notes, Dickens fused what his trip had shown him, what he saw around him in England, and his conception of himself in maturity in *Martin Chuzzlewit*. In its marvelously varied cast, he patterned around himself iridescent mirrors reflecting odd and glittering glimpses of past hopes and current tendencies. Some are farcical, some pathetic, some monitory, some hortatory, all in their self-consciousness ironic.

To judge by the advertisement for the opening installment, his original intentions for the novel were simple, perhaps a return to the youthful bounce of *Pickwick Papers* and *Nicholas Nickleby*. It promises merely Pickwickian fun focused on the title character and his greedy relatives:

THE LIFE AND ADVENTURES OF MARTIN CHUZZLEWIT; His Relatives, Friends, and Enemies. Comprising all His Wills and His Ways; with an Historical Record of What He Did, and What He Didn't: showing, moreover, WHO INHERITED THE FAMILY

PLATE, WHO CAME IN FOR THE SILVER SPOONS, AND WHO FOR THE WOODEN LADLES. The whole forming a Complete Key to the House of Chuzzlewit. (*Examiner*, December 3, 1842, p. 783)

But Pecksniffian England and the American trip, with its time for reflecting on his life, extended the tone and substance. After the opening history of the Chuzzlewits as opportunists through time (echoing Fielding on Jonathan Wild's antecedents), he quickly abandoned the bantering tone.

In *Barnaby Rudge*, Dickens had learned to shape his form around a central obstacle. Here, freed of the constraint and the solemnity of a historical event, he could conceive first the English Pecksniff and then the American Eden, both resident in himself as in us, blocking the road of his projected contemporaries with more baleful inevitability than the Gordon Riots had their ancestors'. These beasts across his path arrest his imagination's first clear, steady, and precise perception of the large danger most persistently before it, illusory goals and their deluded pursuit: great expectations.

Anticipation of the American trip no doubt stimulated fantasies of a tonic revival at thirty to outdo Barnaby's resurrection, though not so simply as *American Notes* or the Martin and Mark sequences in the novel suggest. According to an American who wrote in 1867 of visiting Dickens in 1841, his study was full of books on America and he conversed knowledgeably about American writings.[20] Like any alert Englishman of the day, and more than most, he would have had cause for ambivalence in the months he debated the question of going. There were wonders to be seen, in the famous natural phenomena and social institutions of the great, open experiment in democracy. But he knew that some Americans, like some American mountain passes and rivers, were notoriously untrustworthy, as he hinted in his editorial introduction to *Bentley's Miscellany* (I, 3) by thanking the Americans for reprinting and disseminating his *Sketches* all over their nation "without charging me anything at all."

Under his editorship, *Bentley's* published a fair amount of material relating to America, as did other general-interest magazines: straight travel pieces by English writers, descriptions of life in particular areas, essays or stories commissioned from Americans like Cooper, and comic exaggerations of Yankee habits and characters. Volume 4 (July-December 1838), for example, contains in July and August pieces on the mid-Atlantic states and upstate New York and a series on "Uncle Sam's Peculiarities. A Journey from New York to Philadelphia and Back"; in September, another on "Uncle Sam's Peculiarities" (pp. 294-300) and "Wild Scenes among the Appalachians" (pp. 306-12); in October, "American Lions" (pp. 405-12), on Washington Irving, Fenimore Cooper, and a pride of politicians; in November, "The Ghost-Riders. A legend of the Great American Desert" (pp. 471-82); and in December, "Uncle Sam's Peculiarities. American Boarding Houses" (pp. 581-90)—this last a subject of endless fun for Dickens in both *American Notes* and *Martin Chuzzlewit*.

Though like any sanguine visitor he would have discounted much as prejudice, he knew about the darker side of American life from such books as Mrs. Trollope's *Domestic Manners of the Americans* and Captain Basil Hall's *Travels in North America*. But if reading about the comic and eccentric aspects of the society prepared him to tolerate pigs in the streets, tobacco spittle on the Senate floor, and personal discomforts while traveling, it did not lighten the penalties of celebrity and the bitter attacks on his campaign for international copyright—which he plausibly blamed on chauvinism and greed—to say nothing of slavery. With all his forewarnings and indeed with all his pleasure in the many good things and people he met, he necessarily ended, as his whole life's pattern required, disappointed as well.

Coming to cadge unconsidered trifles at the Pecksniff house, the swindler Montague Tigg tells *Martin Chuzzlewit*'s two most obvious Dickens projections, young Martin and Tom Pinch, " 'You are a pair of Whittingtons, gents, without the cat' "(vii,101). Still at fifty, from an assured eminence, Dickens was to describe himself precisely at the time of *Martin Chuzzlewit* as "A Young Man from the Country," the generic Whittington whose unexpected reward in the metropolis for writing *American Notes* was savage attacks (*AYR*, March 1, 1862). As the folk myth of the poor country boy rising to wealth and honor in the metropolis led Dickens's contemporaries to form a Whittington Society complete with dinners and awards, so it permeated his characters' psychological experiences as it had Dickens's own. Beginning with Nicholas Nickleby if not Oliver Twist, Dickens liked to play his projections ruefully against the myth, as he does repeatedly with Walter Gay, the jeune premier of the next novel, *Dombey and Son*. Like *Great Expectations*, *Martin Chuzzlewit* explodes the myth with half painful comedy.

As a young journalist with the usual scornful response to politics, as a liberal with unsatisfied hopes of reform, as a lover rejected by his first grand love, as a husband enfolded in domestic routine, as a son and brother with old resentments and recent wounds, as an erstwhile sensational success immediately subjected to exploitation, he had sufficient examples of the uncertainty and insubstantiality of rewards. But he had kept expecting wonders. Like most of the characters deluded or fooled in his novels, Dickens had built his castles in the air long before the mirage of renewing vitality in the American cauldron.

If this theme, great expectations mocked, gained distinctness from his time in America and from the England he left and returned to, he knew its pains from childhood. Like Jonathan Swift, who in his sixties wrote a friend that losing a fish off his hook as "a little boy . . . vexeth me to this very day, and I believe it was the type of all my future disappointments,"[21] Dickens remembered all his life an early disappointment of the sort all children have and most forget. In "New Year's Day," a piece in *Household Words* of January 1, 1859, he recalled as a child being taken to Soho Square to buy a toy, selecting a Harlequin's wand, and never managing to work magic with it: "The failure of this wand is my first very memorable association with a New Year's Day."

1

As in *Barnaby Rudge*, among the range of faces in the mirror the young men of approximately Dickens's age in *Martin Chuzzlewit* most obviously reflect himself. But none of them play merely conventional roles. Rather, through Tom, young Martin, Mark, and Jonas, he offers varieties of complex youthful selves, who face opposing selves in the middle-aged Pecksniff and Tigg and the aged, departing sources of character models and selfish desires, the old Chuzzlewits. The conventional gentleman Edward Chester has become two more persuasively imagined characters, the structurally handy and sometimes even animated John Westlock, and the changing, central projection Martin. Though with some loss of poignancy, Joe Willet has picked up wit and originality as Mark Tapley. If Jonas Chuzzlewit lacks the attractive qualities of the Maypole's Hugh, he retains the individuality and adds a social context that helps universalize his brutally rebellious side. And Tom Pinch grows into aspects of Barnaby's function more personally appropriate to Dickens and more easily assimilated to the reader.

Of these, young Martin, the nominal hero, is most a generic everyman and most immediately Dickens's parallel, a retrospect on the process of growing to manhood begun in the child Oliver Twist, continued in the late adolescent Nicholas Nickleby, and touched on in Joe Willet. At twenty-five, about the age when Dickens started life as a newly famous novelist with *Pickwick Papers* and a new family man with his first child, Martin is old for a beginning Whittington. But as Dickens had implied in *Barnaby Rudge*, he was imagining his own maturity to have begun at that point. As if to emphasize this identification, for Martin's journey to London after his expulsion from Pecksniff's, Dickens adds the pathos suitable to the abandoned of any age, a reawakening of the twelve-year-old's sensations in the blacking warehouse (ch. xiii). Moreover, the novel's pattern assumes a new seriousness as an image of life, despite the comedy. As against *Nicholas Nickleby*, where the adventuring hero always finds a culture he can swim in—a theatrical troupe needing a plagiarist familiar with French, upwardly mobile customers for cheap French lessons, philanthropic businessmen to sponsor surrogate sons—*Martin Chuzzlewit*'s world presents struggling humanity with Peer Gynt's Boyg: " 'What am I to do?' " Martin asks his beloved Mary, if not try America (xiv, 236).

Through authorial comments and flashes of self-observation by Martin—even when he congratulates himself on "what a winning fellow he must be to have made such an impression on Tom" (xiii, 214)—Dickens moves the ironic self-vision of his letters into the character of the conventionally adventurous youth. In the course of leading Martin to manhood and self-knowledge, Dickens undertakes to expose his deluded vanity—a danger specially threatening adolescents and authors—first to us and then to him. But it is ambitious, pitiable, hopeful, self-aggrandizing rather than destructive of others: "Poor Martin! for ever building castles in the air. For ever, in his very selfishness, forgetful of all but his own teeming hopes and sanguine plans" (xxi, 350-51). On the way to America, where Martin will repeat a number of Dickens's ludicrous experiences and share his disillusion with the noble political experiment, Martin's injured sensitivity suggests a recollection of the child's mood in the blacking warehouse or a reflection on it. Chided on the ship for not stirring, he also hints at possibilities for change new in a Dickens projection: " 'I lie here because I don't wish to be recognised in the better days to which I aspire, by any purse-proud citizen, as the man who came over with him among the steerage passengers. I lie here, because I wish to conceal my circumstances and myself, and not to arrive in a new world badged and ticketed as an utterly poverty-stricken man. If I could have afforded a passage in the after-cabin, I should have held up my head with the rest. As I couldn't, I hide it' " (xv, 252).

What Martin finds in Eden, essential America as universal deception, serves with equal appropriateness as the heart of darkness everyone who grows into humanity must face within himself. Like Pecksniff for all or the Anglo-Bengalee Insurance swindle for Jonas, this is the culmination of the falsities imposed from within and without, the thing itself, the spirit of negation clothed in matter, to which devils like the American Zephaniah Scadder and the English Montague Tigg sacrifice hopeful men and women. Sensing the approach of death in this trial, Martin asks what he has done to deserve " 'this heavy fate?' 'Why sir,' returned Mark, 'for the matter of that, ev'rybody as is here might say the same thing; many of 'em with better reason p'raps than you or me' " (xxiii, 380). Here, Martin faces the primordial swamp which—when he manages to survive—will redeem him, as the already redeemed Mark rises from it confirmed in his faith. And when he does survive, having paid the dues demanded by grand material expectations, he seizes his redemption by nursing

Mark. Nearly mortal illness and recovery had been regular
plot devices for Dickens from *Oliver Twist* on, I would think
as versions of the psychological deaths he associated with the
blacking-warehouse days and the rejection by Maria. But not
before, not even in Dick Swiveller's nursing in illness by the
Marchioness in *The Old Curiosity Shop* and his resurrection
with love for her, had Dickens made the condition both
universally purgative and morally determining.

Concentrating and intensifying his own disillusionment
with America in the young adventuring self, Dickens also
conceived renewed energies with which to take up again the
challenge of England. To his virtuous or potentially virtuous
projections, disillusionment from the great expectations brings
salutary self-evaluation and suffering, growth, animation,
forgiveness, and reconciliation: the only way for a young
Martin or an old Martin to participate in a happy ending.
Returned as a chastened Whittington, having learned of his
normality rather than his uniqueness—though Dickens can't
forbear having his design for a school win the prize—Martin
has the secure love of his Mary and can study virtue in her and
Tom. Mocked in arrogance and pitied in distress, the Martin
side of Dickens is to live a fulfilled, respectable, unexciting
life with no great psychological gains or losses to anticipate.

But Mark Tapley immediately (as Martin's ironic double)
and the other young men in the novel as they develop show us
other sides of Dickens. As a projection, Mark has the
irreverent wit that Dickens had poured through Sam Weller,
the shipboard nursing duties Dickens had found himself
performing for his wife and her maid on his own voyage to
America, and Dickens's talent for organizing, for getting
things done. Threatened by a murderous bully in Eden for
exposing American hypocrisy, but speaking out nevertheless
as he dangerously speaks out elsewhere, Mark recalls
Dickens, insulted and threatened by the American press,

assuring an American correspondent on October 15, 1842, that "as I have never been deterred by hopes of promotion or visions of greatness, from pointing out abuses at home, so no amount of popular breath shall blow me from my purpose, if I see fit to point out what in my judgment are abuses abroad. And if my being an honest man, bring down caprice, and weathercock fickleness, and the falsest kind of insult on my head, what matters it to me—or to you—or to any man who is worth the name, and, being right, can look down on the crowd, and whistle while they hiss?" (*P*, III, 345).

Mark seeks not secure status but a challenge—the continuous stimulation of the dangerous and new—and in expecting the unimaginable, like Johnson's Rasselas, he must be continually disappointed. However, he has the good sense to know how well he has triumphed over the temptation to give up, having passed his extreme test: serving, nursing, and curing a selfish master and remaining cheerful while himself in deadly peril. He knows that he can now deal with life's worst, and he can therefore accept the best available to him: " 'Then all my hopeful wisions bein crushed, . . . I abandons myself to despair,' " and he decides to settle for contentment with Mrs. Lupin (xlviii, 734). Embodying Dickens's good-humored irony at his own expense, Mark (like Martin) embodies also Dickens's affirmation of cheerfulness in ordinary life, a reassurance that a home in England with Catherine, even if it lacks wonder, need not be as confining to the imagination and the spirit as Rasselas's Happy Valley. Reflected in this mirror, Dickens with his Catherine, like Mark and Mrs. Lupin or Joe Willet and Dolly, could go on creatively, surrounded by children, serving the wayfarer with healthy nourishment, putting up with whiffs of unfulfillment as the way of the world.

If Martin and Mark settle for the ordinary expectations—after Whittingtonian hopes and heroic yearnings—the two other main young men do not. "Conscious that there was nothing in his person, conduct, character, or accomplishments, to command respect," Jonas Chuzzlewit—the most unattractive side of the ambitious self and the one most discussed by psychological critics of *Martin Chuzzlewit*— "was greedy of power, and was, in his heart, as much a tyrant as any laurelled conqueror on record" (xxviii, 448). The tyranny we are shown in dealings with weaker people than himself, notably his father's old clerk Chuffey and Mercy Pecksniff. In Jonas's betrayal of Charity Pecksniff, Dickens combines vengeful meanness with Jingle-like impudence, a squabble between devils in the *Inferno*. But his treatment of her sister Mercy emanates from other elements in Dickens, most consciously the wryly perceived bossiness that led him to sign a recent letter (July 31, 1842) "Bully and Meek" for himself and Catherine. As Dickens wrote his friend Angela Burdett-Coutts on November 12, 1842, he was now "plotting and contriving a new book" and therefore "so horribly cross and surly, that the boldest fly at my approach" (*P*, III, 367).

Jonas's early resentments of his wife suggest lingering memories of irritations in Dickens's own courtships, first of Maria and then of Catherine. To Maria he had written on March 18, 1833, an injured youth bragging of his constancy in the face of provocation: "Under kindness and encouragement one day and a total change of conduct the next I have ever been the same. I have ever acted without reserve" (*P*, I, 17). Writing to Catherine after three weeks of engagement, he had sternly reprimanded similar behavior: "The sudden and uncalled-for coldness with which you treated me just before I left last night, both surprised and deeply hurt me. . . . If you knew [my feelings] you could more readily understand the extent of the pain so easily inflicted, but so difficult to be forgotten" (*P*, I, 61-62). The revenge Jonas exacts has been well noted as Dickens's revenge on Maria.[22] In showing Merry as changed for the better by her suffering, Dickens carries the possibilities of his own self-pleasing fantasy, of a triumph as Petruchio over Kate as guardian and not merely tyrant, a step further.

When Tigg and his Anglo-Bengalee gang went fishing in the pond of London businessmen, Jonas took the lure first because there was money to be made as a partner; second, he could show his superiority to the suckers; and "Thirdly, it involved much outward show of homage and distinction; a Board being an awful institution in its own sphere, and a Director a mighty man" (xxviii, 448). Evaluating his own recent adulation in America as well as the public dinners at home, through Jonas Dickens examines not the achievement of the great expectations but their public acknowledgment: what it means to be a celebrity, a Whittington who has arrived. Somewhere in the puzzle of his private personality a shy man who would not read *The Chimes* before strangers and was to burn his papers to keep them from a snooping public,[23] Dickens was also fascinated and often pleased by his prominence and public esteem from the time of *Pickwick*. Currently and throughout his life he was a frequent speaker at large dinners for charities, he avowedly promoted the cheap editions of his works to influence his readers and elicit their affection, and when he performed his Readings ostensibly for money during his last dozen years, he was at least as much motivated by the universal admiration and the power over his audiences. Through Jonas, he registers this pleasure as well as the ironic self's judgment on its value.

Dickens's acute self-consciousness intensified a favorite image in the Jonas plot, the condition of being seen, witnessed, spied on, first notable with Oliver Twist and Bill Sikes, haunting in "the gaunt eyes in the shutters staring" at the dead Nemo and the heroic finger pointing to the dead

Tulkinghorn of *Bleak House*, deadly in Riderhood's surveillance of Headstone in *Our Mutual Friend*. Always trying to hide his true self and adopt an uncongenial one—as lover, good son, jolly companion—always fearful of slander, Jonas provokes investigation. His career and personality, therefore, spawn the detective Nadgett, the old man "born to be a secret" (xxvii, 446), a conscience that watches over him day and night. His world teems with watchers who keep finding evidence of plans against his father's life, as if Dickens were skirmishing with his own hateful fantasies: in Jonas's confidences to the Pecksniffs in the coach, in his dinner-table mutterings, in Chuffey's warnings of woe, in Lewsome's damning testimony. Looking up from a search for his father's will, Jonas meets the eyes of Pecksniff on the other side of the office transom. Unaware that Tigg and Crimp know of his earlier plan to insure his wife's life, he confirms his viciousness before their watchful eyes at a dinner party. When he hustles her on board a steamer, planning flight or murder or both, the eyes of Tom, Sairey, Nadgett, and Tigg are on him. He might just as well have sought privacy, like Dickens, on an American train or in an American hotel.

At the critical time, from the coach ride of Jonas, Tigg, and Young Bailey until Jonas returns to the "dark room he had left shut up at home" (xlvii, 723), Dickens inhabits the mind of this projection set off before the world as its great antagonist, anticipating and following violent crime with intense sensitivity, as he had done with Sikes, Fagin, Ralph Nickleby, and the Gordon Rioters. For the unredeemable like Jonas, disillusion leads to bitterness, anomie, and rage, psychological states Dickens always recognized with fascination, explored in *Barnaby Rudge*, and made a point of studying first as a reporter in Newgate and later in other English and American prisons. Jonas is the internal blackness, the American Eden that Dickens glimpsed in himself at moments throughout his life and currently when he raged at the slanders in American newspapers: a widely disseminated forged letter attributed to him, he wrote to Longfellow on September 28, 1842, "exasperated me (I am of rather a fierce turn, at times) very much; and I walked about for a week or two, with a vague desire to take somebody by the throat and shake him" (*P*, III, 334).

Having had time to puzzle over his own nature with much greater subtlety here than in his earlier fiction, Dickens raises serious questions about early character formation and change, with a heavy stress on environmental rather than genetic influence. No one of importance has a mother in the novel, for example, but Dickens makes nothing of that. More definitely than the Nickleby brothers, the old Chuzzlewits are seen as having affected the characters of their young heirs by the expression of their own natures, their behavior at home. In his Preface to the Cheap Edition of the novel, Dickens says of Jonas that because of "his early education, and . . . the precept and example always before him, [which] engender and develop the vices that make him odious. . . . I claim him as the legitimate issue of the father upon whom those vices are seen to recoil" (846). Even Anthony's contrition—at about the time Dickens was imaginatively wallowing in the reform of Scrooge—fails to lighten the atmosphere of anger and guilt in which the son moves, an atmosphere shared with Dickens's own thoughts about a father pressing on him while he was writing the novel: to his friend and financial advisor Mitton he wrote on February 20, 1843, "The thought of him besets me, night and day; and I really do not know what is to be done with him. It is quite clear that the more we do, the more outrageous and audacious he becomes" (*P*, III, 444).

Still, Dickens won't insist that Jonas had been helplessly conditioned to selfishness, no doubt because his own

exertions to counter temperamental affinities with his father
led him to advocate resistance. He has thought about
hereditary and environmental factors more than in past
fictions, but still finds reality—and his wish for the freedom
not to resemble his family—too powerful for neat patterns.
Young Martin starts with and retains "a frank and generous
nature" (xxxiii, 524), on which his grandfather at first spread a
veneer of selfishness, though Dickens never tells us how the
intermediate figure—the son of one Martin and father of the
other—escaped the selfishness or acquired the generosity. The
two Pecksniff girls, raised by one monster of selfish
hypocrisy, seem equally vicious up to Merry's marriage, and
yet the older responds venomously to adversity while the
younger is redeemed by it. Jonas's evil far exceeds both the
precepts and practice of his father—whose lessons are mean
but who retains a tincture of humanity to which Chuffey's
love bears witness—and again we can't tell why.

Even from the lowest, most helpless moral environment,
Dickens had always been persuaded that a Nancy might
spring alongside a number of Bill Sikeses, if she had the spark
of goodness and the will. He never says that these qualities are
universal at birth, and even in some of his earlier devils, like
Quilp, he does not try to explain away evil as caused by
environment. By the time of *Martin Chuzzlewit*, he was
becoming more and more certain that the spark and the will
(both of which he recognized in his own triumph), crucial to
civilized humanity, were liable to early extinction in some
temperaments. And a great reason for that extinction, Dickens
says, is bad education. He had hammered away at education
from the beginning of his career in the *Sketches*, presumably
motivated by fears from his Warren's Blacking days that he
would be denied the training by which to improve himself.[24]
Recently, he had delighted in the achievement of education for
all in the famous literacy and intellectual aspirations of the

Lowell, Massachusetts, factory girls (*American Notes*, ch. iv); and he praised their employers and the state for dealing honorably by their wards, as he was to reprobate the attitudes of both at home in his next novel, *Dombey and Son*. Now, more than ever persuaded of education as a national priority, he was stressing its importance in speeches in Manchester and Birmingham while working on the novel (as reported in the *Examiner*, October 14, 1843, and March 9, 1844).

Significantly, Dickens at this stage does not make class a major environmental obstacle in the way of any important projection. As his Memoir was to imply, and as Martin shows on the ship, he knew the Englishman's horrible fear of sinking; but he did not now imagine himself as having risen. Among the major projections, only Jonas in his gullibility, and partly in his envious rage, hints at class striving. Aristocracy is merely irrelevant. Snobbery remains, but only as a joke on both Americans and Englishmen, a delusion of superiority in America where equality was the slogan and in England a crude emblem of high living and power to dazzle Jonas, Chevy Slyme, and other suckers. Dickens had never respected the upper classes as a separate breed, and now as their casual associate at a self-sufficient thirty-one he was warning himself not to take them seriously.

Through the Jonas-Anthony plot, Dickens also comments on the more central and more universal relations of the two Martins, the established independent power and the arriving ward. With new vigor and range, Dickens can inhabit both. As the owner of riches he must soon relinquish, old Martin is the self-conscious personification of great expectations, both for his grandson and for all the family hangers-on: a condition Dickens had experienced early with the phenomenal success of *Pickwick*. In that capacity, old Martin is primarily aware of stimulating evil desires: "'I have been . . . a lighted torch in peaceful homes, kindling up all the bad gases and vapours in their moral atmosphere' " (iii, 40). From the conversations of Brownlow and Grimwig in *Oliver Twist* to Boffin's troubles in *Our Mutual Friend*, Dickens was sensitive to the moral danger a prominent man faeed among an uncertain mixture of the needy and the predatory. As recently as *American Notes*, he had played with the fantasy of wealth and depredation, imagining old men so sick of rapacious relatives that they turned philanthropists, and by leaving money to worthy institutions "in pure spite helped to do a great deal of good, at the cost of an immense amount of evil passion and misery" (iii, 29). In the midst of the novel, the pressure on him from his brother Alfred and his father grew intolerable. "He, and all of them, look upon me as something to be plucked and torn to pieces for their advantage," he wrote Mitton on September 28, 1843. "They have no idea of, and no care for, my existence in any other light. My soul sickens at the thought of them. . . . Nothing makes me so wretched, or so unfit for what I have to do, as these things. They are so entirely beyond my own controul, so far out of my reach, such a drag-chain on my life, that for the time they utterly dispirit me, and weight me down" (*P*, III, 575-76).

Forced to disguise himself in feebleness to sift the expecters, old Martin acts like Dickens digging beneath British and American hypocrisy, or like the novelist generally probing mankind for the truth. Like other good people in the novel, and presumably like the Dickens who wrote *A Christmas Carol* concurrently, old Martin finds the principles of decency still alive. Purged by intimacy with the extreme of hypocrisy in Pecksniff and the extreme of integrity in Tom Pinch—like Dante redeemed by crawling over the devil's body as he strove toward eventual radiance—he undergoes a parallel conversion from selfishness with his grandson. By the end, he admits his error in assuming universal corruption—an error that had made miserable his brother and double

Anthony—recovering the hope that the virtuous young in the novel retain after their great travail. As Dickens reaffirms and accepts his current domestic world, maturity, and his sometimes burdensome responsibilities, old Martin moves (like Scrooge) right around from bitterness to altruism—defined as using his money to serve his wards.

In the plot involving Jonas as another sort of son to another sort of father, Tigg, Dickens develops a comment on a devastating central familial issue in the novel, Tom's discovery of Pecksniff's falsity. Although most of the *Martin Chuzzlewit* characters share in Dickens's pain over exploded expectations, the world-weary Tigg, aged somewhere between Charles and John Dickens, has no hopes to be emptied beyond the enjoyment of a few sensual pleasures. Ironically poking fun at the sides of Dickens that delighted in showy dinners and high living, as well as at his facility in designing schemes (plots) and at his recurrent temptation to decamp, he is also the John Chester devilish side that must be repudiated. His alienation—as the hated sole outsider at the Chuzzlewit family conference of predators at the beginning and the exploiter of any gull whom he can identify—marks him as the cold, non-human observer, amiable in manner but a devil nonetheless. Insouciant, resilient, and a quintessentially bad guardian (of the company's subscribers) like John Dickens, he agrees with Jonas that the insurance scheme must crash when the demands on it come with full force—when numbers of insured people die—but we know that he expects to run off laughing at the heirs, fleeing the country like Dickens's embezzler grandfather.[25] His delusion, that no one can really take the world seriously enough to harm him, that he will be able to ride out the storms of the swindled and fool governmental and universal justice, dies under Jonas's bludgeon. And having Jonas commit the crime, on a side of Dickens recalling John Dickens, ties the parricidal Jonas more tightly to the darkest element of Dickens's fantasies.

Tigg's other Whittington, Tom Pinch, develops the greatest individuality in the novel, sharing its concluding emotional charge only with Jonas. They are the book's poles of selfishness and selflessness, creativity and destructiveness, love and hatred, in their (and Dickens's) generation. Tom is the one Jonas hates, not young Martin, and the two confront each other like no other opponents but Pecksniff and old Martin, or Pecksniff and Tom. Dickens has them fight physically; drags Tom from a casual stroll to carry the message that frustrates Jonas's sinister scheme on the boat; and plays Jonas's widow Merry before us as a plausible prospective wife for Tom, conspicuously *not* making the match. Dickens might well enjoy imagining a Maria-Beadnell-type attracted to his projection, but not before the end of *Great Expectations* does he have an impassioned projection marry a widow. Serious surrogates for Dickens get virgins or no one.

Tom's tie to Dickens comes early, and lasts. We learn right away that Tom's grandmother was a "gentleman's housekeeper" (ii, 22), just like Dickens's. As Dickens then believed his family had been freed from prison (and perhaps he from the blacking warehouse) through her bequest to his father, so Tom tells John Westlock that "'my poor father was of no consequence, nor my mother either. . . . we both became a charge upon the savings of that good old grandmother I used to tell you of'" (xxxix, 608). A psychologically youthful if balding thirty-four when the story begins to Dickens's imminent thirty-one, he contemplates sharing Westlock's apartment "in Furnival's Inn, High Holborn" (xxxvi, 564), Dickens's old bachelor lodgings.

In presenting Tom as gullible with respect to his hypocritical surrogate father Pecksniff and in treating him on his visit to Salisbury with urbane condescension, Dickens compounds the kindly irony appropriate to an adult looking back on his childhood self. But he does not make Tom simpleminded. As Dickens now understands the world, not Jonas but Pecksniff is the greatest danger: not brutal, overt selfish ill will, but hypocrisy so great that the intelligent self Tom could be taken in and that even an innocently altruistic Tom must in time see. Where the devil Tigg preys openly on the avarice and pride of the universal character, the devil Pecksniff betrays the best side of us, Tom, for he dresses himself in the appearance of its proper object, the good. Externally the world's false face, he embodies also the greatest internal danger, delusion—the wish for self-pleasing creations to exist. He is the most dangerous of all the devils, for when successful he dehumanizes his victims by manipulating their wills and even when he fails—is exposed—he can lead them to despair and isolation. Expressing a basic moral health, Tom can survive this discovery of evil in the father and the self, as the sturdy adventuring Martin and Mark can survive Eden.

Tom's shock into reality through the exposure of Pecksniff comes at a reasonably climactic time, a bit more than half way through the book (Installment XII), between stages of Martin's disillusionment in America. The explosion of Tom's great delusion about a kind of father (reliving the child Dickens's shock in the Marshalsea-Warren's Blacking episode over his father's fall) could shake his whole world, as Willy and Biff Loman's audience realized in our century: "It was not that Pecksniff: Tom's Pecksniff: had ceased to exist, but that he never had existed" (xxxi, 491). Conversing with Cherry soon after, Tom senses the discovery of evil: "An uneasy thought entered Tom's head; a shadowy misgiving that the altered relations between himself and Pecksniff, were somehow to involve an altered knowledge on his part of other people, and were to give him an insight into much of which he had had no previous suspicion" (xxxvii, 580). For Tom,

Pecksniff had been a moral ideal, an assurance that mature, active virtue succeeds in the world, and his exposure carries the discovery of evil.

For whatever it is worth, Pecksniff's exposure before Tom, deriving from the paternal figure's gross behavior to a beautiful woman for whom Tom has an idealized love, has the emotional weight of a classic Oedipal crisis: as if the parental differences first over whether young Charles should go to work in the blacking warehouse and then over his returning to it after the family's discharge from the Marshalsea were classically sexual. But only the conflict has this characteristic, not its resolution—neither gets the woman, and the father's defeat comes at the hands of the grandfatherly guardian. Still, besides identifying Tom with Dickens's critically and artistically important, powerful sense of his childhood self, the situation identifies the woman, Mary Graham, not only with his dead young sister-in-law Mary Hogarth but also with Dickens's image of his mother up to the crisis. If this is so, it seems to help explain Dickens's long delight in dreams of Mary Hogarth as a version of his early mother, which ended in the later 1840s, when he was reconciled with his parents. After the disillusionment at twelve, that image of his young mother was part of a past, alive only in the mind, for as his Memoir says he never could forget his mother's wish to deprive him of an education and a future. What Dickens does with Tom's love of Mary Graham suggests that the ideal of unchanging young womanhood, from Oliver Twist's young mother and Rose Maylie on, memorializes the loss of the Elizabeth Dickens of her son's innocence, to be replaced by a series of foolish or peremptory mothers, beginning with Mrs. Nickleby, after he discovered evil.

As against the brilliant succession of two-dimensional American counterparts culminating in the literally two-faced priest of Eden, Zephaniah Scadder, the projection Pecksniff takes on rich emotional emanations from Dickens. He is a kind of artist, as the bachelors' lyrics at Todgers's party describe him (xi, 188), an architect who (like a novelist) copies life and organizes patterns. Cheered by the crowd for the design he has stolen from young Martin, he stands triumphant in his profession (xxxv, 554), a grotesque joke on the nation's foremost novelist Dickens. Willing to chance misconstruction of his noble motives, as he assures old Martin, Pecksniff projects Dickens's ironic glance at the figure he had made in American newspapers. When the Chuzzlewit parasites break up their conference at Pecksniff's house by attacking him, his consolation—like Dickens's in the face of American displeasure with *American Notes* —is that they have all hated him completely before, and he them, so there's nothing lost in any direction (iv, 62). The suspicious side of the self conceiving others as selfish, greedy, and profiteering, and well pleased to point this out to them, he nicely shares energies with the novelist as occasional satirist. Still, like Dickens answering American objections, he complains that old Martin's test has been a trap: " 'To have been deceived, implies a trusting nature. Mine is a trusting nature. . . . There is hardly any person present, Mr. Chuzzlewit,' said Pecksniff, 'by whom I have *not* been deceived' " (lii, 807).

The incurably self-centered are incurably deluded, like Pecksniff, though unlike him the others court desperation. Chevy Slyme and young Moddle, and the tribe of Chuzzlewit parasites, always absurdly expecting what they cannot earn, always go back to that expectation, hopeless and unlovable. Shams and snobs—like Ruth Pinch's employers, "the wealthiest brass and copper founder's family known to mankind" (ix, 135), and the American general shocked to find in his society a man who crossed in steerage—betray their smallness, constantly encountering the barrenness of their egos. Always scratching their open sore, American jingoes must expose their wilful delusion every time they profess high ideals, as happens to the Watertoast Association (no exaggeration, as Dickens insisted, of the actual Brandywine Emmet Association reported on in the *Times* of July 7, 1843), when its idol Daniel O'Connell attacks slavery. Even the resilient Sairey Gamp, a less pernicious cynical parallel to Tigg, always to be revived by alcohol and a good bit of cucumber in this wale of sorrow, needs her comforting invention Mrs. Harris and faces deflation by worse cynics who " 'don't believe there's no sich a person!' " (xlix, 752).

For their part, some of the good female characters have consciously made their adjustments from romantic or other delusions, usually after deprivation. Mercy Pecksniff Chuzzlewit, the only woman to undergo the process of painful disillusionment like the men, purged by her marriage, will dispense charity all her life, rich enough now to emulate Dickens's Miss Coutts in her smaller sphere. Mrs. Todgers, who had learned her disillusioning lesson long ago, had stayed enough beyond cynicism to exercise rare, gratuitous charity. Although Pecksniff calls her double-faced because she must lie for mere weekly room-and-board rates of eighteen shillings to survive, cajoling one boarder, deceiving another, scrimping in wages and provisions, "gazing at the sisters, with affection beaming in one eye, and calculation shining out of the other" (viii, 127), Dickens makes clear that her sins are venial and her virtue deep. Mrs. Lupin, widowed, had earned the responsible Mark, and with him could humanely participate in society after abandoning fantasy: dispensing charity and tolerance, maintaining hope without great expectations.

The two ingenues, more objects of desire than projections, have been chastened in another important way, as dependents in youth, protected only by integrity. Now, as wives of genteel, active men, Ruth Pinch and Mary Graham not only inspire their husbands and prove ties to the future but are themselves sources of charity. Ruth, from the first references a universally responsive female symbol (like the subject of Browning's recent "My Last Duchess"), reflected you in her eyes as "such a capital miniature of yourself, representing you as such a restless, flashing, eager, brilliant little fellow" (xxxix, 616)—a Dickens, in fact. Mary Graham, easily passing Pecksniff's test of her integrity, always faithful to Martin and rewarded by a matronly future with his reformed self, remains for Tom and Dickens the memory of the ideal, the novel's guarantee of meaning.

Through his variety of positive projections, primarily the young men Martin, Mark, John, and with important qualification Tom, Dickens imagined himself going through the pain of disillusion in this Pecksniffian world and moving toward realistic accommodation. Tom, the chief projection by the end, has indeed had the practical satisfaction of cataloguing and shelving thousands of books, putting a so-far chaotic curiosity shop into a system to make sense of human life—Dickens's central undertaking as novelist and man—to furnish what the work-place walls cannot, "wanting language to relate the histories of the dim, dismal rooms" (xl, 618). But instead of joyful fulfillment in marriage, his reward is dwelling mentally with the changeless, even serenity of his music in the novel's coda.

For Tom, the loss of Pecksniff is a painful expulsion from a false eden; but unlike Martin, who replaces great expectations with ultimately hopeful realistic prospects, he finds that an incorruptible ideal suits him more. The arbitrary, such as the embodied ideal's previous commitment of her love to Martin, cannot now hurt him, for merely knowing her affirms the existence of meaning in the world. As he tells Ruth, he has learned to retain his love for various good people, beginning with Ruth herself, without fear of delusive selfishness: " 'The world about me, is there less good in that? Are my words to be harsh and my looks to be sour, and is my heart to grow cold, because there has fallen in my way a good and beautiful creature, who but for the selfish regret that I cannot call her my own, would, like all other good and beautiful creatures, make me happier and better!' " (l, 764). But Dickens never has him consider the other men's kind of fulfillment, a practical, worthy, traditional future available through the newly worthy Merry PEcksniff. Despite Tom's disclaimer, he himself remains a romance, the self that does not settle for compromise and the ordinary, the self for whom there is no earthly completion: the self projected by a yearning for grander requital than good work, Catherine Dickens, and domesticity.

2

The pattern Dickens saw in himself as a representative individual he also saw in the nation (and for that matter in humanity), hence the greater focus than ever before on *Martin Chuzzlewit*'s revealing it in both. The first chapter romps through time and space, leading the Chuzzlewits from Adam and Eve to the present; and though there he stresses the family's opportunism, in the actual novel he ranges morally from Pecksniff, Jonas, and Tigg through the redeemable Martin and Merry and the pure Tom and Mary, sketching a wide, busy human spectrum. But not a wide one socially. Concerned to show an actual world in which most people live, and I would guess reacting against the artificial conventions of his last novel, he devotes no imaginative energy to Sir Mulberry Hawks or Sir John Chesters.

Within his recreated realistic society, he centered the national delusions generally in what he saw as business-as-usual Toryism disguised as reform, in his (and his friends') sense of the new Prime Minister. According to Forster, Dickens's "notion of taking Pecksniff for a type of character was really the origin of the book; the design being to show, more or less by every person introduced, the number and variety of humours and vices that have their root in selfishness" (Forster, 291); and I believe the origin of Pecksniff was Sir Robert Peel. Though in time Dickens was to respect Peel, in the early 1840s he shared liberal Whig suspicions of the Tory leader. In "Subjects for Painters. (After Peter Pindar)" in the *Examiner* of August 21, 1841 (p. 537), shortly after Peel's accession as Prime Minister, Dickens shows him as Sheridan's model of duplicity in *The School for Scandal*, taking his list of cabinet nominees to Victoria as "Joseph Surface, fawning cap in hand." Even if Pecksniff's appearance and manner reflected someone Dickens knew, a journalist named Samuel Carter Hall (Forster, 318, n), he was in essence a social and moral vision of Peel, the anti-hero dragging his society down just as Carlyle's recently celebrated heroes elevated theirs.

Whig journals tended to locate Peel's distinguishing quality in bland falsity. At almost its first opportunity, the newborn *Punch* on August 14, 1841, proposed "The State Doctor. A Bit of Farce" starring Peel as "Rhubarb Pill (a travelling doctor)"—i.e., a snake-oil salesman (p. 53); a week later, it captioned a full-page cartoon "ANIMAL MAGNETISM: Sir Rhubarb Pill Mesmerizing the British Lion" (p. 67). The *Examiner* regularly referred to him for years as the Deceiver General, beginning in April 1842, when it also printed a verse satire on him as "Sir Joseph Surface." Once *Martin Chuzzlewit* was under way, the *Examiner* occasionally headed attacks on government actions "Pecksniffery," and its review of the completed novel asked, after noting an old English tendency to admire a hypocrite in government, "does anyone believe that the reign of Cant and Convenience, and their attendant morality, has declined?" (p. 675). An ostensibly objective profile of Peel in the January 1843 *Monthly Magazine* (the month of *Martin Chuzzlewit*'s first installment), observed that "The modern statesman practises chicanery without the slightest fear of losing caste by its exposure; and exults in hypocrisy as the strongest test of his merit, because he finds it the surest medium of success. . . . Of this race of politicians Sir R. Peel is the type" (IX, 8). Pecksniff even looks and sounds like Peel, to judge by the *Mirror*'s description of Peel a few years later: "He rises, the very personification of candour, the incarnation of courtesy; he speaks, and his persuasive plausible tones allure your attention, and almost win your confidence, and you admire the colour of the fish which you think you have caught; and while gazing, it slips through your fingers. . . . He is tall and well proportioned, but rather inclining to corpulency" (April 1847, p. 275).

Returned with some expectations exploded from America, Dickens found corruption and self-interest flourishing in Peel's England. The struggle for education continued unfulfilled, the struggle for poor relief had few victories—as witness Dickens's Christmas books, first conceived during this novel with *A Christmas Carol* and soon followed by the bitter *Chimes*—in short, social injustice throve. Even his church seemed to be trading humanity for the Anglo-Bengalee kind of surface glitter, as he wrote to an American friend on March 2, 1843: "Disgusted with our Established Church, and its Puseyism, and daily outrages on common sense and humanity, I have carried into effect an old idea of mine, and joined the Unitarians, who *would* do something for human improvement, if they could; and who practice Charity and Toleration" (*P*, III, 455). As he claimed in a burlesque report of a Parliamentary committee "Appointed to Inquire into the Condition of the Persons Variously Engaged in the University of Oxford"—a title patterned on one that had detailed the suffering of children in mines and factories—"the intellectual works in the University of Oxford are, in all essential particulars, precisely what they were, when it was first established for the Manufacture of Clergy Men" in the middle ages (*Examiner*, June 3, 1842, p. 339).

As to insurance fraud as practiced by Tigg and Crimp in the Anglo-Bengalee Disinterested Loan and Life Assurance Company, I found no sign of a major scandal at the moment, but the possibilities spring to notice. A typical issue of the *Examiner*, say the one for September 7, 1842, featured large advertisements for the "Economic Assurance Society," "Victorian Life Assurance and Loan Company," "Eagle Insurance Company," "Freemasons' and General Life Assurance, Loan, Annuity, and Reversionary Company," The "Britannia Life Assurance Company," and "Mutual Life Assurance Society." The "Britannia" text is signed by a "Resident Director" like Crimple and notes "A Liberal Commission allowed to Solicitors and Agents" (p. 60). Perhaps conveniently for Dickens beginning the novel, *The Handbook for Life Assurers* appeared in time for a long, approving excerpt in the *Mirror* of October 1, 1842 (pp. 217-20). Everywhere in the land, Pecksniff and Tigg, the hypocrite and the entrepreneurial cynic, cheerfully lured their prey by providing as reality the expectations of Pecksniff's childhood, " 'that pickled onions grew on trees, and that every elephant was born with an impregnable castle on his back' " (vi, 86).

Earlier, Dickens had attacked specific social diseases through their virulent symptoms—the new Poor Law in *Oliver Twist*, vicious Yorkshire schools in *Nicholas Nickleby*, the industrial infernos of Birmingham in *The Old Curiosity Shop*. But he had been seeking for several years a way of catching the more general evil in society and man, the inescapable Boyg or heart of darkness—as the old curiosity shop of all England, as the exploding sore of the Gordon Riots—and now for the first time he was aiming directly and at large at it, at Pecksniffery and the Eden that Mark and Martin saw before returning to the everyday of England: "The log-house, with the open door, and drooping trees about it; the stagnant morning mist, and red sun, dimly seen beyond; the vapour rising up from land and river; the quick stream making the loathsome banks it washed, more flat and dull: how often they returned in dreams! How often it was happiness to wake, and find them Shadows that had vanished!" (xxxiii, 529-30). Exposing this delusive barrenness in the self as in society was a necessary step in the redemption of both.

Even if old Martin's presence and power at the novel's end imply some faith in an older, perhaps an eternal pattern of integrity somewhere, in the nation Dickens could see no one more powerful than the novelist himself willing to negate the soapy hypocrisy that covered the swindlers with the smile of reform while the public suffered. Like two earlier precocious literary wonders, Pope and Byron, he affirmed his maturity by acting the people's tribune, assuming even more insistent social intentions than in the past. He trumpeted the injustice of unprotected copyright all through the American trip and after, wrote letters to the papers on the duplicity of mine owners, spoke at meetings to improve educational institutions for workers, urged in a prologue that playwrights attack social abuses from the stage, and lectured the rich and powerful in his Christmas books.

In Martin-Mark-Tom of *Martin Chuzzlewit*, as in the central actors of the Christmas books, he admonished himself to keep at the world no matter how intractable it pretended to be, to measure it by an eternal standard, and to stay jolly. As the persistence belongs to Martin and the jolliness to Mark, the eternal standard, Carlylean reality, is Tom Pinch's province in the novel: the goal of his visionary music and reveries, the gold into which he is to transmute the larger illusions of time, distance, and change as they burden innocence and destroy union. And to admonish and teach the nation by exposing the falsity of Tigg, Pecksniff, and the American pretensions, Dickens develops in old Martin an early version of the universally observant, indignant older self of the later novels. Retaining the moral and secular power of the older virtuous figures like Brownlow of *Oliver Twist*, the Cheerybles of *Nicholas Nickleby*, and the old officers and king of *Barnaby Rudge*, the grandfatherly types to invoke against encroaching parents, he is like the novelist the mover of whatever fates he chooses, the source and reward of the characters' expectations. More importantly, willing to challenge his own prejudices, old Martin unmasks both good and bad, doing in the imagining mind of the novelist what the novelist does in society.

We can easily see the social message of the novel, but we are drawn into it, I think, by Dickens's personal admonitions, by the vitality with which he expresses these—through characters that stand alone, vigorously, comically, pathetically—by a synthesis of his conceptions of himself consciously drawn in private letters and censored from the public into the imaginative. Recognizing the delusions of eternal youth and romantic fulfillment as dreams, the business of historical romances, he was admonishing himself to accept time, his place as son-brother-father-husband, act within the limits of humanity, enjoy the fruits of ordinary life, and clear out his own Pecksniffery with the fresh wind of his thirties. To his embrace of both the ironic and the melancholy implications of this acceptance, we owe Mark Tapley, Young Bailey, Montague Tigg, and above all the imaginatively luxuriant Sairey Gamp—the plain speakers, the impertinents, the deflaters—as well as Tom Pinch, the self yearning beyond pragmatism.

To judge by the most effective and critical conflicts in *Martin Chuzzlewit*, one powerful impulse giving it life was again Dickens's sense of his current relations with his father, relations more complex and more ripely understood than in *Barnaby Rudge*. That novel, when he was approaching thirty, imagined two young selves in direct conflict with their fathers, one (Joe Willet) triumphing and one (Edward Chester) successfully asserting independence; two others, Hugh and Barnaby, in ambivalent relationships ending with deaths; and two with surrogate fathers, Simon and Lord George, stranded in delusions. Sons, fathers, and surrogates there showed their connections with Dickens, but not in highly individualized ways.

In *Martin Chuzzlewit*, however, Dickens focuses on the growth of the young men in clarity, independence, and maturity—on the process by which figures and conditions only sketched in *Barnaby Rudge* became complex participants in the actual world of contemporary England. Changes sensed in himself, discoveries in both the leisure and turmoil of the American trip, led him to undertake what people rarely see in his work, transformations in major characters—in the jargon of the criticism trade, "roundness" as well as "flatness." Responding to current pressures from his father as well as the weight of remembered ones, merging with them thoughts and feelings about guardianship and independence that touched him also as tribune to England and America, Dickens conceived several versions of the father, and elaborated four effective sides of his own growth: Mark and Martin casually leaving beloved women to pursue self-improvement and discovering its immense difficulties; Jonas, embodying and evacuating the murderous hatred that destroyed first the Tigg side of the father (with John Dickens's manner and varying conditions) and then himself; and Tom, the most sensitive, shocked by the father down to his sexual core and recovering to transmute his experiences into the ideal.

By the end, Dickens's current resentments toward his father—and toward all the other manifestations of duplicity, frustration, intractability—have been discharged in Jonas's rage, Tom's half-comic shock, the death of Tigg, and Pecksniff's reduction to an abject caricature of John Dickens. From a new conviction that he could transcend them, he draws the positive tendencies toward maturity, in the fruitful lives of Martin and Mary, Westlock and Ruth, the purged grandfather Martin—who overthrew the worst father and affirmed proper guardianship—and the redeemed ordinary woman Mercy Pecksniff, and above all the sensitive artist Tom. With the power and complexity of intimate memories, dredged from as far back as the shock at twelve, the jilting in youth, and the death of Mary Hogarth in 1837, and now considered and assimilated, Dickens's private emotions at thirty-one give a new life to these relationships. They shape the imagination toward a coherence unconnected with any artificial plot of the *Barnaby Rudge* sort, an inner intensity unified as none of the previous novels had been.

Concluding with Tom's yearning in the lyrical coda, Dickens seems to be drawing special attention to his shift in the novel's focus from Martin, the pattern Whittington turned Candide and then Tom Jones, to the Wordsworthian soul with melancholy intimations of immortality. But neither Dickens nor his characters were Balzac's Lucien de Rubempre or Rastignac reaping only death or cynicism from lost illusions. For Dickens, the shock of disillusion carries both adjustment to a diminished thing and—for the fortunate like Tom Pinch—

a new awareness of a greater one. Wordsworth and Shelley knew to start with that earthly goals are insufficient, lamenting instead the loss with time of something higher, fearing the triumph of the earthly, whether in bourgeois prosperity or the flesh's decay. But Dickens's projections, tossed into the materialistic sphere of Whittington, must learn to progress from Whittington's goal as well as his condition.

To a modern taste, Dickens sentimentalizes the ethereal self at the end, elaborating lush vagueness for Tom and his sister Ruth from the mismatch of Carlyle's *Heroes and Hero Worship* with *A Christmas Carol*: "From the Present, and the Past, with which she is so tenderly entwined in all thy thoughts, thy strain soars onward to the Future. As it resounds within thee and without, thy kindling face looks on her with a Love and Trust, that knows it cannot die. The noble music, rolling round her in a cloud of melody, shuts out the grosser prospect of an earthly parting and uplifts her, Tom, to Heaven!" (832). But the early condescension with which he had treated Tom as Pecksniff's gull, a timid countryman excited and frightened by the metropolis Salisbury (a tone repeated near the end for Tom's introduction to London), reminds us that Dickens also looked with irony at his own self-pity for expectations impossible to achieve. After all, he has that same Tom affirm his freedom from romance stereotypes and from complaints of unfair fate. Like Tom, he knows the world owes no one perfect happiness.

But unlike Tom, he had always expected disillusionment at the very height of anticipation, as in admonitions not to slight him that he included in letters of courtship and as in preparing for the American trip. To teach or spare himself, Dickens made a special point of warning his own delusive tendencies, as Fielding habitually admonished his willingness too easily to accommodate others, and Jane Austen the lure of throwing oneself away. Past thirty, with a growing family on his hands and settling in with his standard little wife, Dickens felt time irresistibly flooding over him, carrying away with it delusions of fulfillment, discovery, achievement, permanence. Just as he mocked the early fame that he took pride in through his procession of American baby journalists, each "one of the most remarkable men in the country," so his coda on Tom carries the ambiguities of his self-vision: in one mirror, Gilbert's Lord Chancellor dealing out girls, one for him (John Westlock), and one for he (Martin), but never, oh never a one for me; in another, the noble spirit never to be satisfied of Tennyson's dramatic lyrics. Welcoming a vigorous, fruitful life despite emotional unfulfillment (his overt complaint in his forties), Dickens turns a Barnaby of unusable visions into a Tom Pinch reaching for a reality denied to the grasp of common day.

IV. *David Copperfield*:
Memory and the Flow of Time

May 1, 1849 - November 1, 1850

However much of the past had earlier surfaced unconsciously, by *David Copperfield* Dickens knew of its contributions. At about thirty-five, he had begun defining his past in the Memoir, breaking off in sight of the Maria affair because, he was to write her in 1855, he couldn't bear to relive it. In the novel of that time, *Dombey and Son*, he brought the imaginative fruit of that search into a new richness in the development of the lonely child Florence and her emotional relations with her father; and in *The Haunted Man* (1848), the Christmas tale between it and *David Copperfield*, his projection poured out past guilts and wrongs almost uncensored, discovering however that life without memory was horror, empty of all, both good and bad, that tied him to other people. From *Dombey and Son* and the Memoir through *The Haunted Man* and *David Copperfield*, a dominant vision is of the author or his projection sitting alone, in a reverie, eliciting and reconciling elements of that past.

Entering the mind of his hero absorbed in a current novel of his own, Dickens gives precisely the complex blend of thoughts Dickens was to examine in his response to a letter from Maria Beadnell more than twenty years after she rejected him. When David recalls his young self walking past the Steerforth house long after the shattering elopement of Steerforth and Little Em'ly, he writes: "Coming before me, on this particular evening that I mention, mingled with the childish recollections and later fancies, the ghosts of half-formed hopes, the broken shadows of disappointments dimly seen and understood, the blending of experience and imagination, incidental to the occupation with which my thoughts had been busy, it was more than commonly suggestive" (xlvi, 568).

When an author says such things through his characters, he licenses us to ask how his current emotional world, necessarily suffused with individual memories—living impulses from the past—shapes his creation. It is, after all, Dickens's question in *David Copperfield* from the other end: how had he recreated that past to lead to his present? Like Wordsworth in the contemporaneously published *Prelude* turning selected visions of his literal past into metaphors for his mental movement, Dickens tried fictionally to explain how he came to be who he was.

Direct echoes of the Memoir of two years earlier, and the other parallels between David's and Dickens's life, suggest a beginning in retrospective search for meaning, which author and character so deeply share. For both, there is not one symbolic obstacle to overcome, like Pecksniff or the American Eden in *Martin Chuzzlewit*, but the whole of life to portray. Like Wordsworth's imagination, Dickens's works to introduce his past existences and future possibilities into the present, and to fit personal crises into a mythic conception of growth. Combining his urge toward self-exploration in his closing thirties—the traditional midpoint in life—with a rich coloring of universality to turn the idiosyncratic Dickens into

Everyman by way of the mature novelist Copperfield, Dickens consciously fueled his imagination with passions and experiences summoned from his past.

For David in the novel summing up a life approaching middle age, the effect of the recurrent pauses to contemplate himself at moments in the past is to affirm the memory as man's weapon against death, and thereby to affirm the value of the book he is writing: to solidify the memory, make its public testimony, and even help delay time's flow to oblivion for himself and his readers. Vividly recalling David's (and Dickens's) sensations guarantees that they have happened and that they mean something. Walking in the garden with Dora, David had absorbed sense impressions for later assurance, like Proust's narrator: "The scent of a geranium leaf, at this day, strikes me with a half comical half serious wonder as to what change has come over me in a moment; and then I see a straw hat and blue ribbons, and a quantity of curls, and a little black dog being held up, in two slender arms, against a bank of blossoms and bright leaves" (xxvi, 338). Intensely jarred by memory into a sense of his dead child-wife, in a scene echoing his last view of his child-mother, David evokes for us an equation of innocences, and perhaps an intimation of immortality.

Memory has shown David that time's flow, specially adapted by his character and circumstances, through himself and the figures mixed with him, has shaped him now into a man of early middle age, a novelist, settled in a family and generally admired: as we and Dickens know, a version of Dickens. But the years that David brushes past in the final chapters, the times from his first successful book to his current calm eminence, were not so smooth for Dickens. As we look at Dickens's life from *Martin Chuzzlewit* to *David Copperfield*, we find most of the 1840s, essentially Dickens's thirties, a period of stress, wandering, difficult self-exploration. For some of the agitation and reflection there were sufficient external reasons. Along with exhilaration, his great successes had earned him a position where—as he had noted of the literary profession as early as *Pickwick Papers*—gossip and denigration were sure to mingle with the praise. *Martin Chuzzlewit*'s sales were disappointing, the *Christmas Carol* didn't provide the money its popularity promised, and the later Christmas books received mixed reviews, sometimes (as the *Mirror* said of *The Battle of Life* in its own favorable notice) for extra-literary reasons. The great quarterlies generally disregarded him,[26] and less austere journals were fickle. With friends like *The Critic*, for example, a magazine for the book trade that claimed to revere him, he didn't need enemies. In January 1844, *The Critic* mentioned the current fashion to call "Chuzzlewit a failure, and his writings vulgar" (p. 62), it condemned *The Chimes* as venal on January 1, 1845, and on November 8 and December 6, 1845, it ran a translation of a quintessentially German critic who proved Dickens artistically disorganized, a maladroit inventor of characters, and below grade in humor (pp. 562-64, 643-45).

The intense activity of Dickens's late teens and twenties, the perseverance and continuous outpouring of energy that he has David recognize in himself (xlli, 517-18), gave way now to a year in Italy for reflection and for absorbing another world, and to various experiments. Italy provided what he had hoped for, but it also seems to have aggravated the growing sense of emptiness for which he later blamed his wife. Even as early as *Martin Chuzzlewit*'s unfulfilled Tom Pinch he had been aware of a central emotional deprivation; and in Italy in the year after that novel, he had seriously resented his wife's jealousy of a friend, Augusta de la Rue, whose hallucinations he was treating with his recently acquired powers of mesmerism. According to Fred Kaplan, "She insisted that her husband tell the de la Rues that she was distressed by what seemed to her the impropriety of his relationship with Augusta. . . . He spoke to the de la Rues, but insisted on apologizing for Catherine's state of mind, calling her both over-sensitive and insensitive to others. In his eyes, it was demeaning, irrational jealousy."[27] He nursed his resentment, writing her from an Italian trip after *Bleak House* (on December 5, 1853) that though he wouldn't think of pressing her to write tenderly to the de la Rues (whom he had just seen), if she neglected to do so, "your position beside these people is not a good one, is not an amiable one, a generous one."[28] In the later 1850s, he complained to others as well.

In his teens and early twenties he had been—as he loved to remember—a notable success as a journalist, and he had toyed plausibly with the thought of professional acting. Now in these middle thirties, he deliberately experimented with changes in the pattern of his life. Besides the great novel *Dombey and Son* that turned his life in several ways, between *Martin Chuzzlewit* and *David Copperfield* he invented the new genre of Christmas book; created and briefly edited a great daily newspaper; planned and supervised Miss Coutts's halfway house for reforming prostitutes, Urania Cottage; managed and starred in amateur theatrical productions; and considered a run for parliament. On June 20, 1846, he even applied to a friendly minister, Lord Morpeth, for "some public employment—some Commissionership, or Inspectorship, or the like. . . . I have hoped, for years, that I may become at last a Police Magistrate, and turn my social knowledge to good practical account from day to day" (*P*, IV, 566-7).

Like his character Morfin in *Dombey and Son*, he wished to jar himself out of the routine. When we meet the unexpected, Morfin says, we are shocked and experience a kind of rebirth, into an awareness of disorder and injustice. Overhearing a bitter conversation between his colleagues the Carker brothers, Morfin himself had been so shaken that he had had to reconsider what he knew about them, actually to think about it, which is to say learn how families behaved in fact rather than in theory. " 'I was something less good-natured, as the phrase goes, after that morning, less easy and complacent altogether,' " he says (liii, 712). As Dickens's imagined world at the time, *Dombey and Son* jars various representatives of the self—notably Dombey and his daughter, but also his second wife and the manager of his firm—from their limiting preconceptions.

Turning to *Dombey and Son* signaled Dickens's resumption of his calling after the culminating diversion, the mistake of the *Daily News* (as he said in the preface to *Pictures from Italy*), and that novel's great rewards in prestige, popularity, and money—Forster says the arrangement it began made Dickens financially secure—confirmed that calling. In his advertisement for the cheap edition of his works, at the same time as *Dombey and Son*, he now defined himself primarily as a writer of novels amply rewarded by their welcome into the daily life of his fellows. This edition, he said (*Examiner*, March 6, 1847, p. 160), will not only bring him into the homes of all his responsive readers, but also—curiously like Browning's Bishop of St. Praxed's sensing the ambience of his tomb—let him absorb the life around him:

> to be well thumbed and soiled in a plain suit that will bear a great deal, by children and grown people, at the fireside and on the journey: to be hoarded on the humble shelf where there are few books, and to lie about in libraries like any familiar piece of household stuff, that is easy of replacement: and to see and feel this—not to die first, or grow old and passionless: must obviously be among the hopes of a living Author venturing on such an enterprise.

Without such hopes it never could be set on foot. I have no fear of being mistaken in acknowledging that they are mine; that they are built, in simple earnestness and grateful faith, on my experience, past and present, of the cheering on of very many thousands of my countrymen and countrywomen, never more numerous or true to me than now.

In the novel begun two years later, he could have his hero also, after success as a journalist, find that the reception of his first book and the prospects of his second gave assurances of his calling: "Without such assurance I should certainly have left it alone, and bestowed my energy on some other endeavour. I should have tried to find out what nature and accident really had made me, and to be that, and nothing else" (xlviii, 589).

1

Dickens publicly advertised his identification with his autobiographical narrator by making him a successful journalist-novelist and implied it privately by using almost verbatim passages from his recent fragment of a Memoir in the Murdstone-and-Grimby sequence. In later years, he frequently mentioned his closeness to the novel and its hero, sometimes—as when he was jarred into memories by Maria Beadnell's letter of February 1855—stressing the equivalence of their feelings in intense situations. Through David, Dickens traces his growth into the present, absorbing the time at Doctors' Commons, the journalistic writings, shorthand reporting of Parliament, continental travel, and acclaim as a novelist. Yet he organized the novel so that two of its three critical points, the ends of Part X and Part XV (respectively,

Em'ly's elopement and her imminent return) concern not David's actions but the actions of others that strongly affect him.

Like the end of Part V, when he has been adopted by Aunt Betsey and begun his residence with the Wickfields and attendance at Dr. Strong's school, these external events define stages of David's growth. From "Scenes," Chapters 6 and 7, of the *Sketches by Boz* to the comments in his will on Georgina Hogarth's value to his growing children, with conspicuous examples along the way in his Christmas stories, Dickens often sensed life as a series of stages. Everyone will recall the stages of Scrooge's psychological career under the guidance of the three spirits; and anyone who runs through the Christmas stories will also notice "A Christmas Tree," in the Christmas number of *Household Words*, 1850 (right after the novel); "The Child's Story," Christmas Supplement, *Household Words*, 1852; and "The Ghost in Master B's Room," Christmas Supplement, *All the Year Round*, 1859. David's narrative reflects that sense. In Dickens's working notes for the novel, for example, his hints for No. V include "I make another beginning"; for No. VI, "The Progress from childhood to youth"; for No. XV, "David's New State."[29] Indeed, Dickens identifies even an external version of the hero at a stage before a recoverable consciousness, having David observe of the last vision of his dead mother and infant half-brother, that "the little creature in her arms, was myself, as I had once been, hushed for ever on her bosom" (ix, 115). Like little Paul Dombey, the baby images Dickens's (everyman's) fantasy of dying before achievement, but still leaving a symbolic, consoling trace of himself as marker, a memory of having existed.

After Mrs. Copperfield's death, Dickens relives memories of his recent Memoir through his hero: "I can recollect, indeed, to have speculated, at odd times, on the possibility of my not being taught any more, or cared for any more; and growing up to be a shabby moody man, lounging an idle life away, about the village" (x, 116). Almost literally experiencing in the Murdstone-and-Grinby warehouse and its familial context details Dickens recalled from Warren's Blacking, David in his desperation can do what Dickens's imagination had compelled earlier projections to do but he himself as a boy could not, escape to another world: a version of the alienation from his parents that Dickens could not deal with until the reflective, reconciling period of the mid-1840s. Under the guardianship of Aunt Betsey, David's path to late adolescence seems relatively smooth—like the peaceful gap in Dickens's recollections between the blacking warehouse and Maria—as his involvement with the boat people, Heep and the Wickfields, Steerforth, the Micawbers, and the rest suggests universal social and psychological patterns Dickens derived from his own life. Sometimes the connection of the two comes to the surface, as with "the stipendiary clerks" (xxvi, 331) at Spenlow and Jorkins's, like the teenage Dickens and his mates; or with Aunt Betsey's apparent impoverishment that forces David to scramble for a living, allowing Dickens to imagine himself again the energetic young shorthand reporter turning novelist in the years of courtship and early marriage.

For each stage of the developing self, Dickens provided David with a young female symbolizing his ideal, as he provided alternative guardians (David's young mother and Peggotty, the Murdstones, Aunt Betsey) and alternative projections (Heep, Steerforth, Traddles) for his states of mind. They are not mutually exclusive in time, for Dickens was alert to the variety of pressures on the mind, particularly amid the tensions of youth; and he was creating them primarily as rich, plausible, imagined human beings in his story rather than allegorical states. Just as importantly, Dickens here, for the first time in his novels deliberately remembering and evaluating his past, also for the first time deliberately ranges over the possibilities of the feminine as fulfillment for himself; perhaps, as Alexander Welsh says, as possible sexual partners.[30]

David's mother, the first female and (along with Peggotty) guardian, leaves her son a clear and loving memory of her innocence, playfulness, beauty, and affection. A child herself, she mirrors David's childhood in her need for affection, her fearfulness, her limited responsibility, her inability to judge the master she marries, her enforced submissiveness to that goblin and his sister. On his way back to school after her last embrace, David stores a vision of her that symbolizes his protected early childhood: "I was in the carrier's cart when I heard her calling to me. I looked out, and she stood at the garden-gate alone, holding her baby up in her arms for me to see. It was cold still weather; and not a hair of her head, or a fold of her dress, was stirred, as she looked intently at me, holding up her child. So I lost her. So I saw her afterwards, in my sleep at school—a silent presence near my bed—looking at me with the same intent face—holding up her baby in her arms" (viii, 104). Dreams, almost hallucinations, of the beautiful mother as emblem of the loved stage of childhood keep David going in his flight from the chaotic warehouse, as the adult David was to need an emblematic woman to inspire him and help him order his life. The innocent mother recalled from childhood—as Michael Slater says, Dickens's idealization of the mother dead to him after Warren's Blacking—remains symbolic of her child's own stage of purity at least until *A Tale of Two Cities*, where Jarvis Lorry speaks of how " 'My heart is touched now, by many remembrances that had long fallen asleep, of my pretty young mother (and I so old!), and by many associations of the days when what we call the world was not so real with me, and my faults were not confirmed in me' " (III,ix,295).

Baffled by the addition of the Murdstones to the world of his mother and Peggotty, the child David responds to it only intuitively. But among the boat people he asks questions and makes judgments, testing his tie to them. The emblematic female of this new state, Little Em'ly, similarly testing the outer world, accompanies the complex change in the boy who needs to understand and act as he moves from innocence into social activity. A figure not sexually significant to David, or far beneath conscious acknowledgment of sexuality (like Dickens's memories of his sister Fanny, recently dead, as a child), Em'ly inhabits a society magically isolated in its completeness, filled with virtuous eccentrics united under the bachelor patriarch Daniel Peggotty. The only hint of dangerous external pressures in this early idyll is the difference in class between this group and David, a difference only Em'ly wishes to overcome. In his sense of a slow maturing before the turmoil of late adolescence, Dickens says that nothing varied noticeably in this archetypal society but "the tide, which altered Mr. Peggotty's times of going out and coming in, and altered Ham's engagements also" (iii, 35).

Through Em'ly's catastrophe at the climactic halfway point in the novel, the idyllic pastoral fishing world yields to modern England's intrusion in the form of Steerforth and social class, and also to David's own necessary psychological change: the shock of sex, a betrayal of romance like the child's abandonment by his mother, the end of innocence, revulsion against the arrogant romantic self Steerforth. Pitied and rejected in a retributive world, the eager young spirit Em'ly must recede as David progresses to adulthood, to a daily reality that David (for Dickens) asserts to be richer in its necessary limitations, struggles, and compromises, and that we can agree is more complex. After her return, the start of redemption, and the elimination of both her brother-betrothed and her despoiler, Em'ly rejects numerous marriage offers in Australia. Her destiny is special, emblematic, to remain for David a memory of his richest ideals of youth, like the emigrant ship on which he last saw her, "a sight at once so beautiful, so mournful, and so hopeful . . . ." (lvii, 695).

In Mr. Peggotty's report on their emigrant history, Dickens carefully notices the marriage in Australia of the reformed prostitute Martha, to assure us that celibacy and good works were Em'ly's deliberate choice and not her doom. As Em'ly lives the sensitive union of social aspiration, spiritual nobility, and sexual attraction, her townswoman Martha constitutes the ordinary danger among the poor, the lives Dickens had pitied from without as a young reporter and was daily trying to improve at Urania Cottage. Jarred out of a suicidal reverie at the river's edge, she could expect no more than to live on "and to see the day break on the ghastly lines of houses' " (xlvii, 583)—perhaps a thematically intended echo of the famous ending of Number vii of the just-published *In Memoriam*,

And ghastly thro' the drizzling rain

On the bald street breaks the blank day.

Succumbing out of desperate boredom to temptation, failing and returning to convention through determination, good will, and the help of the religious conscience personified in Mr. Peggotty, Martha seems to reflect David's psychological growth past the danger of the ordinary. Another side of David's adolescent ambiguities, the tension of adult sexuality, becomes externalized in Rosa Dartle, the bitter, scarred companion of Mrs. Steerforth. Cut from the cloth of Fielding's Lady Booby and Dickens's own Edith Dombey, the damaged Donna Elvira to Steerforth's Don Giovanni, in her resentful passion she fascinates and frightens the developing David. All three of these fantasies of David's sexually developing years he needs to grow out of: the ideal renunciation of Em'ly as much as the self-destructive obsession of Rosa and Martha's drift into degradation.

For David's puppy yearnings—in the stage from thirteen to twenty-three, when Dickens said he had been constantly in love (*P*, IV, 346)—Dickens provides a succession of embodied fantasies that culminate in Dora Spenlow. Ready for attachment, David settles on a sweet and childish recreation of his mother, complete even with Miss Murdstone as her warder. Dickens several times said she was based on Maria Beadnell, and passages in the novel about the courtship were to reappear, lightly modified, in his letters to Maria in 1855. But he had been rejected by Maria, so that the fictional marriage was wholly imagined, in its deficiencies a judgment of probabilities and perhaps a revenge. A year after *Copperfield*, in the Christmas supplement to *Household Words* Dickens made that inference himself. His persona in "What Christmas is, as We Grow Older" recalls losing "the priceless pearl who was our young choice" and thinks that "we really know, now, that we should probably have been miserable if we had won and worn the pearl, and that we are better off without her." After the Memoir began the purgation, *David Copperfield* helped free Dickens of the pain in the memory, allowing him the emotions of the affair strained into nostalgia.

But if David's early married life reflects fantasies of what Dickens's would have been with Maria, it also incorporates recollections of his actual life with Catherine and his sense of her deficiencies. Very early in the marriage, soon after their first child was born, his sister-in-law Mary wrote in terms that would fit Dora in the same situation: "Poor Kate! it has been a dreadful trial for her. . . . Every time she sees her Baby she has a fit of crying and keeps constantly saying she is sure he will not care for her now she is not able to nurse him. I think time will be the only effectual cure for her—could she but forget this she has everything in this world to make her comfortable and happy—her husband is kindness itself to her and is constantly studying her comfort in every thing."[31] That is exactly the sort of thing Dickens would have summoned to memory in his reflections on his marriage in Italy. And precisely as he was working on No. XVII of the novel— Dora's dying days, during which she apologizes for her wifely incompetence—he wrote to Catherine, "I think of you all day" (*P*, VI, 151). A half year after *David Copperfield*, when Dickens was preparing to take her to a specialist in nervous illnesses, his notes to her were as tenderly paternal as to a young daughter—as David's attitude to Dora perforce became after he had given up treating her as an adult equal.

When Dickens years later justified his alienation from Catherine, he sometimes complained of domestic incompetence and indifference—the qualities in Dora that David had to grin and bear—or in sympathetic retrospect blamed the youth of both. We may or may not accept his position of September 1857, that there had been irreconcilable incompatibilities as far back as "when Mary was born" in 1838 (*N*, II, 888), but we do have the evidence of negative attitudes on his part going back a long way: condescending jokes at the expense of young wives from the Kenwigses of *Nicholas Nickleby* on; his assumption from the Italy trip of 1844 that her sister Georgina, not she, was managing the children and the household; and his stern resentment of her jealousy of Mme de la Rue.

In directing Dora's character and destiny, then, Dickens moves from memories of his first love to a combination of paternal tenderness and irritation toward Catherine. And when Dora's approaching death leads David to Dickens's old question of the irrevocability of chance—what if David had never seen her, she wonders (xlii, 522)—he suggests more than the artist's admission that in depicting reality he must always consider accident. Rather, their immature involvement was inevitable, because the independent, controlling, humanly sensitive, middle-aged autobiographer—the imagined other self—could not live without some infusion of Dickens's youthful affair with Maria and uncertain youthful marriage to Catherine.

Of the significant young women, Agnes is the one that David looks back on as offering stimulus and inspiration to lead him from adolescence to mature hope without delusion, from the start "my sweet sister, as I call her in my thoughts" (xviii, 229). If Dora recalls Dickens's emotions for his first love Maria and his wife, Agnes as ideal, sister, sensible manager, and finally helpmeet, seems to blend hints, strained through the censorship of conscious thought, of his sister Fanny and his two sisters-in-law, the dead Mary and the current director of his household Georgina. From Rose Maylie of *Oliver Twist* on, the dead Mary had been his version of Dante's Beatrice, a guide to heaven. Memories and dreams in which she cheered and inspired him had recurred for years, taking a form he described in a letter to Forster of January 29, 1842, on his grand reception in Boston: "I feel, in the best aspects of this welcome, something of the presence and influence of that spirit which directs my life, and through a heavy sorrow has pointed upwards with unchanging finger for more than four years past" (*P*, III, 35). Participating in Dickens's private myth of Mary Hogarth, Agnes animates a version of such a scene (developed more fully for Dr. Manette in *A Tale of Two Cities*) for David: with "that solemn hand upraised towards Heaven!" (liii, 658), she combines inspiration to go forward with the news of Dora's death. If Traddles's Sophia—one of ten sisters, burlesquing the collection of Hogarth girls—is the supremely good-natured, housewifely, managing version of Georgina, then Agnes is Georgina with the beauty and spirituality of her dead sister Mary. With neither Mary nor Georgina Hogarth could passion be an acceptable thought, and indeed it does not seem to have existed. Agnes, therefore, cannot be the goal of great emotional expectations, of the excitement stimulated by Dora. The heaviest cost of adulthood, Dickens shows from Tom Pinch to Pip, is abandoning such expectations—perhaps the reason that readers have so often found Agnes dull.

2

Although all the achieved characters in the novel, including these young women, seem to some extent projections of tendencies within Dickens, his clearest alternative selves after David, the selves he fantasied as partial or cautionary fulfillments of old images he had shed, were David's male contemporaries—Heep, Steerforth, and Traddles—and more distantly the older men like Micawber, Mr. Dick, Murdstone, and Mr. Peggotty. Presumably because Dickens had been mercilessly examining his past for several years and discovering the sources of desires and revulsions he had earlier overlooked, he now makes class a sensitive issue for these imagined selves. From Oliver Twist through the Dombeys and Walter Gay, the main projections had been bourgeois-genteel, like David Copperfield. But those subordinate ones played against them had either been of the same class, like Quilp or Jonas Chuzzlewit, or figures from the other classes only distantly imagined as admonitions, like Sir Mulberry Hawk and Lord George Gordon far above, or Noah Claypool and Simon Tappertit sufficiently below. Squire John Westlock and Tom Pinch, the grandson of upper servants, had no chasms of class between them.

Now, however, Dickens projects from recollected sides of the self the great opposing dangers subverting his female emblems and ideals, Steerforth as the Byronic arrogance of youth and Heep as selfish opportunism and bitter envy. Of these, the greater danger in the plot, to the adult even more than the boy—the personality perceived as more deeply embedded—is Heep, the lower-class self desperate to rise and twisted toward vicious means by his nature and by a society that imposes great obstacles. He again reflects what Warren's Blacking might have done to the child abandoned to it: "I fully comprehended now, for the first time, what a base, unrelenting, and revengeful spirit, must have been engendered by this early, and this long, suppression" (xxxix, 491). Although David responds with shock and guilt to the elopement of Steerforth and Em'ly, it does not deprive him of sleep, as does the possibility of Uriah's thrusting his impurity on Agnes.

A side of Dickens that he had recognized only as otherness and attacked and exhorted as far back as the "Sketches of Young Gentlemen," in his opportunism and obsession with battling through life without quarter, Heep is a caricature of qualities that Dickens still wanted to admonish in himself. At fifteen, when David meets him, the already repulsive Heep has Dickens's virtue of dedicated industry and Dickens's teen-age employment, work as a law clerk. The intensity continues, but its goals become worse and worse, the imagined consequences of a life without redirection: " 'I've got a motive, as my fellow-partner used to say; and I go at it tooth and nail. I mustn't be put upon, as a numble person, too much. I can't allow people in my way' " (xlii, 520), he says, preparing to ruin the Strongs' lives because he suspects Mrs. Strong of contempt. With a will and energy like Dickens's, Uriah had long been taught to cover them, at the cost of intense resentment: " "People like to be above you," says father. "Keep yourself down." I am very umble to the present

moment, Master Copperfield, but I've got a little power!' "
(xxxix, 491).

In developing Heep, Dickens follows one startling thread
from the great weave of myth, opposing to a heroic David an
enemy named Uriah. By such naming, Dickens courts
psychological intrusiveness. No one, except a believer much
simpler than the Heeps, would name a child Uriah. Uriah the
Hittite has one function only in the Bible (2 Samuel 11), to die
so that King David may conveniently appropriate his wife
Bathsheba. While Uriah was away on duty in David's army,
David saw Bathsheba bathing, made her his mistress, and got
her with child. To make sure of having her without
interference, David ordered that Uriah be put in the front lines
of battle and abandoned to his death, after which David made
the widow his favorite wife. At the very least, Dickens's
villain's name suggests that the hero's is not accidental; at
most, it hints at great status and achievement for the hero but
also—another farewell to Whittington—guilt.

If Dickens did not plan the biblical parallel consciously, his
subconscious was mining in full view. Entering gentility
gracefully, his chief projection takes the wife that Uriah, the
rejected grubby self, thinks he has legitimately earned. And
Dickens projects the biblical prototype's sovereign
indifference to conventional justice: David gets the girl, the
mark of maturity and social solidity, not because he has
worked for her, as the apprentice may be said to have done,
but because he's God's choice and ours. Already frustrated in
the earlier novels (Walter Gay married the *rejected* daughter
of his soon-to-be bankrupt boss in the last one), here the
Whittington self becomes a mere exploded scoundrel, rightly
sacrificed for David's social ease. The self scrambling upward
at all costs—not our view of the young Dickens, but one he
knew held by some (like his old publisher-adversary
Bentley)—has been cast out disdainfully in favor of that much

nobler person, a distinguished novelist who has left Bathsheba dangling till he can use her.

The David-Uriah myth also has a slanting applicability to the romance plot, where Dickens kills off both Steerforth and Ham to preserve Em'ly as a distant ideal for David alone. There too Dickens provides a parallel for Uriah, a mirror that helps justify Uriah's frustrations. Littimer, Leporello to Steerforth's Don Giovanni—or, considering Dickens's current references to the *Vicar of Wakefield*, an unregenerate Jenkinson to Steerforth's Squire Thornhill—created a servile tool like Uriah by the class system and ending as Uriah's mate in a model prison, helps connect the two eminent bad projections. Em'ly's marrying Ham would have been plausible and tolerable, but she would have dwindled into a model working-class wife like *The Haunted Man*'s Milly Swidger, not soared as the angel of youth. The marriage to Littimer that Steerforth tried to force on her, like Agnes's to Heep, would be gratuitous, distasteful degradation, the rule of chaos in the world. Her seduction by Steerforth without either the workaday or the sordid aftermath leads her from the edenic myth to redemption, by way of a fall through a mythic romance, maintaining their different kinds of ideality

In Steerforth, the bad angel (as Agnes calls him) who complements Heep from the other end of class, Dickens undertakes his most complex fantasy of aristocracy. That fantasy focuses the goal of upward mobility that had been blurred in Dickens's first serious novels: Oliver's and Nicholas's relatives and models, the romance figures of *Barnaby Rudge*, the grand and sinister ladies beginning with Edith Dombey. By now, Dickens had long been at home among the nobs, sharing a speaker's table with the earl of this and a committee with the marquis of that, and he was aware of ambiguities he had not earlier considered. Class feeling in the ordinary social world, surfacing here in the idiotic toadies at the Waterbrook dinner—"'We see Blood in a nose, and we know it'" (xxv, 320)—always disgusted him, but aristocracy as an attribute of superiority in a universal adolescent fantasy, fed when he was young by Scott and Byron, fits Steerforth high in the melodrama with the enchanted maiden Em'ly and the stalwart yeoman Ham. Like Ham, he is some years older than David, a model for the boy's future who can be observed, admired, exposed, and stored away in memory rather than imitated.

In his manner and governing attitude, Steerforth seems deliberately conceived to show sides of Dickens opposite to those assigned to Heep, to fill that paradox of one's own extremes that needed smoothing and reconciling in David's growth to maturity. Established as domineering and yet bravely protective, warm to naive admirers and brutally willful in asserting class privileges, he can handle all classes and situations with the charm Dickens joked about in letters where "the Inimitable" soothed customs officers and innkeepers on the Italian travels: "There was an ease in his manner—a gay and light manner it was, but not swaggering—which I still believe to have borne a kind of enchantment with it" (vii, 89). As this charm balances Heep's exaggeration of Dickens's occasional diffidence in society, Steerforth exposes the aristocrat's indifference, even passivity about directions in life against Heep's singleminded opportunism. He laughs at the thought of excelling at Oxford, finds all professions equally barren, and commits himself to nothing but guilty libertinism. To a central question in the novel, whether there is any point in going on in a world that imposes compromises and defeats, Steerforth's suicidal daring of the great storm gives the answer of one familiar side of Dickens.

Both the charm and the superiority to competitive striving turn out mere symptoms of a cynicism like Heep's. In retrospect, David can see its root in frivolity as self-serving as Uriah's pursuit of the main chance: "all this was a brilliant game, played for the excitement of the moment, for the employment of high spirits, in the thoughtless love of superiority, in a mere wasteful careless course of winning what was worthless to him, and next minute thrown away" (xxi, 265). When he appears to say his mysterious farewell to David while plotting the seduction among the lower orders, he coldly reports that Barkis is dying. We can't stop to worry about others, he says: " 'No! Ride on! Rough-shod if need be, smooth-shod if that will do, but ride on!' " (xxviii, 364). Dickens, like Browning, tended to picture life as a battle for the good, but he kept admonishing himself against the extreme of the attitude: recently, in the Christmas book *The Battle of Life*; here, in Dora's tearful response to the very idea and in Murdstone's and Steerforth's savage use of it. Like Heep, Steerforth must be eliminated for David to achieve adult humanity.

Of the main parallels to David, Traddles, his closest contemporary, constitutes Dickens's assessment of his own real prospects if he had lacked artistic talent—and in his recent retrospect Dickens must have marveled at its unexpected manifestation in his twenties. Of the three young law students at the Waterbrook dinner, David lives with his generous aunt's help and Heep has usurped his benefactor's property, but Traddles takes the central way—Dickens's way—cheerfully struggling up through poverty. At the great Heep explosion, he calmly takes charge, like the managing side of Dickens, explaining exactly what everyone must do, and making sense of the confusion Heep has created.

In Traddles, Dickens imagines himself as a man raised with indifference, objective about himself and humanely just to others, who plows his way honorably to distinction (an imminent judgeship) in a traditional field: a David Copperfield without artistic talent, spared from the beginning Dickens's fears of sharing the selfish cynnicism of Heep and Steerforth. Universally respected, harried by large responsibilities and handling them well, Traddles shows the world Dickens the flourishing model citizen, to accompany David Copperfield as Dickens the sensitive artist. Steerforth and Heep, purged from his present nature, remain in memory, partial selves looming over the flow of time as lifelong admonitions.

3

Confident at this stage of his life, Dickens affirms through David and Traddles the first principle of his faith in character, that a good beginning, health, and freedom from damaging obligations are all that any able, willing, hopeful young man needs. But the excitement of the novel also reflects his memory, sharpened by current domestic concerns, of how close the central self can be to destruction in childhood despite its marvelous resilience. Much depends on the guardians through the stages of development, Dickens always wrote, but he still neglects to explain exactly how this is so. Murdstone's way of improving a child or a childlike wife is surely wrong, but what way is right? And the speculating writer, surrounded by eight small children with a ninth in process and uncertain of his wife's ability to guide them, was not posing a hypothetical question.

How much does the way in fact matter, if a frivolous, venal meddler like Mrs. Markleham could produce the virtuous Annie Strong? What besides Agnes's innate character makes her go right when Steerforth, no more worshipped by his mother than Agnes by her father, goes so wrong? Writing in the *Examiner* early in *David Copperfield* and later in *Household Words*, Dickens kept insisting that those denied participation in civilized society were being groomed to plague it; and he shows it not only in the distorted Heeps but also in the abandoned poor of *David Copperfield*, trifling in Murdstone and Grinby's warehouse or viciously preying on the helpless child David in his flight. But to the continuing annoyance of socially exigent critics, he knew from the world he saw that there was more to the problem. Why did Mell, even poorer than Uriah and with a foolish mother to burden him, turn out well? Why, if great trials evoke unexpected power in the boat people, do they bring out the worst in Mrs. Steerforth and Rosa Dartle? Why does more ordinary adversity lead Traddles and Micawber on very different paths? Faced with the world's complexity, Dickens will not force it into conventional patterns, always—unlike the usual popular sentimentalists and even his great contemporaries Balzac and Eliot—giving observation precedence over theory.

Still, despite this mysterious, capricious obduracy of individual character, Dickens asserts the possibility for moral and emotional influence, negative and positive. Mrs. Mell was proud of her son's genteel accomplishments (like flute playing) for their own sake, not to avenge her on society. The boat people had long been inured by the conditions of their world to face catastrophe by drawing together, and they were heartened by a superlative leader steeped in the ideals of that world. As a father of growing children brooding over his responsibilities to them, as a social reformer since his youth, and as director of an institution for rehabilitating prostitutes, he was specially alert to the needs of those too weak to go it alone and familiar with the roles of those expected to guide them. Complementing the memory that projected him into the novel's young, his current age and situation helped him animate the older guardians, the mediators between the developing person and the rights of others..

   David's are of course the most vividly drawn guardians, beginning with his mother. While surrogate fathers are greatly important in the novel, David and his most evident alternatives or doubles, Heep, Steerforth, and Traddles, all lack living fathers. Evil fathers, conspicuous in the novels at thirty when Dickens was constantly complaining of paternal exploitation, have now—after the reconciliation—been replaced as dangerous influences by mothers, doting and otherwise. No doubt an unconscious intrusion of reflections and recollections into Dickens's imagination, this bias comes into consciousness (as Harry Stone reminds us) in Dickens's note to No. XV, presumably on Mrs. Markleham's tricks, as "Shew the faults of mothers, and their consequences." [32] All of David's mother's instincts are loving, and she provides him with a love that warms him through life, but she gives no guidance past infancy, and demonstrates her acknowledged bad judgment by marrying Murdstone. Supporting her and extending her early gift of love, Peggotty as nurturing woman threads the boy into the archetypal human society of the boat people. Limited in power, she and her brother stand, like Tom Pinch's grandparents, as models and assurances of parental virtue to the projected David.

   Murdstone and his sister are the corresponding models of socially approved bad parents, making evangelical theories minister to their own sadistic natures as "firmness," which David early understands to be "another name for tyranny" (iv, 42). After six months of their rule alienate him and render him "sullen, dull, and dogged" (iv, 48), they throw him to a school whose master, socially appointed to civilize the young (recalling the master of Dickens's own old Wellington School[33]), was an ignorant rascal. When David's mother dies,

Murdstone caps his bad guardianship by refusing to guard at all. Washing his hands of the child, he sentences him to hopeless labor in the warehouse, on the ground that " 'What is before you, is a fight with the world; and the sooner you begin it, the better' " (x, 131). As everyone has said, the Murdstones reflect Dickens's memories of resentments against his own parents for Warren's Blacking and its bleak prospects.

By contrast to the Murdstones, Aunt Betsey, who starts as an eccentric witch out of folklore, becomes a model of guardianship when the boy flies to her, taking his part from the very first in her confrontation with the bad guardians and exposing their justifications as selfishness. Herself abandoned early by the handsome young husband who should have protected her, she has developed maternally by nurturing Mr. Dick. Dickens does not explain her change, which continues into warmth for Dora after early sharpness to Clara Copperfield, but has her imply that the years of guardianship have enriched her, lessened her oddity, increased her responsiveness to emotional complexity. If I may push my thesis a bit, as a projection of Dickens she had been long since betrayed by a proper protector (as he had been by John and Elizabeth Dickens of past years) but had found an aging and responsive ward, Mr. Dick (John Dickens of late) to care for. Her wish, the good guardian's creed, is " 'to provide for your being a good, a sensible, and a happy man' " (xxiii, 296), and therefore, unlike Elizabeth Dickens, she places her young ward's education first.

Besides embodying David's own growth in vision from childhood's simplicity as a grotesque turned normal, Aunt Betsey—in part a recollection of his great-aunt Elizabeth Charlton[34]—also suggests Dickens's growing tolerance of his past. The very fictionalizing of his development tends that way, for David is also Everyman in the fiction, and he is also an approved human being: if no more than what Shaw describes as a walking gentleman in a play, still a good man. We can therefore join David and Dickens in awarding good and bad grades to the people who affected him. We know, however, that no matter what the grade they have all contributed to his productive, stable, relatively contented middle age and perhaps to his sense of lacking some final fulfilling thing. If we want to play a popular game and pretend that this fictional creation is a real person subject to psychoanalysis, for example, we can say that the absence of a proper father and therefore of a traditional Oedipal mess led to that faint but certain permanent emptiness. But wouldn't Dickens's point, that the lack is Everyman's lot, that expectation cannot be fulfilled in this life, where even Sairey Gamp really has " 'no sich a person' " as her loving Mrs. Harris, forestall such a conclusion?

The guardians of the three main alternatives to David and of both his loves share a variety of disabling deficiencies, from nonexistence to the extreme of pliability. Traddles's parents died before we meet him as a schoolboy, and when he grows up his invisible uncle arbitrarily drops him. Mrs. Heep is an exhausted mother dragon of her fire-breathing son, an ineffective familiar in his time of need. Mrs. Steerforth responds to her son's misdeeds as badly as she had prepared him: when she speaks with Mr. Peggotty, "all that I had ever seen in [Steerforth] of an unyielding, wilful spirit I saw in her. All the understanding that I had now of his misdirected energy, became an understanding of her character too, and a perception that it was, in its strongest springs, the same" (xxxii, 401). Though Mr. Spenlow loves his daughter, he lives the unexamined life and is like her too thoughtless to make provision for the future. Intending her for the frivolities he knows, he sends her to France for an education in uselessness, and with no more judgment than Mrs. Copperfield hires Miss

Murdstone to be her " 'companion and protector' " (xxvi, 334). Like him, his sisters contribute to the infantile quality of Dora that requires guardians in her husband, his Aunt Betsey, and Agnes. Not surprisingly, in these situations Dickens blames the guardians for the failures and credits character for Traddles's great success.

A more elaborately imagined pair than the other secondary guardians and wards, Wickfield and Agnes, again suggests the ambiguities of Dickens's personal retrospect. Brooding over a loss (of a first love like Maria Beadnell, an ideal like Mary Hogarth) causes even greater paternal irresponsibility than heedlessness. In Wickfield's self-blame, Dickens poignantly mixes old griefs of his own with one side of the swelling theme begun in *Dombey and Son* and pushed to its extreme in *The Haunted Man*, of memory as destructive and redemptive: " 'Weak indulgence has ruined me. Indulgence in remembrance, and indulgence in forgetfulness' " (xxxix, 493). For Wickfield, memory has the seductive pull to death attracting Little Paul Dombey and his father, the side that for David recalls his parents' graves in Blunderstone, but not the compensating inspiration for the future provided by his mother's intensely maternal look at their final parting or by Agnes's pointing hand.

Abetting memory's negative tendencies, consolatory port wine quite removes Wickfield's ability to deal with the outside world on his own and his daughter's behalf. Although Dickens concurrently (October 27, 1849) wrote a leader for the *Examiner* arguing that drunkenness was mainly a social disease incurred by those caught in hopeless poverty, he said it was their response, despair, that led them to it. Despair, in Wickfield's case inability to end grieving for his wife and fulfill responsibility for a ward, is his motive in drinking too. The Wickfield side of the self cannot pull free alone to resume the struggle of life; but Agnes reverses roles—carrying her father's weight, Dickens's lot in his twenties and early thirties—early enough for him to revive with the discoveries and actions of Micawber and Traddles.

As a contrast to all of these stands the rocklike father, the unworldly ideal, the childless patriarch Daniel Peggotty. When we meet the Yarmouth boat family, we see immediately how well he has preserved his nephew and niece in their ark; and we know that no blame can attach to him when, like the child of his prototype, Goldsmith's Vicar of Wakefield, she falls in her trial by the corrupt embodiment of wealth and class. The worst fall comes to the ward of the best guardian, but through him she also achieves her grand redemption. In their responses to her fall, not only she and Ham but even the elderly ward Mrs. Gummidge prove the value of Mr. Peggotty's early guidance. And he himself, in a pattern Dickens had tried more lightly through Sol Gills's search for Walter Gay in *Dombey and Son*, outdoes Goldsmith's Vicar in his demonstration of selfless care. Wandering through Europe exposed to all dangers to reclaim the lost child, he confirms his moral eminence. Moving from his despoiled arch, this Noah also leads his family through watery dangers to safety. In pastoral Australia, he recreates the innocent childhood world, guiding the strayed lamb to sainthood and preserving others in virtue. As Em'ly and Agnes are idealized goals for Dickens, Mr. Peggotty is the ideal projection of himself as a father, literally of children approaching adolescence and needing guidance, figuratively of the lost daughters at Urania Cottage whom he was preparing for redemption in Australia.

By making the bachelor Daniel Peggotty and the separated wife Betsey Trotwood the book's successful guardians, Dickens seems to suggest that the complexities of ordinary life (like his own) work to undermine this chief parental function. The sifting of memory provides various conflicting versions of Dickens's parents in the novel to suit different portions of his life, but like other figures of the past they yield precedence to those complexities, which were centered in the great constricting knot of his marriage. The current couple, whether David and Dora, David and Agnes, the Micawbers, or the Traddleses, necessarily occupies the center of its own concern, and it will now in turn create a world for new wards.

No outsider can fit a couple to each other's hopes and desires once they are married; all that anyone can do for their intimate life (as Aunt Betsey makes clear to David) is to help them talk to each other, as Mr. Dick and David help the Strongs. Given the difficulty of finding the perfect match of Agnes and David—which in life would be foiled by the continuing marriage to Dora—we are left with the normality of the imperfect. The Christmas books, repositories like his short magazine fictions of Dickens's least censored reveries, tell story after story of good marriages missed, or eccentric marriages succeeding against odds, to go with their conventional swarming Cratchits. From their perspective, David's pursuit of compatibility with Bathsheba seems worth any guilt it incurs.

After Mr. Dombey's huge unresolved mistake in marriage, David's troubles with marriage and the troubles of other couples in this novel confirm the prominence of marital pain in Dickens's imagination. In the *David Copperfield* world of bourgeois possibilities, a man may honorably pursue many careers, not only novel writing but various forms of law, teaching, business, overseas colonizing, farming, even—a long step from *Martin Chuzzlewit*—medicine and undertaking. With prudence and industry, anyone not badly handicapped can make his way, starting again if one or another path fails him. But marriage, which no one can drop as David (or Dickens) dropped law or journalism when he found his calling, and to which people often commit themselves immaturely, requires the cooperation of another person, undefinable and uncontrollable psychological qualities, and the wholly indeterminate future. Something will turn up for Micawber, and after an unsuccessful law case or novel Traddles or Dickens may hope for a happier one. But in nineteenth-century England, only ruinous expense and scandal, or death, can cure a sick marriage. Reflecting Dickens's wish imaginatively to understand how he came to his present situation, the remarkably unsensational plot of *David Copperfield* allows him to offer several studies of marriage, between Murdstone's two dreadful lessons in how not to treat a childlike wife, as comments on David's and his own.

The novel's most conspicuous and endearing couple, the Micawbers—in personality famously based on Dickens's parents—live companionably despite their precarious finances and endless fecundity. As Forster says, "While the book was in course of being written, all that had been best in [John Dickens] came more and more vividly back to its author's memory" (Forster, 538), and we may add that the author's memory now tolerated Elizabeth too, somewhat less generously. To maintain the positive, Dickens limited their connection with the parental Dickenses to some events and to temperamental affinities, not including emotional family relationships. They are never made David's guardians or debtors. The Murdstones bear all the guilt of the warehouse episode, while the Micawbers share the sympathy and parallel suffering that Dickens was now willing to concede to John and Elizabeth in the Marshalses days. In all the details from the Memoir—the child's wanderings during lunch breaks, his pawning their books, the arrest and consequent dissolution of the household—David is a victim, but not theirs. For the adult son, Dickens substitutes his hard-working, equable, practical, vaguely comic side Traddles to be their milch cow. Finally, to preserve his fond, expurgated fantasy of his parents—and of his in-laws, as Doris Alexander has shown them to be (pp. 100-105)—Dickens exiles the Micawbers to Australia, the furthest conceivable repair shop for damaged people.

Despite being no longer young when we first meet them, they are endlessly youthful, pre-Warren's Blacking parents, parents without responsibilities we need consider: Mr. Micawber like the young Charles Dickens still searching for a career, and Mrs. Micawber always nursing a new baby. The pair are perfectly matched, always ready to dream a fulfilled life together at the hint of an opportunity, always starting life like David and Dora. In this way, Dickens makes them— roughly his and Catherine's current age—congenial analogues, gently ironic, condescending comments on his own marriage. As Forster says of Dickens, "Anything more completely opposed to the Micawber type could hardly be conceived, and yet there were moments . . . when the fancy would arise that if the conditions of his life had been reversed, something of a vagabond existence . . . might have supervened. It would have been an unspeakable misery to him, but it might have come nevertheless" (Forster, 636n). Dickens in fact liked to play at identifying with Micawber, as in writing Forster on August 15, 1850, about Catherine's overdue pregnancy with their ninth child, "Mrs. Micawber is still, I regret to say, in *statu quo.* Ever yours, WILKINS MICAWBER" (*P,* VI, 148).

As the Micawbers and Traddleses illustrate happiness for evenly matched couples in different kinds of poverty, the Strong marriage offers the possibility of happiness despite the obstacle of a great difference in age. When we meet them, the sixty-two-year-old Dr. Strong doesn't realize that there is talk

about his young wife Annie and her ne'er-do-well cousin Jack
Maldon, and left to himself he never would know. But when
Uriah Heep deliberately brings it up to cause disruptions, the
husband, now over seventy, takes all the responsibility for any
wrong. Insisting on his wife's honor (like Peeribingle in *The
Cricket on the Hearth* and Sir Leicester Dedlock of *Bleak
House*), he tells those interested that any fault in the marriage
is his, for marrying a beautiful girl so much younger than he.
But Annie affirms her devotion and gratitude to him, the
father-husband who had lifted her from relative poverty and
ignorance through spontaneous love. In the process, her
speech, clearly reflecting Dickens's brooding on his own
situation, illuminates David's problem with Dora.

As with the Murdstone marriage, Dickens uses the Strongs
to explore the possible relations between a young woman and
a socially stronger older man. But the Strongs may expect
happiness, because the man will not abuse his authority and
the woman perceives his virtue and has the character to profit
from his guardianship. She shows that character by citing the
importance of temperamental and intellectual compatibility,
which far outshines the physical compatibility between herself
and her frivolous cousin. Two other odd but unmarried
couples again show the cheerful prospects when the stronger
voluntarily guards and the weaker willingly follows: Mrs.
Gummidge (with the neurotic self-pity Dickens was to
complain of in Catherine) and the saintly Daniel Peggotty; and
Aunt Betsey and Mr. Dick, an ironic version of Dickens
himself. Always trying to explain himself in a Memorial,
sending off his writings on kites as an author commits his
books to the winds, he also shares a name Dickens had been
using himself in letters since February 1844 (e.g., *P*, IV, 56,
70-71, 528). All of these couplings, and the congenial Barkis
and Peggotty too, are of people who have worn into

compatibility despite their oddity—and they affect our perception of David's marriages.

Since David is the representative of Everyman, Dickens imagining himself in that role, David's marriages are central. The first one, studied in joyous and painful detail, shows Dickens's dissatisfaction in what he must have considered a gentle form. With all her poignant charm, the affectionate child-wife, lacking " 'more character and purpose, to sustain me and improve me by [and] power to fill up the void which somewhere seemed to be about me" (xliv, 552) cannot be a help meet for the adult man. Like Dickens in the succeeding years, David finds subversive refrains to judge his marriage by in Annie Strong's speech, agreeing that " 'There can be no disparity in marriage like unsuitability of mind and purpose' " (xlv, 564) and regretting " 'the first mistaken impulse of an undisciplined heart' " (xlviii, 595). Realizing after conscientious, comic, desperate efforts to "form her mind" "that perhaps Dora's mind was already formed" (xlviii, 592-93), David could only resolve to endure without fulfillment: "It remained for me to adapt myself to Dora; to share with her what I could, and be happy; to bear on my own shoulders what I must, and be happy still" (xlviii, 596). Freed of burdensome parents, and now burdened by his wife, Dickens turned his marital discontent into a poignant element in his projection's knowledge of life.

Eliminating this obstacle to David's completeness as earlier he had eliminated David's and Dora's inconvenient parents, Dickens even indulges the pleasing fantasy of having the wife gracefully abdicate into death, accepting David's judgment and her own deficiencies. On her death bed, she tells him that she had been very happy but realized that " 'as years went on, my dear boy would have wearied of his child-wife. She would have been less and less a companion for him. He would have been more and more sensible of what was wanting in his home. She wouldn't have improved. It is better as it is'" (liii, 657). Enriching the fantasy, she privately appoints Agnes to be David's next wife; and when David finally proposes to Agnes he assures her that "'even out of thy true eyes . . . the spirit of my child-wife looked upon me, saying it was well; and winning me, through thee, to tenderest recollections of the Blossom that had withered in its bloom!'" (lxii, 739). Imagining away the death, Dickens arranges blameless, painless polygamy for the projected self, fictionally judging and trading off Dora, the combination of his first love Maria and his wife Catherine, for an inspiring housekeeper who would confine her fecundity within reasonable limits.

Nevertheless, a strong sense of guilt accompanies this denouement, a sense that had been with Dickens from the beginning of his literary career and surfaced intensely in *The Haunted Man*, the Christmas book planned soon after dredging up his worst recollections for the Memoir and written just before *David Copperfield*. Before the wandering and soul-searching that lead him to promote Agnes from sister to wife, David has suffered a series of guilts: for biting Murdstone, informing on Mell's social status, introducing Steerforth to the boat eden, costing more than Aunt Betsey could afford to prepare him for life, bringing out the gossip about the Strongs, and resenting his wife's limitations. Most of these stings are more or less comfortably soothed, but not the last. Even Dora's farewell speeches could not whitewash his insufficient magnanimity toward her. Dickens must still cope with his thoughts about his own wife even in the culminating vision of his projected self as talented, virtuous, successful, and domestically not merely suited but inspired.

The replacement for David's wife Dickens has chastely been calling a sister, in a pattern he had used before and prepared for in this novel. Among the adult brother-sister pairings, the Murdstones and Spenlows, like the Nicklebys and Brasses of earlier books, are merely identities in conventionally different clothing. Between David and Agnes, however, the same punctilios (to use a pertinent word from *Clarissa*) develop as had obtained between Walter Gay and Florence Dombey, the fears, hopes, and guilts of pushing companionship toward all the complexities of marital fusion. The melodramatic Em'ly plot also rests on such tensions. On the Peggotty boat, where the terms are metaphorically used for a boy and girl growing up side by side, great complications of feeling develop. The Ham-Em'ly relationships involve some of the guilt of the David-Dora-Agnes, Dr.-and-Mrs. Strong situations. Em'ly's guilt in abandoning the innocence of brother and sister is overt. But Ham after his turmoil demands his share, for the apparently virtuous step of turning brother into would-be husband (li, 630), as Dr. Strong has blamed himself for moving from paternalism. Dickens, wrestling with the uncertainties of his own feelings for his wife, odd thoughts about her sister Georgina, considerations about his growing daughters, and lack of serenity despite his apparent cornucopia—a victim like his hero of *Rasselas*'s "hunger of imagination"— cannot escape the father-brother-husband-lover-creator labyrinth, but he can share it with us through what only looks like a conventional concluding vision.

Perhaps because of such emotional complications, rooted in Dickens's life, this novel as he approached forty directly raises questions about the point of going on, of always beginning again. Publicly, he affirmed his own resolve to re-form and go on in the cheerful "Preliminary Word" in the first number of *Household Words* of March 30, 1850, in the midst of the novel: "We seek to bring into innumerable homes, from the stirring world around us, the knowledge of many social wonders, good and evil, that are not calculated to render any of us less ardently persevering in ourselves, less tolerant of one another, less faithful in the progress of mankind, less thankful for the privilege of living in this summer-dawn of time" (I, 1). Sharing national and international hopes that were waxing and waning while the book took shape, he wrote an eloquent appeal for a committee helping Italian refugees in London (*Examiner*, September 8, 1849, p. 564), was a participant in a dinner for Polish freedom, and no doubt with the *Examiner* supported the aspiring Hungarians and Prussians. Moreover, while writing the novel installments, he plunged into more forms of hopeful work than we would expect even of him: planning and controlling the new weekly *Household Words* with microscopic care, overlooking everything—personnel, admission, discipline, building maintenance, even color of clothing—in Miss Coutts's Urania Cottage, participating in committees to improve London sanitation and the prospects of needy writers, and arranging the schooling of his sons and the care of his parents.

So also in the novel, Dickens's chief projection—along with Traddles, the Micawbers, the Peggotty group, and other good people—renews himself despite remembered losses and discovered limitations. With Dora's death and the Peggottys's departure, David has faced the finality of the past for the Dickens of the painful Memoir, suffering a "hopeless consciousness of all that I had lost—love, friendship, interest; of all that had been shattered—my first trust, my first affection, the whole airy castle of my life; of all that remained—a ruined blank and waste, lying wide around me, unbroken, to the dark horizon" (lviii, 696). And at the height of his vigor as David, Dickens affirms the renewal, putting aside the desires for Em'ly and Dora as immature though creditable. Agnes, therefore, must be wrested from Uriah, lifted from the grasp of the sordidly opportunistic self, to guide the evolved, purified David. Consciously evaluating what had gone before in his own life, Dickens conceives David's life in stages; and as the stages recede, each with its feminine emblem—his mother and Aunt Betsey as guides, Em'ly and Dora as child-models, wards—the maturing self requires a replacement. For David, renewal means Agnes, nominal ward and actual guide, pointing up and on.

Through David, Dickens focuses his need for the undefinable fulfillment—Faust's and Ahab's vast ambitions in his century, Henderson the Rain King's private "I want" in ours—on what he had been missing and was biblically justified in desiring, a helpmeet to share the rich mature years. It is true, as Orwell and others have complained, that in providing this vision of a wife ideally united with his projected self Dickens indulges in a kind of casuistry, an accommodation with popular models of bourgeois complacency. Searching for happiness through marital compatibility, Dickens does manage to have and cat all kinds of cake in the novel, grafting Agnes on Dora to feed David with affection, status, and even complacent integrity.

But the pathos that survives the shedding of old dreams and old selves hints at an awareness of emptiness even while the future lies open to the confident, honorable artist. Those old selves, old dreams, even old instants held before David's eyes in the novel, preserved against time by memory, still proffer troubling urges and questions. Steerforth and Heep, eliminated from the present, remain as admonitions to a spirit that cannot—like the saved in Dante's Purgatory—have the very inclinations to Pride and Despair wiped away. Something of what they desire must still remain, and rightly so, to the living man, something beyond the wholesome Traddlesian satisfactions. As Dickens wrote in an often quoted letter to Forster of several years later, he and his hero shared a recurrent mood: "Why is it, that as with poor David, a sense comes always crushing on me now, when I fall into low spirits, as of one happiness I have missed in life, and one friend and companion I have never made?" (*N*, II, 620-21).

At life's middle, the hero of *David Copperfield* surveying his past finds grounds for encouragement and reconciliation, but also for atonement. To cope with his discovery of memory's great truth—the finality of the past—Dickens can give him a friend and companion, even one "pointing upward," to help memory's other truth, the past's vitality. In taking her for this David from a Uriah, however, he reflects irreconcilable intensities within himself. As Mrs. Micawber's refrain tells us that she has been considering deserting her husband, David's insistence on marching ahead forces on our attention the seductiveness of chucking everything. As Dickens's complementary grand projections with David the arrived son, the universal patriarch Daniel Peggotty and Micawber the feckless, beloved father-son—both featured in the *David Copperfield* Readings uniting Dickens and his audiences a decade later—can fill their emblematic roles only in the Australian world after the flood. The result is an ambiguity of tone mirroring the ambiguity of Dickens's imagination of the world and himself at forty: an annoyance to even the best-disposed social critics (like Orwell and Shaw), but a criterion of honesty to the rest of us.

V. *Bleak House:* Passing the Bog

March 1852 - September 1853

A t first glance, Dickens at forty seems to conceive a world antithetical to his last one: a world where the individual fails under the pressure of massive social forces and the only hope lies in isolated places and a few good people. Where in *David Copperfield* he had traced the development of an individual mind and exposed only collaterally the social horror in store for Martha and Little Em'ly and the social waste of the Proctors Court, now he overtly and at length attacks national ills, bitter injustices. His perspective changes, both inevitably and intentionally. Even technically, in its wide social range, its tightly organized plot centering on Lady Dedlock's secret, its stress "upon the romantic side of familiar things,"[35] *Bleak House* challenges or answers *David Copperfield.* For Dickens as for any serious artist exploring reality, the themes that fundamentally probe that reality recur, particularly in temporally close works; and if they are not ruled by mere ideology, they necessarily reflect a dialogue in his mind. The central impulse here remains Dickens's conception of his situation after an additional year of brooding and a series of external shocks and gratifications.

The grand theme of *Bleak House* directly responds to the issue Dickens had consciously raised for himself in his Memoir at thirty-five, how the past had led him to his present world. But in place of a general acceptance of that past, modified only by a sense of incompleteness, *Bleak House* begins a series of novels (*Hard Times, Little Dorrit, A Tale of Two Cities*) in which past wrong or sin breaks with scouring effect upon present corruption. All of them center on social issues. Yet all of them reflect Dickens's preoccupation with what he was to call the skeleton in his closet (*N*, II, 765), his sense of a terrible mistake in his own past: his growing unhappiness with his marriage. Secrets that surface after long submersion—revelations of parentage, the identity of criminals, the sources of wealth or disintegration—had forever been staples of romance fiction and were endemic in his own and other people's nineteenth-century novel. Now, however, he conceives the explosion of past into present epically, fusing the condition of the individual in mid-century England with an understanding of who he was and where he had come from.

In Dickens's domestic world, painful events pitted the period from *David Copperfield* (last installment, November 1, 1850) to the end of *Bleak House*. After a horrible operation, John Dickens died, having been visited often in the last days by his son, in March 1851. A month later, Dickens's ninth child, the baby Dora whose birth in 1850 had been so difficult for Catherine, died suddenly. Among his close friends, no fewer than three died while he was at work on the book: Richard Watson (whose estate provided some hints for Chesney Wold), Count D'Orsay, and Mrs. Macready, all in summer 1852. Catherine herself had suffered for months from an illness, apparently nervous, that required an extended stay at a private sanitarium.

All this was in context of his usual busy life of attending, addressing, and chairing meetings for good causes, organizing and participating in theatricals for more good causes, supervising Urania Cottage, and painstakingly editing his weekly *Household Words.* In addition, when he bought Tavistock House, he undertook extensive remodeling to accommodate his large family. When the idea for the new novel began working in him, he seems to have used it as a vent for still unexhausted nervous energy, an explosion rather like its own climactic and culminating events. "I am wild to begin a new book—and can't, until I am settled" in the house full of disturbing workmen, he wrote his friend Thomas Beard on October 6, 1851 (*P*, VI, 506).

In its relationship to the external world, *Bleak House* is everywhere suffused with Dickens's concerns as social reformer. The editors of the Pilgrim Edition of his *Letters*, Volume VI, note some of the major ones: "His practiced and important concern with sanitary and housing questions has obviously close links with his appalling descriptions of Tom-all-Alone's, the brickmakers' hovels, and the horrors of metropolitan graveyards. What he saw as sham philanthropists, with a single universal panacea for the ills of society, are stigmatized in 'Whole Hogs' [in *HW*] and reflected in the novel, though imaginatively transmuted, in the entourages of Mrs. Jellyby and Mrs. Pardiggle" (p. xi). Some of his incidental publications of about that time document his absorption in these issues. Repeating points in his review of George Cruikshank's *Drunkard's Children* in the *Examiner* of July 8, 1848, his leader in the *Examiner* of October 27, 1849, "Demoralisation and Total Abstinence" (pp. 672-73), insists that the way to a cure for drunkenness among the poor is not prohibition but eliminating the filth and degradation of slum lives and providing air, light, and decent schools. He pursued the need to improve housing in "Health By Act of Parliament" (*HW*, August 10, 1850) and in a speech on May 10, 1851, before the Metropolitan Sanitary Association (in which he was deeply involved).[36] Aside from other reasons for doubting the value of missionary zeal in

Africa, he particularly condemned it as an evasion of responsibility to the English poor: "The work at home must be completed thoroughly, or there is no hope abroad," he wrote in a review of Allen and Thompson's *Narrative of the Expedition sent by her Majesty's Government to the River Niger in 1841* (*Examiner*, August 19, 1848, p. 533). He wrote the same thing on December 16, 1850 (*P*, VI, 237), to the reformer Lord Denman.

And of course he had long shared the bitterness of reformist contemporaries against the Court of Chancery as a symbol of the failure of Government's most obvious function. A few years earlier, to cite a casual expression of a widespread attitude, the *Mirror* of January 3, 1846, had defined Chancery as "A kind of judicial rat-trap, or mouse-trap, which it is very easy to glide into, but from which it is very difficult and often impossible to recede" (p. 15). His own exasperation with Chancery, presumably beginning with his work as a shorthand reporter decades ago, had been aggravated by a decision he long resented. On November 12, 1861, he wrote to an editor of a South African paper whom he had stopped from running *Great Expectations* that "I have a special reason for protecting my property, on principle, . . . derived from the Court of Chancery. Some years ago when I made application there for relief from a new kind of piracy, which if it had not been successful, would have established a comprehensive system of fraud before unheard of, I heard it gravely argued that because I had submitted to be pirated before, I had lost my remedy in equity" (*N*, III, 254). Recently, he had taken two nips at the Court in *Household Words* ("A December Vision," December 14, 1850; "The Last Words of the Old Year," January 4, 1851) and twice attacked it at length, in "The Martyrs of Chancery" (*HW*, December 7, 1850) and "The Martyrs of Chancery. Second Article" (*HW*, February 22, 1851).

But despite his commitment to improved sanitation, housing, education, law, and other causes, and despite his intention to expose the pernicious frivolity of aristocracy, he based the novel on the individual and the common lot of individual life whatever the pressures of society. Through spokesmen for the self (Esther) and the world (the omniscient narrator), he undertakes not only a picture of society ranging over England (and briefly France), from Jo through the world's workers to the clans of Boodle and Buffy, but also a move from innocence to adult participation in society that fuses with movement in that society through its dependence on time. Esther recalls a past, limited like David Copperfield's, that helps her to understand character and process and shocks her through catastrophes and revelations; the omniscient narrator surveys the present, an ironic camera recording busy scenes, aerial views over housetops, and miles of road at home or abroad, able to reproduce character history and to film individual people and the whole society on stage before the imagining mind.

But if their narratives illuminate and comment on each other, indeed persuade us of their integral tie, they leave us without telling us what that tie is. Everything, the omniscient narrator implies for Dickens, is related, but he implies it with the question Prufrock warns against: "What connexion can there be, between the place in Lincolnshire, the house in town, the Mercury in powder, and the whereabout of Jo the outlaw with the broom, who had that distant ray of light upon him when he swept the churchyard-step? What connexion can there have been between many people in the innumerable histories of this world, who, from opposite sides of great gulfs, have, nevertheless, been very curiously brought together!" (xvl, 219). Under this aspect the arbitrary had long concerned Dickens as a key to what his own life could mean, as in Dora's question how it was that she and David had met and loved, and he was to worry the arbitrariness of human contacts obtrusively in *Little Dorrit* and *A Tale of Two Cities*. Here, combining the intimate Dedlock secret (part of Esther's business) with the universal obstructive world imaged in Chancery (the omniscient narrator's), he conceived it in a world of projections who affected each other inevitably.

1

Among the characters sharing attitudes and circumstances with Dickens, the young—those who face the challenges he so often recalled as prefiguring his current condition, and also those reminders of his paternal concerns at forty—engage us immediately in the person of Esther Summerson. The child opening to full humanity, the victim of crisis and its survivor, Esther is Dickens's central conception and projection now as representative youth struggling toward maturity. Sharing an identity with Dickens as his first-person narrator, she also forms the heart of the novel's great family secret and represents him as the child outsider—seemingly parentless, like Oliver, Little Nell, and Pip, even illegitimate like Oliver and Clennam—in his series from Oliver to Pip coming to engage London and life.

A female version of his own underlying character with some qualities of his congenial sister-in-law Georgina, Esther leaves the Murdstonian rule of Miss Barbary, the blacking-factory-stage mother, for school and a notable start in life at about Dickens's factory age, if in the more genteel pattern of the recently popular Becky Sharp and Jane Eyre. This pattern of un-Dickensian youth, as Doris Alexander has discovered, owed much to Dickens's delight in a young ward of several years earlier, Esther Elton. After her father, the actor Edward William Elton, died in a shipwreck on March 13, 1846,

Dickens brought the plight of his children (of whom Esther was the oldest) to the attention of his rich friend Angela Burdett-Coutts, who provided suuport on the condition that Dickens direct its use.[37]

As the major action begins, in London when she is twenty (his age for suffering love and loss) she brings order to the Jellyby children like Georgina among the little Dickenses, complete with the story-telling talent Dickens had remembered in himself and lent David Copperfield. At Bleak House, she receives the household keys as a mark of adulthood and as a "methodical, old-maidish sort of foolish little person" (viii, 92) superbly exerts Esther Elton's, Dickens's, and Georgina's talents for establishing order. As the passage of time informs the epic in the cycles of weather, law courts, and seasons, in the centuries that matured the Chesney Wold ghost's resentment, in the eons that equated Chancery with the Megalosaurus, so it marks the stages of Esther's life, most critically in her illness.

Through that illness, like Martin Chuzzlewit at the edge of death in Eden and Florence Dombey exiled from home, she is reborn into the new world where she can learn who she is, what she needs from others, and how she can know them: "In falling ill, I seemed to have crossed a dark lake, and to have left all my experiences, mingled together by the great distance, on the healthy shore" (xxxv, 488), she writes. Deliberately created a representative outsider to do and suffer in the world, to encounter life's inevitable obstructions—Dante's beasts in the forest, Peer Gynt's Boyg—Esther shares her catastrophe in Number X with the socially significant catastrophe of Krook's spontaneous combustion. The second half of the novel provides the consequences of these climactic events, new stages in Esther's emotional life as in the dissolution of both the Dedlock family and the great law suit.

Of her illness, Esther writes, "Dare I hint at that worse time when, strung together somewhere in great black space, there was a flaming necklace, or ring, or starry circle of some kind, of which *I* was one of the beads! And when my only prayer was to be taken off from the rest, and when it was such inexplicable agony and misery to be a part of the dreadful thing?" (xxxv, 489). Much exegesis can be, and has been, grown on such an image, some of it gratuitous. But by indicating at the very least, as Garret Stewart says, "a passionate wish for divorce, for removal,"[38] it does seem to suggest Dickens's specially current brooding through his chief embodiment of responsibility, relationship, human ties. That sensation is, however, in Esther's worst stage of an illness notable for its isolating the sufferer from those still innocent of it. Even through delirium and confusion, Esther manages to reintegrate herself after the illness, like the young Dickens psychologically pockmarked by his rejection by Maria, and like the mature Dickens going on with his soured marriage. But he needed relief, as he gave Esther time to recuperate at Boythorn's. As soon as possible after finishing the novel, he was off on a long tour of Italy—without his family.

As the painful wish for separation also indicates, Esther shares Dickens's and David Copperfield's guilt, though unlike them she has done nothing to deserve it: "Knowing that my mere existence as a living creature was an unforeseen danger in [my mother's] way, I could not always conquer that terror of myself which had seized me when I first knew the secret" (xliii, 591)—a gentle version of Dickens realizing that he hated his marriage. Because of her, she thinks, the ghost paces out the fate of the Dedlocks, and because of her, her godmother had doomed herself and Boythorn to sterility; but through the adverb in her exclamation, "what sorrow have I innocently caused!" (xliii, 605), Dickens rejects that guilt for her, and for her share in himself.

As for her mature, adult stage, Dickens rewards her with both the satisfaction of requiting the worthy old lover Jarndyce and moving guilt-free from him to Allan Woodcourt. When she accepts Jarndyce's marriage proposal, she cries "as if something for which there was no name or distinct idea were indefinitely lost to me" (xliv, 611): the condition of yearning incompleteness Dickens said he regularly shared with David Copperfield. If left in this situation, Esther would lose the emotionally and intellectually fulfilled love of which the middle-aged Dickens felt he had been deprived by chance and time. But Dickens has her pass through a second great physical and psychological trial, a heroic, epic journey to the underworld under Bucket's guidance to seek her mother. This way, in a confused mingling of sleeping and waking, fainting and reviving, night and day, snow and mud, he projects her earning birth into new life.

Esther's reward and male complement, Allan Woodcourt, must also pay for passing life's Bog with a shipwreck, a plainer love than he had won, and a life of obscurity. A kindly walking gentleman like David Copperfield, Woodcourt also demonstrates in extreme form Dickens's order-making qualities, in the shipwreck acting with the authoritative calm prudence Dickens was to show in a dreadful railroad accident in 1865. Like Traddles an alternative Dickens with great ability but without the arbitrary talent and good fortune, Allan among the poor in Yorkshire will be, as Jarndyce says, " 'a man whose hopes and aims may sometimes lie (as most men's sometimes do, I dare say) above the ordinary level, but to whom the ordinary level will be high enough after all, if it should prove to be a way of usefulness and good service leading to no other' " (lx, 816).

In contrast with these successfully adult laborers for good in private life, Dickens develops at length the emblematic permanently adolescent young lovers at the center of the Chancery Bog, the novel's purest form of False Hope. From the beginning, when he speculated in the *Sketches* ("Scenes, Chapter 7. Hackney-Coach Stands") how a coach, given the power to speak, would chronicle the fall of "the country girl" to prostitution or "the raw apprentice" to theft, Dickens had considered defeat the easy path for the youth impatient—as he had been impatient—of long, dull labor for mediocre rewards. In *Dombey and Son*, according to Forster, he had planned to have Walter Gay exemplify "that common, everyday, miserable declension of which we know so much in our ordinary life" (Forster, 473). *Bleak House*'s most carefully studied victim of great expectations, the young man from the country recalling "my namesake Whittington," Rick abandons medicine, law, and the army to pursue the unmodified delusion, thinking himself likely to succeed where others fail because " 'I am young and earnest; and energy and determination have done wonders many a time. Others have only half thrown themselves into it. I devote myself to it. I make it the object of my life' " (xxxvii, 527).

Besides Dickens's residual fears from the blacking-factory time and recollections of his father's career, fears for his oldest child accompanied his conception of the Rick side of the self. On August 22, 1851, not long before he mentioned thoughts of the novel, Dickens wrote Miss Coutts that Charley only "wants . . . a habit of perseverance. With that, he could do anything. He wants it as a fixed purpose and habit of his nature. He gets on at Eton, with credit, so easily that he merely takes short rides on his Pegasus and jumps off again, when he ought to be putting him at great leaps" (*P*, VI, 467). But significantly more like Dickens than his son, Rick Carstone suffers from intensity rather than the "indescribable lassitude of character" that Dickens thought Charley inherited from Catherine.[39] Great hopes dashed or dissipated, from Martin Chuzzlewit's and Tom Pinch's through Pip's, were Dickens's joy and pain, not Charley's.

Rick earns our sympathy because his battle with Chancery is at bottom ours too. Even for Esther as for Jarndyce, our best selves, Chancery concentrates the murderous chaos with which people must deal, and for which Krook says Miss Flite has named her birds: " 'Hope, Joy, Youth, Peace, Rest, Life, Dust, Ashes, Waste, Want, Ruin, Despair, Madness, Death, Cunning, Folly, Words, Wigs, Rags, Sheepskin, Plunder, Precedent, Jargon, Gammon, and Spinach . . . all cooped up together by my noble and learned brother' " (xiv, 200). As the novel opens, mud and fog centered in Chancery are our universal psychological threat, a cloud we enter when reaching for maturity that dissipates completely only with death and that has its roots so far back that "it would not be wonderful to meet a Megalosaurus, forty feet long or so, waddling like an elephantine lizard up Holborn Hill" (i, 1). If like Jarndyce, Esther, Caddy, and other worthy survivors we repudiate Chancery's delusions or overlook them because of better aspirations, we still suffer its wounds—some by the Court's influence, others by brushes with its metaphoric relatives like the dandyism of the cynical or the insensitivity of false ideals, others still by retreating from the life with which it has mingled.

Rick had won his young love—a more prepossessing though far less developed version of Maria-Catherine than Dora, merging Dora and Little Em'ly—as Dickens had not. But while Dickens makes Ada prominent in Esther's consciousness, she is even there mainly a symbol, of ideal

Victorian girlhood and young matronhood, brushing the Bog most painfully through her love (again like Little Em'ly). Following the possibilities if the irresponsible adolescent self Steerforth had been permitted to live on, she is the guardianship Rick has evaded, the duty abandoned, the good in the world lost in the deluded pursuit of the century's empty quest. The effect was the same as Steerforth's had been, to leave her as a living memorial to an adolescent dream. However, in the adolescent ideal reconsidered, this Steerforth intended no ill, and feelingly repents before dying: again as with Esther, Dickens (like Sophocles inhabiting Oedipus) frees from guilt the victim of an injustice in the human condition.

In *Bleak House*'s third set of young couples, Caddy Jellyby like Esther carries the greater force of projection, becoming a kind of Traddles to Esther's Copperfield. Complementing Dickens's picture of Esther as contented womanhood, she adds the rebellious determination to struggle out of stultification at home that Dickens associated with his own career. Resentment helps motivate her as it did the young Dickens: " 'O! don't talk of duty as a child, Miss Summerson; where's Ma's duty as a parent?' " (v, 47). But as with Dickens, it is not her general state. Sympathetic to her father and eager to be reconciled with her mother—reflecting Dickens's attitudes to his parents in recent years—she chooses for herself in the unfamiliar world and by the end of the novel makes a good life for a crew of dependents, fully supporting her deaf-mute daughter, her lame husband, and his parasitic father, and providing a resort for her own father and all her unregarded younger siblings. Dedicating herself to "a natural, wholesome, loving course of industry and perseverance" (xxxviii, 538), Caddy is hugely attractive, particularly in view of the difficulties we and Dickens know a woman faced. But Dickens considers her, and has her consider herself, secondary to the reflective, large-visioned, order-conceiving, and clear-sighted self Esther. Although this judgment no doubt follows on Dickens's assumptions about the roles of the sexes, it is also true that he had preferred Copperfield to Traddles for pretty much the same reasons: reasons that reflect his sense of what was most valuable in himself.

As *Bleak House* offers Dickens's most substantial projection into a good woman in Esther, it also presents in a woman, the bitterly envious Mlle. Hortense, an extreme of his rebellious qualities far beyond Caddy's. Moreover, Hortense, at thirty-two about halfway in age between Esther and Lady Dedlock when we meet her, can be mistaken for either in shadow, and act the raging scapegoat for any guilts attached to them. Dickens's fascination with physical doubles—earlier, as in the cousins Edith Dombey and Alice Brown, kept within traditional literary limits by family ties, as here with Esther and her mother—which would reach critical focus with Carton and Darnay of *A Tale of Two Cities* and subside into plot in *Our Mutual Friend*, begins with Hortense to assert the mysterious arbitrariness of Providence. Hortense suggests also the horrors open to a courageous self struggling in the Bog: as the passionate Lady Dedlock thinks, if she herself had been differently circumstanced, who could answer for her? for us? Dickens had played with the idea of the violent woman from *Sketches* on, most recently in Rosa Dartle's rages; and now he pours out through Hortense the reckless resentments at life's constraints that had long tempted him as well. When she is caught, she delights in the irrevocability of her deed, the defiant attitude of a Bill Sikes, a Maypole Hugh, a Uriah Heep, or a Dickens who singlehanded took on the American literary pirates and the aristocratic idlers of the Royal Literary Fund.

Among the highly visible young men, Esther's first suitor, the intelligent and energetic Guppy, shares with Dickens

early social class, an early occupation, and an unsuccessful
first love. For Esther, he has gone through the strains of
puppy love, particularly the haunting of the beloved's street,
Dickens's recollection of mooning after Maria that amused
him in creating David's and Pip's pains: " 'I have walked up
and down, of an evening, opposite Jellyby's house, only to
look upon the bricks that once contained Thee' " (ix, 125).
Like Kit Nubbles of *The Old Curiosity Shop*, Uriah Heep of
David Copperfield, Josiah Bounderby of *Hard Times*, and
Bradley Headstone of *Our Mutual Friend* as well as the
young Dickens, he shows the negative signs of ambition to
rise from low social status. But if the elements that compete
for Guppy's soul—and he has one—on the battlefield of class
may surface comically as with Kit Nubbles, they don't
discredit him. He refuses to take money from Lady Dedlock
for keeping her secret or searching for the compromising
letters, stands up to Tulkinghorn's menaces for her, and
unselfishly comes to warn her that her secret is out. Though
his curiosity in practicing cross examination of Jo seems
gratuitous and impertinent, it suggests the intense dedication
to a calling that Dickens believed the most essential element
of his own success all his life. Something of an answer to the
most recent lower-class suitor for the heroine, Uriah Heep,
Guppy shows a Dickens aware that he himself had not really
been so bad, so absorbed in rising at all costs. A half amused
and half rueful farewell to part of Dickens's young self, if
Guppy were not so clearly headed for success—perhaps as
Stryver of *A Tale of Two Cities*—he would deserve our pity
for the upbringing that vulgarized his mind.

Much more stunted by their family than Guppy, the
predatory, obsessively avaricious Smallweed teenagers
represent a greater danger to society than Hortense. Young
Bart, "now something under fifteen, and an old limb of the
law" (xx, 273), unattractively revises the Artful Dodger of
Oliver Twist and Young Bailey of *Martin Chuzzlewit* as a

version of what might have become of the Dickens abandoned in childhood to the wholly practical. He and his sister Judy come from the same creative impulse as Dickens's contemporaneous "Where We Stopped Growing" (*HW*, Jan. 1, 1853) on the need for the imaginative, as contributed by fairy tales, adventure fiction, and mystery, to enrich the growing mind. By contrast with them, little Charley Neckett illustrates the saving qualities of love, which had been encouraged by a loving mother and by opening her to the feelings of her father and little siblings acts like a heightened form of imagination. In her Dickens revived some of his early feelings for his sister Fanny as well as his sense of his own childhood self dealing with the younger children.

Jo the crossing sweeper stands at the extreme of the servant-and-youth group, as insistently a representative human as Rick engaging the Bog and Esther rising from her shrouded origin. At his deathbed, Allan Woodcourt makes the omniscient narrator's point by leading Jo through the Lord's Prayer, affirming his share in universal humanity despite society's rejection. In him, Dickens projects a self abandoned in childhood under the worst circumstances, Oliver Twist without even the poorhouse scraps of food and schooling, this novel's Phil Squod or Guster without even the exploitive tinker or workhouse: "No father, no mother, no friends. Never been to school. What's home?" (xi, 148). After testifying at Snagsby's, he sits looking ignorantly up to the cross on St. Paul's dome, like the childhood self Dickens recalled in the *Household Words* reminiscence a few months later, "Gone Astray" (August 13, 1853). But whereas Dickens remembered himself as a small child thinking, acting, seeking help, he imagines Jo as just sitting in the midst of passing life till he must move on.

Affirming Jo's right to human treatment—thereby using him as he had Barnaby Rudge, to test the humanity of those who encounter him—Dickens ties him to the chief projection in the novel, Esther, by bastardy, by her unknown father's interest in him, and by the illness they share as a consequence of her sympathy. A reverse Robinson Crusoe, barbarous and alone in populous civilization, a joke Whitington to the heartless Skimpole, Jo gains his power as a projection contrasted with Esther, a young self not providentially saved like her but wholly abandoned. As a unifying figure who knows nothing of the story but registers its pain (like Barnaby, or their grandchild Faulkner's Benjy), he embodies the mystery of human experience.

2

As the hopeful young must approach the Bog more or less unprepared—unless they have been prematurely aged beyond hope like the Smallweeds, evading the struggle and its reward of humanity—so the middle-aged wander, search, labor, and flounder in it. These, Dickens's contemporaries, occupy as prominent a stage position as the young, even more evidently than in *David Copperfield*, and appear before the omniscient narrator as equals. They are not primarily fathers and mothers, like Spenlow and even the Micawbers, but possible friends or enemies, without absurdity lovers. Where middle-aged women in the earlier novels were expected to look and act sedately like Mary Rudge or pay the penalty of silliness like Mrs. Varden, here Mrs. Jellyby is pretty and Lady Dedlock, the acknowledged queen of fashion, "has beauty still, and if it be not in its heyday, it is not yet in its autumn" (ii, 10).

Among the contemporaries that Dickens inhabits imaginatively, those offering cautionary lessons in life to himself and Esther, Lady Dedlock—originally almost as

much an outsider among the Dedlocks as Esther and Jo in
their worlds—takes precedence. Recalled through a chance
encounter with a handwriting from the past, her old passion
generates the novel's romance plot, and she remains the
heroine of that plot. In her twenty years or so at the top of
fashion (a fair parallel to Dickens's public position), she has
always wandered in the Bog, martyred by a forced separation
from her first love. Through her, Dickens insists that the past
(like the fruits of his own mistaken marriage) must burst out
in her lover's letters and her daughter's existence, as the
Jarndyce v. Jarndyce case must erupt in combustion and
Esther's contact with the corrupting Bog in smallpox. Like
Dickens, Lady Dedlock must stay in an unsatisfying domestic
situation to prevent a dreadful scandal; but unlike him she has
a compromised past, in that respect being the object of
Dickens's fantasies, the woman a romance self could have
loved, as well as his projection.

Though Lady Dedlock's farewell note is more final than
Little Em'ly's, and she flies not into joy but from shame, she
ends fulfilling a similar romantic archetype, emblematic
union with a dead love, and forgiveness by a husband mixing
Ham and Mr. Peggotty. Having savored the one pleasure to
be derived from her past, discovering and embracing her
responsive daughter, she yields to the call from the past to
become an idealized memory for her daughter and her
husband. For Esther she has been the beautiful mother briefly
resurrected and eliminated, like Dickens's recollections of his
mother in childhood, to offer some security and remove guilt.
For the omniscient narrator and the lonely Jarndyce,
Dickens's most obvious projections, she is mature humanity
lost like the immature Rick among mankind's most painful
delusions.

Though Esther's father Captain Hawdon appears in the
novel's present only as a corpse, his influence is the pressure

of the human past and human individuality. As critics have
pointed out, one major aspect of that past was an intense love
affair of some twenty-one years before that was broken off
because, like Dickens at the same time, the lover was poor
and socially unsuitable. Now resurrected through his
handwriting—an idiosyncratic quality to which Dickens was
sensitive, as when the address on Maria's letter three years
later took him back a quarter century—this past self stirs
Lady Dedlock to intensity, to renewed life, as he stirs people
and processes that finish the downfall of the Dedlocks.
Moreover, just before the novel's present, as an alienated
Nemo, a no one, he had been a rudimentary father to the
other alien, Jo; with Esther and Lady Dedlock (to whom Jo
shows his grave) forming a family of emblematic guilts,
loves, and mortal interactions. From the underworld and the
past he claims Jo and Lady Dedlock, and twice reaches out
for Esther, once through Jo and then through her mother.
Such effects affirm a kind of universal Justice transcending
class and time, one answer to the arbitrary: evidence that a
life picked almost at random will reverberate after it has
dropped the infinite distance into death. As an emanation
from that well, through Lady Dedlock he leads the heroic
Everyman Esther to her trials and therefore her triumphant
normality.

Among the other middle-aged pairs, Dickens's
preoccupation with his domestic irritations makes the
women's characters determine the happiness of the men. The
Jellybys, for example, function badly as a family, for the man
has been neutered and the wife has rejected domestic
responsibilities. In part based on Caroline Chisholm, whose
helping poor emigrants to Australia Dickens approved of
while he laughed at her housekeeping,[40] she seems also the
imagination's hit at Catherine Dickens, even physically
resembling her as "a pretty, very diminutive, plump woman,

of from forty to fifty, with handsome eyes, though they had a curious habit of seeming to look a long way off" (iv, 36). Grace Greenwood, who met Catherine at this time, described her as a "plump, rosy, English, handsome woman, with a certain air of absent-mindedness, yet gentle and kindly."[41] As Dickens had imagined versions of his parents in different distorting mirrors from *David Copperfield*, here the Snagsbys are another reflection of Dickens and Catherine. "In his way, rather a meditative and poetical man," Snagsby also shares with Dickens a wish to buy relief for a social conscience, in his case by dispensing half crowns. Uncertainly seeking and giving honorable affection, pricked inwardly by others' misery and his own attitude toward his wife, Snagsby joins the people of good will—ranging from dim Jo to bright omniscient narrator—self-consciously wandering in the fog. As to Mrs. Snagsby, her sole function is to cause trouble mainly through groundless jealousy, one of Dickens's charges against his wife.

Less central middle-aged couples project more distant speculations on a possible Catherine. Although the piously philanthropic Chadbands are well matched in loathesomeness, the female has actually done her nasty worst sharing post-Warren's Blacking motherhood for Esther, and the female Pardiggle is worse than the male; both couples, predators pretending to be guardians, hover over the Bog looking for prey.

By contrast, the sensible and loving female Badger and Bagnet—both with something of Betsey Trotwood's comic eccentricity—create light by which to lead their husbands and their wards. In this female-centered complement to *David Copperfield*, Dickens assigns to Mrs. Bagnet, the constructive, affectionately responsible wife and mother contrasted with Mrs. Jellyby, the role of Mr. Peggotty, to

redeem the wandering middle-aged child Trooper George by
a desperate journey. As is frequent in *Bleak House*, the
husbands are primarily the wives' mute annotation,
amusingly distorted images of Dickens the courteous man of
distinction (Badger) and Dickens the bluff father (Bagnet)
playing concerts with his like-minded son and fondled by his
two loving daughters.

Through the Rouncewell brothers, one a bachelor and the
other with an unseen wife, Dickens plays into realistic
middle-aged antitheses old fancies about brothers divided in
their paths of life: most conspicuously the older Nickleby
men, Little Nell's grandfather and grand-uncle, and the
morally opposed John and James Carker of *Dombey and Son*.
Dickens uses the Rouncewell men to symbolize important
aspects of his world, imagining one as incapable of
independent movement through the modern chaos and the
other as the book's best possibility of fitting it with roads, but
he also shapes them to reflect passionate aspects of himself.
One side, Trooper George, is the direct, "manly"—a positive
word in Dickens's time—unfulfillable outsider who regards
with unenvying love the happy, bustling Bagnet family,
blames himself for worrying his mother, and gladly accepts a
niche as surrogate son and support of old Sir Leicester. The
other strives for autonomous achievement for himself and his
heirs, like the novelist who has gained eminence and
advanced society, granting precedence to no one. Although
Dickens makes them emblems in an integrated vision of his
time, the military retainer of the past and the manufacturer
presaging the future, he bases them in tendencies he knew in
himself. " 'You are not used to being officered; I am.
Everything about you is in perfect order and discipline;
everything about me requires to be kept so' " (lxiii, 850),
George tells his brother, thankfully refusing an offer to join
the firm.

Like the omniscient narrator, Bucket the detective is both a formal voice for Dickens in judging other characters and a figure of the present, discovering old secrets hidden in bosoms and families: "Time and place cannot bind Mr. Bucket. Like man in the abstract, he is here today and gone tomorrow—but, very unlike man indeed, he is here again the next day" (liii, 712). A gifted impersonator, a humorist, and a sympathizer with the oppressed whom he must control, "in his humble way a public man" (xlix, 676), Bucket is in every respect but prolific fatherhood an offshoot of Dickens. Moreover, despite Dickens's parade of investigative scientism for him, he divines the killer's identity through artistic intuition, indeed by way of a key image in the recent *In Memorian* xcv: " 'By the living Lord it flashed upon me, as I sat opposite to her at the table and saw her with a knife in her hand, that she had done it!' " (liv, 739). Like the novelist an agent of providential justice, like him also he guides others to relatively firm ground in the morass and explains and relates people to each other. Translating the omniscient narrator's exposition for the benefit of the novel's characters, he registers and judges society's views of Gridley, the Bagnets, Jo, and George, opens reality to Sir Leicester, exposes Skimpole to Esther, and leads her to her final test and triumph.

Another middle-aged man, as a false guide Bucket's opposite, the lawyer Vholes has yielded to the Bog by way of Chancery long ago, internalizing it as his own soul: "Mr. Vholes, quite still, black-gloved and buttoned up," looked at Richard "as if he were looking at his prey and charming it" (xxxvii, 535). An imaginative burlesque of Dickens as family support, Vholes has three daughters and an aged father, who—even after a centenarian grandmother lightened the load by dying—"'render it indispensable that the mill should be always going'" (xxxvii, 534). Butt and Tillotson note that "he was originally intended to support an aged mother: 'father' is a correction in the manuscript"[42]—evidence that Dickens consciously wanted to disguise the connection to his own situation.

Helpless in the Bog though more vociferous than his fellow victims, Gridley, the best joke in Chancery, "the man from Shropshire," represents—like Miss Flite, or the people in Dickens's *Household Words* articles on Chancery—Everyman ravaged in the prime of life by the disease of law, Jo raised to middle-class victim of society. Like Dickens in his quixotic battles, " 'I made a fight for it, you know I stood up with my single hand against them all, you know I told them the truth to the last, and told them what they were, and what they had done to me' " (xxiv, 351). Sensitivity to his wrongs leads him to imprudence, even an impression of violence, a quality Dickens recognized in himself. A few years later, he was to write to Henry Chorley that if like rioting Italians he had grown up maltreated by the church, the government, and the military, "I should not, I am afraid, if I know myself," behave better than they. "Such things would make of me a moody, bloodthirsty, implacable man, who would do anything for revenge" (*N*, III, 149-50). As patterns of behavior based on class and money destroy Lady Dedlock, Chancery destroys Gridley, as it concentrates one form of obstructiveness in life and he one temperament engaging it.

Among Dickens's contemporaries in the midst of the struggle, the ironmaster Rouncewell and Mrs. Bagnet, both relatively simple, move with honorable, clear-eyed confidence. The ironmaster has had the good fortune and the talent to find a way to disregard the Bog, though as we know only his public manner—which includes a portion of insensitivity Dickens often associates with a rise in class—we can only guess the serenity of his domestic life. And we can infer, from Dickens's image of party politics, the predatory game of Boodle and Buffy, that Rouncewell has yielded to that delusion even in rightly opposing the Dedlock interest. Mrs. Bagnet has also removed herself and her family as far as possible from the Bog, through devotion and integrity, as well as an ability to judge the small talent that gives them independence: curiously like Prince and Caddy Turveydrop, with whom the Bagnets share a precarious hold on the rim of danger.

For the Dickens contemporary at the center, Lady Dedlock, the ambiguous defeat of her first engagement long ago leads to the ambiguous end, democratic death with her lover and shrines in the memories of her daughter and husband; and the others like Hawdon, the Snagsbys, the Jellybys, Gridley, and Trooper George have left or will leave the world no less confused and unfulfilled than they are now. Even Bucket, the only trained guide in the Bog, can interpret the omniscient narrator to his clients only through those simple patterns open to his profession.

3

Through the older people, Dickens's prospective selves, he projects guides and victims around the Bog and its willing servants, those aspects of its nature that move within it to draw and torture its prey. As his obituary for Sergeant Talfourd in the March 25, 1854, *Household Words* reminds us, Dickens had arrived so young that a number of his most notable friends, among them the lawyer-playwright Talfourd, the actor-manager Macready, the novelist Bulwer, and Count D'Orsay, were a good deal older than he, and some, like Leigh Hunt, Landor, Sydney Smith, and Lord Jeffrey, were of quite another generation. Though only forty, Dickens had long sat with the chiefs of his tribe; and in the past few years he had aged greatly in appearance[43] to suit his position. Since his father's recent death, he himself was now the main father figure both to his own large family and the families of his brothers, with age and decline before him. Imaginatively exploring the possibilities for himself in the stage of life he was approaching, and responding to a past from which they rose, Dickens makes an unusual number of old people significant in this novel. A world in the eternal present as against *David Copperfield*, *Bleak House* shows the concurrency of the entering young, the entrapped mature, and the variedly surviving, damaged, inevitable old.

Where David never needed to consider anyone for long, even in her own half of the narrative Esther always knows that she must consider her guardian. Like her, and like her unsuspected collaborator the omniscient narrator, Jarndyce judges life for us and Dickens. Like her, he also acts for a part of Dickens: a part for which we now have vivid confirmation, thanks to Doris Alexander's discovery of his guardianship of Esther Elton. Casually sharing with Dickens "a handsome, lively, quick face, full of change and motion" (vi, 63) and a horde of would-be parasites hawking expensive causes, he is connected to other characters almost generically, like a novelist: not an uncle to Rick and Ada, as the Lord Chancellor guesses, nor a grandfather, but that universal relative a cousin. With the equality inherent in such a relationship comes also the ambiguity, as he cannot settle on his role toward Esther or enforce his enlightened fatherhood on anyone. Where he has some formal authority, the ward for whose good he exercises it considers him " 'the embodiment of the suit' " (xxxix, 552): the Bog itself. Identifying with Jarndyce as Laius as he identifies with Rick's Oedipus, Dickens shows that with or without literal parenthood the

Bog entails inevitable differences of perception, perhaps even alienation, on father and son.

With his Rick adolescent self headed for ideal memory (paired with the ideal adolescent Ada, a version of the dead Mary Hogarth) and the Hawdon self dead with the old passion for Maria, Dickens infuses the melancholy of his current emotional life into Jarndyce. Into his relations with Esther, Dickens projects mental play about Georgina and himself in which he had been indulging since Ruth Pinch and would continue to indulge through Pip's Biddy. About this time, Dickens was facing the possibility of Georgina's marrying and leaving his household. Informing Miss Coutts in a letter from Italy of October 25, 1853, of Georgina's refusing his friend the artist Augustus Egg, he added, "whether it is, or is not a pity that she is all she is to me and mine instead of brightening up a good little man's house where she would still have the artist kind of life she is used to, about her, is a knotty point I never can settle to my satisfaction. And I have been trying to untwist it in my mind on the road here, until it will perish in ravelling itself out on this paper."[44] Doomed never to fulfill reveries about his version of Georgina, the Jarndyce self in *Bleak House* is left as the archetypal father and guide for Ada and her baby son in the original Bleak House and for Allan and Esther's growing family in the Yorkshire duplicate: like Dickens with two daughters to console him for lacking a true wife. " 'Let me share its felicity sometimes,' " Jarndyce says of their home, " 'and what do I sacrifice? Nothing, nothing' " (lxiv, 859).

Sir Leicester Dedlock also projects the admonitory prospect of unfulfilled aging and also formally affirms responsibility as a guardian for those around him. But unlike

Jarndyce he lives in delusions, able to offer his parasitic wards only the vestiges of family privilege—the material goods for which Dickens had so long been pestered by parents and brothers. Sir Leicester's remaining public responsibility, dueling Rouncewell for parliamentary representation (the conflict of squires and mill-owners that Disraeli had taken seriously in *Congingsby*), Dickens exposes as a dishonest children's game played for Boodle and Buffy. Deprived of his Guinevere (significantly named Honoria), "a main fibre of the root of his dignity and pride" (liv, 744), he becomes in private life what Mlle. Hortense calls him, not a guardian but a " 'poor infant.' " Though attractive models in the family, both Sir Leicester and his chief support at Chesney Wold, Mrs. Rouncewell, the best representatives of an aristocratic past Dickens in general scorns, are blind guides turned victims in the Bog.

Boythorn, Dickens's tribute to both the character and manner of his friend Landor (whereas he said Skimpole showed Leigh Hunt's manner only), seems sufficiently symbolic too, but he's more fun than the old aristocrat. Always opposing Sir Leicester's false Camelot, as a harvest god surrounded by fertility Boythorn belongs in ideals even farther from the daily 1850s than his neighbor's. After his fertile impulses had been blasted by Lady Dedlock's inveterately pious sister, " 'He has never since been what he might have been,' said Mr. Jarndyce, 'and now you see him in his age with no one near him but his servant, and his little yellow friend' " (ix, 121), the bird on his head. Like the other virtuous old people, he serves mainly as an exhortation—to continue open, warm, and good despite early rejection in love and the lifelong deprivation of love.

Among those good old people, Miss Flite, along with the young Rick and middle-aged Gridley emblematic of the effect of Chancery, has managed through a touch of madness to color if not cushion reality. Her expectations are so great that she can live in her mind, birdlike above the ordinary world except when drawn to pain by her ready sympathy. The madness prevents her suffering Rick's despair and Gridley's suicidal rage: " 'I expect a judgment. Shortly. Then I shall release my birds, you know, and confer estates' " (xxxv, 499). Having discovered that " 'the sixth seal mentioned in the Revelations is the Great Seal' " of England (iii, 33), she expresses the side of the mind envisioning horror, like Barnaby Rudge, but also like him she cannot save herself or—except in their response to her—others. Standing at the entrance to the morass, she warns them that Chancery draws people, as it had drawn her father to misery, want, and death in a debtors' prison; her brother " 'to drunkenness. And rags. And death,' " and her sister " 'Hush! Never ask to what!' " (xxxv, 499). But she has no better success than Dickens's other projected visionaries, for her warning and example deter no one.

Arrayed against Jarndyce are the Bog's servants and representatives, the devils busy in the Inferno. As benevolent in aspect as Dante's Geryon and congenially youthful to his youthful prey, Skimpole offers fashionably proper advice in the service of an evil Dickens dreaded in himself: throwing everything up for freedom. An eternal constituent of human nature, he claims irresponsibility, moral as well as financial, as the artist's fair recompense for displaying himself. He would gladly submit his talents and himself to any patron who supported him, he tells Boythorn, showing himself Dickens's professional caution and aversion, the artist as cynical, resentful prostitute. With great natural talents that enabled him to acquire both the science of medicine—since Dickens treated Mme. de la Rue with mesmerism, respected in Dickens's fiction—and various arts, with a charm that gains him friends and a cheerful family, he combines the diabolical indifference of an elderly Steerforth, essentially

choosing a self-willed, uncreative loneliness much worse
than the loneliness of the good old people. Like Wordsworth,
they know by the lack what their souls deserve. He defines
the lack as his soul.

Turveydrop, the practitioner of deportment, is a simpler,
theoretical parasite, and less dangerous, for his form of
dandyism has lost adherents in what he calls " 'this weaving
and spinning age' " (xxiii, 329). Like Skimpole, in such
phrasing he appropriates to his own selfish use an issue that
Dickens was more and more stressing in his speeches and
magazine pieces—as in "Where We Stopped Growing" and
"Frauds on the Fairies," *Household Words* of January 1,
1853, and October 1, 1853—and through Sleary and Sissy
Jupe in the coming *Hard Times*: the need for imagination in
prosaic times. As never before, in Turveydrop and Skimpole
Dickens is warning himself about idleness and parasitism as
the artist's delusive mode and assuring readers about his own
integrity. Aside from Barnaby Rudge, the personified
imagination, Dickens's earlier artists—journalists in *Pickwick
Papers*, actors in *Nicholas Nickleby*, freaks and animal acts
and advertising sloganeers in *The Old Curiosity Shop*,
architects in *Martin Chuzzlewit*—had been arrogant, harried,
and mercenary in their poverty, exploitive in success. But his
caution now at forty, while still featuring pride, was against
idle self-indulgence and artistic atrophy: being uncreatively
frozen, doing Tulkinghorn's bidding.

Looming portentously through the fog, like the three heads
of Satan in Dante's last hell signifying impotence, ignorance,
and hate, are the three great ministers of chaos. The Lord
Chancellor has the least to do of any substantial symbol in
the novel, but he dominates his province as an idea, the
institutional bad guardian, the figurehead at the door of the
trap. Where the muddy streets are muddiest, "in Lincoln's Inn

Hall, at the very heart of the fog, sits the Lord High Chancellor in his High Court of Chancery" (i, 2). Recalling Dryden's heir to the throne of nonsense in *MacFlecknoe*, the Lord Chancellor is most emblematically himself "with a foggy glory around his head." No matter what his formal intentions, at the center of the Bog, where the Court of Chancery weighs heaviest upon the human soul aspiring to justice, he must preside over emptiness and negation only.

Krook, self-consciously his brother in the Chancery-devastated slum, like him suspicious, choosing the Lord Chancellor's obligatory acquisitiveness and inactivity, also contributes to the general harm as guardian of his haphazardly gathered past. An archetypal figure from the lower world, complete with his deadly familiar the cat Lady Jane, "short, cadaverous, and withered; with his head sunk sideways between his shoulders, and the breath issuing in visible smoke from his mouth, as if he were on fire within" (v, 50), he suspects everyone, knows nothing, and cherishes only shards of mysteries from beyond the grave. After his reeking dissolution, his heirs the Smallweeds spontaneously generate themselves among his papers, and grubbing about like the Chancery lawyers in the Chancellor's cartloads discover documents that lead only to emptiness and pain: all burlesques of the novelist searching for evidence of meaning and relationship.

In his apartment filled with dust, "the universal article into which his papers and himself, and all his clients, and all things of earth, animate and inanimate, are resolving" (xxii, 305), the lawyer Tulkinghorn also sits alone, drinking port (like Krook gin) and planning strategy. In the service of the chaos—the old false order—of the class system, Tulkinghorn too is a chancellor, but he rejects the rules that curb his fellows. Sniffing the secret and tracking it down, he wishes

only to hug it to himself, affirm his power to no end, keep the
victim on the rack, fuel his hatred of life. Tulkinghorn's aims
and materials are more intelligible in the normal world than
those of the Lord Chancellor or Krook, but when
contemplated from a distance by the omniscient narrator
quite as empty. When ordering his chief victim Lady Dedlock
to remain in torture at his pleasure, he gibes at her (and
Dickens's) losing gamble in life with the devil's old negation:
" 'most of the people I know would do far better to leave
marriage alone. It is at the bottom of three-fourths of their
troubles' " (xli, 580). Toward the young advancing on life—
within Tulkinghorn's orbit, Guppy who stands up to him and
Hortense who succumbs by murdering him—he acts to force
all into their places in the old diseased flow to destruction.

Like "the something on the ground" (xxxii, 455) that
remains of Krook, Tulkinghorn and his corpse are finally the
embodied secret. After their catastrophic dissolution, the
world could begin to recover and progress. In the open air,
Tulkinghorn's corpse, like the skeleton out of Dickens's
closet shocks everyone; after formal burial, he will be
forgotten for everyone's good.

4

In the plot of the novel, Tulkinghorn is the active villain,
not only in manipulating so many people by the strings he
holds, but also in professing to guard the patterns of the past.
For here, more sharply than ever before in his fiction,
Dickens rejects the past as a model for action, at the same
time granting even more than before its inescapable power
over those who must act in the present. In his preceding
novel, he had offered a conciliatory retrospect in the main,
not forgiving evil in the Murdstones, Uriah, Steerforth, or
lesser oppressors in school or on the road, but triumphing

over them and affirming the good effects of the hero's mother, nurse, friends, guardian aunt, and teacher, and his kindly elders the boat people and the Micawbers, all now largely consigned to memory. But *Bleak House*'s probing into the past, its digging through massed incoherence, finds fragments and bitter errors that must now be brought to light, labeled, and regretted, the past's victims consoled and its ills repaid and atoned for, to make the future endurable. The world of this novel at forty is the present, the stage for the future, the challenge for a Dickens who must not lose himself in nostalgia.

Instead of David's nurturing elders and schoolmates, this past, epitomized in its nature and still noxious power by Chancery, bred bad secrets, bad social divisions, bad choices. When it gives up its secrets, as of Esther's parentage or the last Jarndyce will, they open only on the pain of human passion and the emptiness of great expectations. All the writings studied in the novel remain fruitlessly ambiguous, like the markings of Melville's white whale. Like them, Dickens offers no certainties, though he affirms the value—as well as the temptation to despair—of searching for meaning.

And perhaps there lies the use of the past, even of the shameful Court of Chancery and the more shameful society that bore it, for the novel's present. Although Dickens does not focus here as steadily as in *Dombey and Son* on the drift to death, the stimulus to seek meaning out of the fall of dust addresses the same issue. Hawdon's handwriting and its mysterious associations, irrelevant to the actual case in Chancery, push into our present to help surrounding chaos shape itself into some sort of meaning. Particularly like the great Americans at the mid-century—Hawthorne of *The House of Seven Gables*,[45] and Melville and Thoreau reading nature's runes—Dickens was guessing God's intentions and in his own invention accepting some of His prerogatives. The uncertainty itself gives point. Raising the question, like memory opening the past, constitutes an obstruction to the drift. The consequence is action, pursuit, investigation. If that does not lead to clarity, it does discover possibilities of relationship, connectedness, not only of Esther Summerson's place in the world, but in a sense of all those individuals and multitudes the omniscient narrator wonders about, from Jo the crossing sweeper to the high and fashionable.

By tying the secret of an old passion to the class system and imagining shocking consequences, Dickens opened his conception to embrace the freeing of English society from the past. Throughout history, and particularly in the previous two hundred years, he saw the class system as a device for perpetuating injustice. That is the lesson of the ghost story at Chesney Wold, a major thesis of the *Child's History of England* that he was concurrently writing for *Household Words*, an element of his quarrel with the administration of the Royal Literary Fund in the 1850s, and the gist of some explicit passages in letters to his aristocratic friend Angela Burdett-Coutts in those years, as in one of May 15, 1855, on bitter national divisions: "You assume that the popular class takes the initiative. Now as *I* read the story, the aristocratic class did that, years and years ago, and it is *they* who have put *their* class in opposition to the country—not the country which puts itself in opposition to *them*" (*N*, II, 661).

Chesney Wold has no future, finally succumbing to the rot first revealed in the Civil War, though Dickens allows Sir Leicester, Mrs. Rouncewell, and George Rouncewell to live out its evening peacefully. Like the handsome manor and its grounds, they memorialize its few virtues. But its bad monuments, beginning with its dependent crowds of cousinly Volumnias, extend far beyond the grounds: generally in decay-dealing Chancery and the selfish dandyism of fashion and of parliamentary Boodles and Buffys, specifically in Turveydrop the deluded toady and the parasitic jester Skimpole, who find in it rationalizations for exploiting family and friends, in the embittered lackey Hortense, in the ruined lovers Hawdon and Honoria, and in the devil Tulkinghorn, for whom its ideology provides a mould in which to cultivate his love of power. But it is all on the way out. After Lady Dedlock's death, the fashionable world itself abandons Chesney Wold: "passion and pride, even to the stranger's eye, have died away from the place in Lincolnshire, and yielded it to dull repose" (lxvi, 876); and unlike Yeats, who borrowed "passion and pride" for his aristocratic "Wild Swans at Coole," Dickens is not complaining.

No doubt fashion and power find other estates and less evidently guilt-ridden queens and impotent kings, but Dickens's symbolic intentions are unmistakable. Though Chesney Wold's neighboring grounds and villages (the setting in which it had sparkled) may be beautiful, they are also moribund. Even the pastoral associated with it lacks a core, a base in soothing ideality that Dickens often reserved for the memories of his best characters, from the graveyard of Oliver Twist's mother to Joe and Biddy's forge in *Great Expectations*. Esther, as Lady Dedlock's child the closest to its natural heir, has no rights in it and no regrets; Rosa has been detached from the home-bred servant's loyalty to fuller humanity as an industrialist's wife. Boythorn, its local divinity, makes nature fertile, but he himself has been doomed to emotional sterility by the effects of the Chesney Wold system, a Fisher King paradoxically blighted by class and religion, of Miss Barbary's sort.

With the rejection of class comes also, for the Dickens of forty, a more emphatic rejection of the self as great and distinct, arbitrarily graced above others. In self-consciously examining his talent and his personal life, Dickens refused to play the aloof genius of romantic excess, and even his admiration for Carlyle and his ideas could never bring him to the silliness of hero worship. Reality kept breaking in. Perhaps because he had not discovered his calling until his twenties after cultivating other aptitudes, had not grown up dedicated to the sublimity of literature like a Milton or a Hawthorne, he was proud of what he had done but not persuaded of divinely ordained privileges. He knew, as he wrote Catherine in the lecturing letter from Italy, that his rank was above aristocracy. But he didn't think much of aristocracy. In a variety of public ways—wishing for *Household Words* to touch the lives common to his compatriots, contriving cheap editions of his books, and later reading from his works before large audiences—he reached out for identification with mankind generally.

After easily imagining himself into the distinguished novelist David Copperfield, in the answering world of *Bleak House* he speaks half the time as the indignant conscience of general humanity and the other half as an assertively normal young housewife. The special qualities of special individuals, here associated with the selfish claims of the Chesney Wold parasites, Tulkinghorn, Skimpole, Turveydrop, Hortense, Vholes, and the philanthropists, are as delusive as Chancery promises of special rewards to the Jarndyce claimants or as the old story of Whittington. Every good person loves Esther, but no one, least of all she, aspires to London's summit for her. London's summit is the Lord Chancellor's seat in the fog. The qualities with which Dickens allies himself here are energy, determination, responsibility, and not ambition but good will in a struggle for survival, not preeminence: Caddy Jellyby, Snagsby, Boythorn, Trooper George, the Bagnets, Charley, Bucket within their limits; Esther, Allan, and John Jarndyce as the reader's best selves. The iron-master

Rouncewell, raised to prominence by his own efforts and originality like Dickens, and like Dickens offering a better life, is too special a case, set off too far from the main projections and the large world of the novel's action to reflect Dickens's central conception of his condition. Like Miss Flite in her mad visions, Rouncewell is merely a fragment of a state of mind, a condition to retreat to but not to live in. While the omniscient narrator asserts his role as spokesman for the multitude of decent mature people anonymously, in the young Esther and the old Jarndyce Dickens especially projects a sense of himself as Wordsworth's Milton, choosing to travel on life's common way.

Among the possible selves that Dickens imagined in *Bleak House,* some were recollections, like Boythorn or Guppy rejected by a beloved woman, and some lives that he had escaped, like Jo, Young Smallweed, and Guppy as aspiring law clerk. But others were alive for him, at least metaphorically presented through characters of any age. Although he could not yet go to extremes in his own life, he accentuated the main alternatives by having Lady Dedlock throw everything up and giving Esther the chance to change her most important decision. Imagining himself in that orderly, affectionate young past self of decent domestic and emotional aspirations, Dickens provides the fulfilled wishes that he denies his older self Jarndyce, as he had denied his male projections Tom Pinch, Paul Dombey, and even David Copperfield. It may be that he imagined a woman's mind as finding sufficiency where a man's would not, in a spouse like Agnes Wickfield. In any event, Dickens's novels before and after forty both say through his chief young projection that fulfillment and unfulfillment are functions of the desiring mind, not of its object. And the richness of that mind, its ability to overcome shocks, he imagined more hopefully in Esther than in David. Most of his contemporaries, however, have either made their choices and must live with them willy nilly or take Lady Dedlock's violent path. Esther's contrasting omniscient narrator shows no defining mark of sex or age, though I think most readers identify the voice as a middle-aged man's, a larger minded and therefore less bouncy Bucket, indeed a near equivalent to the actual Dickens. In that capacity, complementing Esther's open dealings with the world that led to a limited, traditional domestic happiness, he has so long battled that world that he expects no solutions, but he indignantly, insistently urges continued action.

Besides blending an emblematic quality with the normal or idiosyncratic, the old are involved in the action as much as the others, in the virtuous Jarndyce and the evil Tulkinghorn and Skimpole at times dominating it. More than ever before, they suggest possible prospects for himself, as at thirty the variety of young were also his fantasied possibilities. Despite the element of projection that gave life to his earlier Pickwick, Fagin, Ralph Nickleby, and old Martin Chuzzlewit, these were powers in his world, like the political leaders or uncles of his youth. But in Dr. Strong of *David Copperfield*, and generally in the old men of *Bleak House*, he imagines figures after the defining struggles of maturity, alternative lives on the slope down as the middle-aged are possible selves right now. As Dickens anticipates for himself, Jarndyce, Boythorn, and Sir Leicester face unfulfillment, losses, even disintegration, with warmth, responsibility, a desire for relationship despite the impossibility of the truest union in marriage. Whether or not Jarndyce's feelings for Esther and renunciation of a selfish marriage convey Dickens's tepid fantasies about Georgina, Dickens surely is playing with thoughts of starting anew with a young, understanding wife. But at the end he conceives for Jarndyce a spiritual bachelorhood, an insufficiency soothed by surrogate daughters and grandchildren like Tom Pinch and

Dombey. All three good old men endure an emptiness that results not just from Chancery but from more deeply seated obstacles, Chanceries of the human condition.

At forty, Dickens was conceiving a large and inevitable bog built into the external world and the human spirit, not the divine testing of Job or the divine malice of Moby Dick, but something closer to the cloggings and frustrations of Shelley's doubt, chance, and mutability or Childe Roland's dark tower. Although we can modify its effects by our characters and behavior—Boythorn's hearty embrace of life, Lady Dedlock's self-sacrifice for a servant girl, Sir Leicester's defense of his wife against his whole world, Allan's direct and Guppy's irresolute magnanimity over Esther's disfigurement, even Jo's attempts to behave well despite his inhuman deprivations—the obstacle makes every one of us pay.

Its mere name and specific attributes in the novel as the Court of Chancery may be due to Dickens's resentment over an old bad decision, his share in the reform issues of his day, or his unhappiness in a marriage that law would not cure. But its roots in a class system rotten for hundreds of years, its magnitude and inevitability, its exactions upon all travelers through life, suggest a larger conviction. Beginning with *Dombey and Son*, Dickens had been haunted by the image of life as a river eternally flowing to the ocean of death. Here, in the dark wood of forty with the river bank below, he knows that warmth and energetic good will can guide a few along the way in relative serenity, but he has felt the unending threat of fog and east wind.

Into this most marvelously complex, coherent vision of surrounding chaos, Dickens infuses the vitality of his mature powers, charged with his faith in that vitality but also with an insistent sense of unfulfillment. In an image he was more and more frequently called on to employ as relatives and friends were swept away, he would keep marching on. Through the reforming drive of his public omniscient narrator and the shining model of private life Esther, he affirms the resolve to keep moving and building. Even if all hell breaks loose under the accumulated pressures of the past, these narrators have identified it and shown that the responsible, perseverant, and loving can hold fast against it.

But after the loss of the young Whittington self Rick and his embittered older extension Gridley, after the different dispositions of the helpless childhood selves Charley and Jo and the different moral and psychological speculations on rising youth in Bart Smallweed and William Guppy, the chief figure in the action, Lady Dedlock, and Dickens's best prospective self, John Jarndyce, enter a different sense of his present and future. In Lady Dedlock's death after the Bog's excavation, as in Rick's after expectations exposed and dissolved, he memorializes passion gone with youth. In Jarndyce—amid the mirrors of fragmented other selves like Snagsby and Boythorn, surviving the loss of old visions and passions and of the rejected festering secret self Tulkinghorn—he faces a kind of godlike loneliness mingled with cheerful, unremitting philanthropy. Opening Dickens's fifth decade, *Bleak House* expresses an imagination newly enriched by time's unforgiving pressure, the world's obstinate resistance, the imminence of explosion, and the obligation to endure—to persevere—nonetheless.

VI. *Great Expectations*. Defining Estella

December 1, 1860 - August 3, 1861

Dickens had experienced enough in those best of times and worst of times his forties, which were drawing to an end when he undertook *Great Expectations*, to justify a second, revised, universalized version of his psychological autobiography. They had been times of great professional exertion and discovery in the four varied, experimental novels *Bleak House, Hard Times, Little Dorrit*, and *A Tale of Two Cities*; of shocked and compassionate evaluation of the personal and national issues these engaged; of social efforts in the Urania Cottage work and in associations for improving slum housing, sanitation, and public administration; of intense escape into tours in England and abroad, theatrical performances for the new Guild of Literature and Art, and public Readings; and a great culminating crisis in his emotional life. Out of that crisis the decade first led him to project a self of almost uncensored fantasy in Sydney Carton of *A Tale of Two Cities*, a persecuted Christ conquering the arbitrary under the guillotine, and then brought the more tempered answer to the "Why Me?" in *Great Expectations*: because you are human. From *David Copperfield* on, he had been trying to define Tom Pinch's consoling reveries and David's elusive pain. Now, after ironies, revelations, explosions, and scandal, he grasped a hint of Pip's "poor dreams" in Lucie Manette and the thing itself in Estella.

As readers like Ruskin, Shaw, and Orwell thought, in his forties more than ever before Dickens affirmed his social responsibilities in his art, addressing a national rot symbolized by and emanating from Chancery (*Bleak House*); industrial strife aggravated by utilitarianism (*Hard Times*); financial swindles and bureaucratic strangulation in a world made penal by delusions (*Little Dorrit*); national injustice so great as to call forth retributory horrors imaged in the Reign of Terror (*A Tale of Two Cities*). In *Household Words* and its recent successor *All the Year Round*, he constantly aimed to educate his huge audience (well over three hundred thousand copies weekly when he serialized *Great Expectations* in it) to face ideas from Carlyle's to Darwin's and problems from the plight of the London homeless in winter to the sources of
~ industrial friction. The snobbish gentility on Pip's conscience, the conditions around and in Newgate, Jaggers's motivation for saving Estella, Magwitch's reflections on his prospects had his childhood world been better, all derive
~ from Dickens's intense social convictions. But they are not the subjects of impassioned lectures like those on financial duplicity in *Little Dorrit* or the selfishness of oligarchs and agitators in *Hard Times* and *A Tale of Two Cities*. In the world of *Great Expectations*, the pressure of the personal, and its relationship to the human lot, so strongly guided Dickens's imagination that social issues become contributory elements rather than bogs and blockages.

In *Great Expectations*, Dickens on his way to fifty looks back not on his continuously successful exertions for acclaim and achievement but on how his projections shaped and were shaped by people and circumstances, how a developing mind arrives at acceptances after a tumultuously normal course through the world. For that, stimuli from his recent life guided his imagination consciously to summon intense responses from his past and perhaps unconsciously to animate his present. Besides the deaths that swarmed on him beginning with his father's and his baby daughter's in his fortieth year, and besides his purchase of Gad's Hill, the manor near Rochester that from his childhood had meant social status and literary associations with Shakespeare, he had experienced two complex emotional sequences in the decade, one private and sweetly ironic, the other impassioned, corrosive, drawn out, inevitably public and scandalous, and at the time of the novel, precariously joyous.

The first was the startling initiation of correspondence, after more than two decades, by the plump matron who had been the love of his adolescence and early manhood. In *Little Dorrit* and *Great Expectations*, powerful elements reflected not only the intense commitment of his energies to Maria Beadnell in that past time, but the revival of those sensations by her writing to him in February 1855. As he said on February 10 in response to her first letter, he vividly remembered places and people associated with their youthful love: "I forgot nothing of those times. They are just as still and plain and clear as if I had never been in a crowd since" (*N*, II, 626). As he wrote Forster in December 1855, "I cannot see the face (even at four-and-forty) or hear the voice, without going wandering away over the ashes of all that youth and hope in the wildest manner" (*N*, II, 716). In *Little Dorrit*, the book begun within months of the correspondence, he took revenge on both Maria and his own youthful self, more or less kindly as the reader judges, through Flora Finching's comic impact on Arthur Clennam as counterpoint to Clennam's feelings for Pet Meagles and Amy Dorrit. But by *Great Expectations*, he was able to give that early love its legitimate place, to recollect the old emotions and melt them into his new one.

The other, greater event was that new love, for the young actress Ellen Ternan, whom he had engaged in summer 1857, along with her mother and sister, to act in an otherwise

amateur production of *The Frozen Deep*, on which he and
Wilkie Collins had collaborated. Consciously from the early
1850s, retrospectively from long before, he had become more
and more alienated from his wife, and his feelings for Ellen
now led to a completebreak. In May 1858, after stormy
negotiations with Catherine's mother and her sister Helen, he
arranged a separation and made the whole event notorious.
By the time of *Great Expectations*, Dickens had rejected an
American reading tour in 1859 to avoid an extended absence
from Ellen and had apparently bought her a long-term lease
on "a sizeable four-story house" in London.[46] Although no
one has absolute evidence of the degree of intimacy between
the two then, scholars generally assume that they were lovers.

1

Planning the novel, Dickens was deliberately exploiting
autobiographical materials for Pip, writing Forster that "To
be quite sure I had fallen into no unconscious repetitions, I
read *David Copperfield* again the other day" (Forster, p. 734).
Not now the settled family man who had written that novel,
he approached fifty as a dignitary oddly perched on the edge
of society, a husband living separated from his wife,
undefinably connected with a girl his daughters' age (or, in
juicier gossip, with the sister-in-law who ran his house),
supporting a senile mother and the wrecks of his brothers'
families, and civilizing vast numbers of magazine
subscribers: the great novelist and squire of Gad's Hill living
in the midst of grotesque ambiguities. Only an assertive
universality could imply meaning in all this, and that is where
Dickens centrally imagines himself. In the course of the
novel, Pip faces the world within his family and outside it,
copes with the complexities of society and the interior of his
own mind, registers others and impinges on them, shares,
achieves, loses, and shares again, not just Dickens's but

everyone's expectations. And as Jaggers implies in letting Pip know that he too had had "poor dreams" in youth, all have imagined their Estellas and known them in middle age as the worn consequences of the first dream.

From the *Sketches by Boz* to *Our Mutual Friend*, eager, delusive expectation—Pip's novel-long motivation—is Dickens's theme. From Nicholas Nickleby on, Dickens had provided young men hoping for such touches from life as he and Pip and the nineteenth century generally expected, and he offered those touches, if not always through Cheerybles at least through Crummleses and Chuzzlewits, as he had himself found them from casual opportunities. The great Reform platform of his teens, the grand American experiment in democracy, the continental revolutions of 1848, these had been largely public expectations he had shared and bemoaned at their dissolution; and privately what he had brooded over was the disappointment of expectation from his parents, of requital from Maria, of a fulfilling marriage, of increasingly successful professional and social ventures, of distinguished sons, of eternal health and love and friendship.

Without delving into details that occupied his always-planning, always-hoping, always-seeking kind of mind, we can see endemic expectation even in the chronic uncertainties of the family's prospects in his childhood, even in the normal conditions of an author continually awaiting responses; and experience had long ago taught him the ambiguity of the very best results. As a reporter he had learned to doubt even while expecting, and he had embarked on the investigation of the American experiment in part inoculated against disappointment by his reading. As he had characteristically written in the *Pictures from Italy*, arrived in Genoa "I stroll about here, in all the holes and corners of the neighbourhood, in a perpetual state of forlorn surprise; and returning to my villa: the Villa Bagnarello; (it sounds romantic, but Signor

Bagnarello is a butcher hard by), have sufficient occupation in pondering over my new experiences, and comparing them, very much to my own amusement, with my expectations, until I wander out again."[47]

Pip's recollections of the progress of his expectations, which constitute the novel, follow the stages of life from childhood to advanced adulthood, a favorite pattern of Dickens's Christmas fictions (as in "The Ghost in Master B's Room" in the Christmas Supplement in the 1859 *All the Year Round*, the last before the novel). Indeed, it is on Christmas eve—as we discover after an opening that shocks us with older archetypes—a suitable time for birth (in Pip) and rebirth (in Magwitch) of sympathy with the human lot, that the mind begins its development. Pip opens to our awareness with the child's universal complement—the self as father or mother—in a graveyard verging on the bleak wild marches, a scene as bare and symbolic as a Becket setting. There, "On the edge of the river I could faintly make out the only two black things in all the prospect that seemed to be standing upright; one of these was the beacon by which the sailors steered—like an unhooped cask upon a pole—an ugly thing when you were near it; the other a gibbet, with some chains hanging to it which had once held a pirate" (i, 4-5).

By that meeting at the beginning of recalled consciousness, the projected self is diverted from a pattern so eventless that no sensitive mind can actually experience it—drifting to the sea of death along smooth, unmarked ways—to a world of arbitrary expectations and ambiguous, life-forming effects, as a deflection in Lucretius's rain of atoms created a living world. In this novel of unforeseen events and people, the universal is always latent. No one really meets a convict in a graveyard escaped from a wicked Noah's Ark and lives through dreams of Miss Havisham, Estella, elevation, loss, and rebirth; everyone really meets a convict in a graveyard escaped from a wicked Noah's Ark and lives through dreams of Miss Havisham, Estella, elevation, loss, and rebirth.

Some years after meeting the primordial father, the child undergoes another great change through a magical mother. At about Charles Dickens's age when John Dickens was arrested for debt, Pip suddenly loses the child's innocent view of his home, its assumptions and plans, its stereotypes, its sense of social sufficiency. Like that event in Dickens's early household, the projected self's change strikes the memory in adulthood as response to a bolt from without: Miss Havisham's whim, mediated through the honorary uncle Pumblechook (a belated revenge on the blacking-factory Lamert), belittling the self and minimizing its status as "coarse and common." Shocked into a sense of class inferiority and possible stultification, as Dickens had been by the Marshalsea and blacking-factory crisis, Pip cannot delight in the next change, achieving his early, traditional expectation as Joe's apprentice: "Once, it had seemed to me that when I should at last roll up my shirt-sleeves and go into the forge, Joe's 'prentice, I should be distinguished and happy. Now the reality was in my hold, I only felt that I was dusty with the dust of the small coal, and that I had a weight upon my daily remembrance to which the anvil was a feather" (xiv, 100). Though Dickens never detailed recollections of his own equivalent year or two clerking in a law office in his middle teens, his escape to journalism—at about seventeen, Pip's age when his formal expectations began with Jaggers's announcement—suggests the same boredom with routine prospects.

Preparing for Whittington's universal adventure, eager for the delusions that masquerade as great expectations before the inexperienced apprehension, Pip believes himself to be specially favored, not by the talent and intense dedication of the young Dickens, but by their magical equivalent, a fairy godmother. Mysteriously, she seems to send him where the young Dickens had gone: to the larger world of class, culture, money, diverse opportunity, interesting people, and as it develops, an ideal and a love. Seizing the opportunity to leave, Pip knows he's going alone on his path, breaking up his household (like Dickens in his recent separation) for an ambiguous freedom. None of the chief Dickens projections before had occasioned such pain on leaving home as Pip did for Biddy and Joe, and none had expectations so grand and open. When at the end of the first section "the mists had all solemnly risen now, and the world lay spread before me" (xix, 152), we know that his eyes dazzle, like Lucien de Rubempre's at sight of Paris all waiting for him.

After Jaggers has provided Pip with chambers at one of the legal inns, Pip makes the adult discovery that obligations attend the great expectations of maturity. Pip's awareness of his corruption in condescending to Joe at the novel's center (ch. xxvii) gains emotional power, I think, from Dickens's reliving his own early fear of being thought arrogant or proud as he became prominent and from embarrassment by his father when he was an aspiring young author. But Dickens arranges for us to exculpate Pip, and himself, by Pip's very uneasiness, and even more by Joe's knowing that their worlds must diverge. Metaphorically, the pain is not occasioned by mild snobbery but by the son's move away from his father— specifically in Dickens's case, by a desire in his twenties and early thirties to free himself from his father.

With the convict's revelation, Pip realizes "how wrecked I was," for there had been no plans by Miss Havisham, no destined marriage to Estella, and "sharpest and deepest pain of all—it was for the convict, guilty of I knew not what crimes, and liable to be taken out of those rooms where I sat thinking, and hanged at the Old Bailey door, that I had deserted Joe" (xxxix, 307-8). In addition to showing Pip both the picture of one kind of reality underneath Miss Havisham's sham and the selfish base of Pip's own tie to it and to him, Abel Magwitch hereby replaces Joe Gargery as Pip's father. In Pip's shock, Dickens's resentment of his own father as a delinquent weight on his striving youth becomes metaphorically universalized.

Like Marley's ghost in the most popular of Dickens's recent Readings, Magwitch, recalled from another world, leads the chief projection to evaluate the life he has been living, and to change it. In the last third of *Great Expectations*, Pip faces the great problems of protecting the convict, which—combined with the agony over Estella, shame for snubbing Joe, and pity for Miss Havisham—will call up Pip's humanity and save him. At the final stage the son, having recognized an identity with the father, needs to participate in that father's good ending, to atone for the childhood fear and the adolescent resentments over status. Magwitch's death with Pip in attendance (as Charles Dickens had been with John) perfectly seals their union as forgiven sinners, with love between them and consciences cleared. The book's first vision, of Pip the child with the gigantic convict of the marsh, and the later shocked discovery of relationship lead to a mythic resolution, Odysseus protecting the old Laertes he has replaced. But with surprised pleasure, we recognize an artistically unifying variation by which Charles Dickens triumphs in magnanimity over John from first to last: in all their relations, even in the first reluctant provision of shelter to the endangered criminal, he has conceived Pip as saving that father.

After Magwitch and all the expectations are gone, Dickens shows again that like the Peggotty boat of David's childhood, the retreat to Joe's forge is not available to adults like us.

Instead of marrying Biddy, Pip can follow Herbert Pocket, who like *David Copperfield*'s Traddles effects a normal compromise with great expectations, to the nineteenth-century middle-class pattern of the acceptable, a trader's clerkship: as with the young Nicholas Nickleby and the middle-aged Arthur Clennam of *Little Dorrit*, a way for alternative selves without special gifts to be psychologically rewarded for striving well. Returning after eleven years of normal struggle, mature in his profession, Pip finds his replica, pointedly called Pip, "sitting on my own little stool looking at the fire" (lix, 457), to begin again the universal cycle. In *A Tale of Two Cities*, right after a domestic revolution that yielded hopes for the future as well as current slander, Dickens had imagined only memories of the hero's merits to keep him alive for his beloved and her children; as Pip now that Dickens was established in a new, unorthodox pattern, he permits himself a revived place among the generations.

2

After Pip (and more limited youthful projections like Herbert Pocket, Wopsle, Trabb's boy, and the brutal Orlick and Drummle), the most important aspects of Dickens in the novel are the early innocent father-brother Joe and the shapers, the exhibitors and symbols of the great world who are also the models of possible consequences, what Pip as young Dickens might become or Dickens may be: the atavistic father-convict, life's first shock to the child and the great shock of truth to the young man, as innocently deluded about the civilized world as the blacksmith and the child; the professional, arrogant, apparently cynical surrogate uncle Jaggers, who lives open-eyed and suspicious in the fallen world; and the embittered, autocratic, mysterious, manipulative, intense witch-mother Miss Havisham, suffering greater and more pernicious delusions than the blacksmith or the criminal.

In contrast with Joe, whose contribution to the bed-rock of Pip's character occurs unconsciously, the deliberate shapers change in Pip's eyes and mind. All of them finally seek to justify themselves, even to apologize, for what they have been and done. To all of them, Pip has to address not only the obvious question that little Paul Dombey asked his father in one of Dickens's most successful public Readings, What can money do? but also the greater questions, Why did you do this? Why to me? Sometimes taking on qualities from Dickens's intimate life, and always acting in a normal moral world between the poles of angelic Joe Gargery and demonic Compeyson, these three figures and the grandest vision of all, Estella, stand out before Pip and us, as the more specialized elderly stand out of the Chancery fog in *Bleak House*, clear above the mist of marsh and time.

The great sympathetic figure for Pip, the model of virtue that he plays up to and against through the novel, is the first father Joe, the John Dickens of colleguial early childhood: "I always treated him as a larger species of child, and as no more than my equal" (ii, 7). Associated purely with a child's world, the mythic spirit of that stage of Pip as Miss Havisham is of adolescence, Jaggers of youth, and Magwitch of maturity, the never-changing Joe is out of place among social complexities, incapable of coping with Miss Havisham, Jaggers, and Pip's new lives. "A good-natured foolish man" in Dickens's first conception of the child's world (*N*, III, 186), Joe (like Magwitch) grows in the maturing view to enforce the democratic lesson, the human equality among the good characters. Where Joe is at home, however, Pip in the complexities of adulthood can only visit. As Magwitch is to

be a vision of both father of the child and adult self in a world
of pain, so Joe is always both father and innocent child.

As the always-adult agent for the father in Pip's maturing
stage, the lawyer Jaggers is Dickens's guide through vanity
fair, recalling as an idiosyncratic character the anonymous
universal narrator in *Bleak House*. Appropriately, he appears
first as one of the many strange figures in the strange society
of Satis House, the incomprehensible local evidence of an
unseen outer and upper world for Pip's villagers. Having
established his authority (at the Jolly Bargeman tavern) on
the sensations drifting down from that world, he promises Pip
a share in it with the news "'that he has Great Expectations'"
(xviii, 130). After the annunciation, Jaggers arranges the
transition and the training for the larger world beyond the
forge's old patterns. But since he is responsible and clear-
eyed like the novelist, inoculated against the large world's
glitter by painful experience, he tries to lead his young ward
to see a bleak reality for himself. Always assuming self-
interest on all sides, he claims aloofness from the human
mess. But like the good novelist or the worldly wise uncle
who supplements the father's better teaching, he has more
than prudential advice and management to contribute. For Pip
growing up to see witches and monsters become people
Jaggers stands as an honorable guide, a self intending good
even while he parades a tamed murderess as his housekeeper
and dares criminals with ostentatiously unchained windows.

One of the book's triumphs is the great emotional scene
when Jaggers responds to a human appeal beyond his
professional obligations and takes on the role of father to Pip,
like the John Jarndyce who can't keep himself within the
limits of legal guardianship for Rick Carstone. Pip pleads
with him for a clearer understanding not of his legal situation
but of Estella's origin. "I wanted assurance of the truth from

him. And if he asked me why I wanted it and why I thought I had any right to it, I would tell him, little as he cared for such poor dreams, that I had loved Estella dearly and long, and that, although I had lost her and must live a bereaved life, whatever concerned her was still nearer and dearer to me than anything else in the world" (li, 390). As the recollected young self Pip appeals to the mature one—to a man Dickens's age—for a concrete truth, a hint, whatever golden bit of meaning the species has dug from the mine of time.

And Dickens has Jaggers reply on those terms, abandoning aloofness to show another life of expectations, of incompletely stifled humanity even amidst the filth of a practice in criminal law. In one memorable act of disinterested good will, he had seized the chance of saving one pretty, still unpolluted little girl from sure destruction: an imaginative rationalization, I think, for Dickens's appropriation of Ellen Ternan. Although Dickens did not describe the respectable Ternan mother and daughters as facing such dangers, his pictures of theatrical life, from the *Memoirs of Joseph Grimaldi* to his last long talk with his daughter Katey, imply a toughening into moral sloppiness from which he would wish to protect Ellen. Jaggers's act has also shown normal human charity, thereby helping Pip to a mature perception of normality around him. He teaches Pip by this revelation that one can live open-eyed in a sinful world and remain honorable, even on occasion compassionate and hopeful. And his confession of old "poor dreams" of his own suggests to us Pip's special good fortune at the end, like Dickens's at fifty, in keeping them alive.

Jaggers's equally middle-aged clerk Wemmick complements him as an active, useful surrogate uncle for the developing youth, a normal side of the professionally dedicated Dickens that the self-consciously mythic Jaggers represses: the cultivator of home and friends, with a playful fancy, affectionate relationships, and a tendency to good works. Embattled like Jaggers in the Newgate ambience, breathing the law's assumption of universal selfishness—where he can at best be a courteous gardener among the doomed criminals, culling them like the novelist selecting characters—he defends himself by as complete a division of mood between work and home as his professional taint allows. At a time when Dickens could not have avoided speculating about such a division in himself, with his usual self-irony he imagines a humanity strong-willed but nonetheless limited by habit, in the toy defenses of the little suburban castle and the collection of grisly relics. In his close ties to the Aged Parent, a cheerful parallel to Pip-Magwitch, Wemmick also reflects Dickens's fantasies about his own dependent parents, as well as the continuing question about maintaining comforting illusions—a question Jaggers pointedly posed to Pip about Estella's secret. I also suspect mild mockery of Dickens's current concerns in Wemmick's middle-aged love and his pretence of going fishing to avoid gossip about it.

While Jaggers mediates between Pip and higher principles and powers and Wemmick teaches Pip the obligations and pleasures of daily life, Matthew Pocket—another avuncular mediating figure—more formally introduces him to his new middle class, imparting the things a beginning gentleman (like the young arriving journalist and novelist Dickens) needed to know, say, and do. Scorning the paraphernalia of the upper class, as his son notes, Pocket expresses Dickens's continuing desire—now sharpened, I think, by the need to polish the Dickens girls and Ellen—to raise Pips and Estellas to the community of the civilized. The harried father of a large family, he extends and burlesques an aspect of himself that had been amusing Dickens for a decade. Bemused by his regiment of children in a household where they tumbled up without their mother's attention, unable to understand why he rather than someone else has them, Mr. Pocket could say with the Dickens of a February 1852 letter, "I begin to count the children incorrectly, they are so many; and to find fresh ones coming down to dinner in a perfect procession, when I thought there were no more" (*P*, VI, 591).

The convict, the human animal, the bare forked, featherless biped itself—but now, unlike Jo of *Bleak House*, fanged and clawed—seizes on the child's mind as a vision of both predator and prey, though the pitiable qualities are first buried beneath the fearful ones. Indeed, those fearful ones, "the revival for a few minutes of the terror of childhood" (xxviii, 217), welled to Dickens's mind from his own childhood as he imagined the novel. In an "Uncommercial Traveller" piece of September 8, 1860, in *All the Year Round*, Dickens recalled stories of his nursery days that featured the giant Captain Murderer, who threatened to eat children. Pip's pity for a fugitive may have had a source as old, for in "New Year's Day" of January 1, 1859, in *Household Words* he had remembered a long-ago New Year's day when he joined with his sister to hide a fugitive in their cellar. Both elements and their associations would have been frequently revived by his public Reading of *A Christmas Carol* that featured Marley's sudden, frightening appearance to Scrooge and included the Cratchits' worry that a Christmas pudding might have been stolen, as the Gargerys' was.[48]

In Dickens's conception of that first brilliant scene, he conveys the sense of dredging the figure out of memories older yet and more universal. When the convict rises from the mist in the graveyard where Pip's family is buried, he seems not only the primordial ancestor of childhood but a representative from the vast assembly of the dead like Esther's father in *Bleak House*: "As I saw him go, picking his way among the nettles, and among the brambles that bound the green mounds, he looked in my young eyes as if he were eluding the hands of the dead people, stretching up cautiously out of their graves, to get a twist upon his ankle and pull him in" (i, 4).

Assuming the blame for looting the blacksmith's pantry and tool supply, and (as we learn much later) reminded by the child of his own daughter, he early stands as a version of protective fatherhood to Pip that is to be his chosen role. When Dickens, pursuing a fantasy endemic in his Christmas tales, casts him back upon England after a long absence—like Clennam and Manette sharing the loss of decades with a Dickens repudiating his married years—the convict is inured to that role. Returned to London at sixty, in great danger of the death in Compeyson's shape, Abel Magwitch realizes the joy of challenging the world through his more powerful recreated self, a rich and genteel son.

Summoning up recollections of his dead father, Dickens stresses the weight that Magwitch lays on young Pip, the weight that Dickens had felt on his back when he was storming the world's gates. "What I was chained to, and how heavily, became intelligible to me, as I heard his hoarse voice, and sat looking up at his furrowed bald head with its iron-grey hair at the sides" (xl, 313). But if Dickens in his late twenties and early thirties had resented his father's irresponsible behavior, for John's last few years their relationship had been warm, and the son's memory since his death even warmer: "'The longer I live, the better man I think him,'" Forster quotes him as saying (Forster, 552). In an apology for his old thoughts about his own father, therefore, Dickens has Magwitch show paternal selflessness and gratitude: "'In every single thing I went for, I went for you. "Lord strike a blight upon it," I says, wotever it was I went for, "if it ain't for him!"'" (xxxix, 305). Arousing Pip's necessary responsibility and involuntary gratitude, respect, and sympathy, he helps Pip to rise to charity: "when I took my place by Magwitch's side, I felt that that was my place henceforth while he lived. For now my repugnance to him had all melted away, and in the hunted wounded shackled creature who held my hand in his, I only saw a man who had meant to be my benefactor, and who had felt affectionately, gratefully, and generously, towards me with great constancy through a series of years. I only saw in him a much better man than I had been to Joe" (lix, 423).

As a final blessing on John's memory, Dickens has Magwitch die with a loving adoptive son at his side and news of a miraculously resurrected daughter. In this respect, as in age, a sense of atonement, and some aspects of temperament, the convict reflects Dickens himself as well as his father, fleshing out the fantasy that the baby Dora had lived—as Esther Summerson and Lucie Manette astonished their parents by existing. Like Joe Gargery and John Dickens, Magwitch cannot guide Pip practically; but despite a criminal education in misconceiving the world, in this filially pious book his moral perception—like theirs—is fundamentally right. Although Pip had been mistaken in forsaking Joe, he had unknowingly done so for a good man· a man who like John and Charles Dickens had "'worked out and paid for'" his sins and now lived honestly, an Abel who deserved better from life than the brand of Cain. Wholly accepting identification with the life-giving, reborn sinner as father, Dickens here for the first time stresses not the father's obligation to the child but the child's to the father. As Jaggers might say, Dickens wanted the children on his side in the separation, not Catherine's.

As Magwitch from the start intrudes intense animal life into the graveyard and the dreary marshes, a criminal and a victim because in youth he had not learned to control his passions, needing almost two decades—about the term of

Dickens's marriage—to labor patiently and then burst back into the dangers of life, so his complement Compeyson is a metaphor for death, a projection in its ultimate form of Dickens's old sympathy with mocking mischief. The seducer and betrayer of Miss Havisham, her half-brother, and Magwitch, the relentless plotter and employer of half of London's criminals, Compeyson had "'no more heart than a iron file, he was as cold as death, and he had the head of the Devil'" (xlii, 330). A symbolic mental state and social quality rather than a character with complex interests, Compeyson appears first as a threat in the graveyard mist attacked by Magwitch, who thereby forfeits his chance to escape from the hulks; then as a shadow of Pip at the theater while a mortal danger to the returned Magwitch; then as the old cause of Miss Havisham's living death and Magwitch's imprisonment; finally as a shrouded doom grappled to the depths of the river of death. First and last he entraps and desperately fears the principle of turbulent life, Magwitch.

The essence of selfish negation, Compeyson haunts Pip in the last third of the novel as the world's agent to punish and represent pride, the novel's special sin. Swelling Steerforth's adolescent Byronism into a personification of superiority to human feeling—of unearned, arbitrary class privilege—he manipulates the puppets in the vanity fair of expectations. Having himself risen from a shabby genteel origin to whatever participation he chose in any level of society, Dickens had been exposing just such puppeteering with increasing contempt from the beginning, never more convincingly than in the novels of his forties, in *Bleak House*'s Dedlocks, Boodles, and Buffys, *Hard Times*'s Harthouse and Mrs. Sparsit, *Little Dorrit*'s Tite Barnacles, Gowans, Mrs. Merdle, and Mrs. General, and the grotesque St. Evremondes and parasitic emigres of *A Tale of Two Cities*. Through Compeyson as pure, motiveless evil, Miss Havisham in her delusive swamp, and the adult Pockets (laboring father and son, lounging mother), he now suggests the avenues available to the gentry after the decline of Chesney Wold: exploitation, suicidal sterility, irresponsibility, or rational turn to the bourgeoisie. And though Dickens usually said, to Miss Coutts as to the working men of Birmingham (in a speech before a Reading reported in the *Examiner* of January 17, 1854), that he was against abolishing the class system, the careers of Compeyson, Miss Havisham, and the Pockets—as of their predecessors in his vision of life in the mid-nineteenth century—suggest otherwise.

Psychologically ruined by the corrupt class model Compeyson, Miss Havisham plays out her share of this vision, enlisting on Compeyson's death-devoted side in the hope of making all society share her misery. When as nineteenth-century readers we consider her abandoning a creative life out of thwarted vanity—one impassioned alternative to Dickens's plunge into work after Maria—her inactive despair rotting everything about her, her transformation of her ward Estella into a sterile facade, and finally her careless self-immolation that almost destroys her rescuer Pip, we know we are better off without what she represents. Presumably as human to start with as Magwitch, she has been more deeply devastated by a culture of obsessive social class.

Hints of Miss Havisham that recur during his maritally troubled forties, from as far back as 1853,[49] had grown into three vaguely maternal figures in *Little Dorrit*, when Dickens's sense of having a skeleton in his domestic closet was acute: Clennam's real mother, who had lived a ghostly imprisonment in the family house for years until her death; the old servant Affery, who sees visions and hears noises; and Mrs. Clennam, confined to her chair by guilt and illness until she breaks out and then collapses to parallel the

disintegration of that house. Fragments of the idea persisted
into the time after he stopped pretending domestic normality.
A year before he began *Great Expectations*, the Christmas
supplement of *All the Year Round* for 1859, *The Haunted
House*, concerns a house with the rotten quality of Miss
Havisham's wedding-breakfast room; and his first piece in
that number, "The Mortals in the House," says that people
asleep suggest death, as "the stopped life, the broken threads
of yesterday, the deserted seat, the closed book, the
unfinished but abandoned occupation, all are images of
death" (p. 2). Still preoccupied with associations of domestic
disintegration and the fear of disastrous consequences,
Dickens centered his 1861 Christmas supplement of the
magazine, *Tom Tiddler's Ground*, on a hermit's turning his
house and grounds into a wasteland and the need to move out
to engage the world.

Evidently Dickens conceived Miss Havisham as a
grotesque third-stage mother: the first stage being the
childlike mother before Warren's Blacking, say Clara
Copperfield; the second the severe Miss Murdstone or
Georgiana Gargery who thwarted him; the third the silly
woman from Mrs. Nickleby on (and including Mrs. Gargery
after Orlick's vengeful assault), now exaggerated by
Elizabeth Dickens's senility. "My mother," he wrote a friend
on August 19, 1860, "is in the strangest state of mind from
senile decay; and the impossibility of getting her to
understand what is the matter, combined with her desire to be
got up in sables like a female Hamlet, illumines the dreary
scene with a ghastly absurdity that is the chief relief I can
find in it" (*N*, III, 172).

The immediate grotesque embodiment of the upper world
for the village and the willing medium of its appeal, Miss
Havisham looms before Pip, Dickens, and the reader as the

fairy godmother turned witch, and then turned again to distraught normality. Following a thread of misdirecting helpless children that Dickens had been trailing since Fagin, Miss Havisham first shows Pip—at about Dickens's blacking-factory age—his contemptible place in a world of class and wealth, and then helps lead him to his delusions in it. In all her attributes, she symbolizes the stage of Pip's delusive expectations, the genteel society he hopes he is entering: its decay indicated by the dissolution of the family business, the house, the grounds, even the wasted wedding breakfast; its parasitic poor relations; its manipulative selfishness; its suicidal tendencies that finally arouse the mature Pip's compassion. Pip realizes, observing her desolation, what has been the core of her deficiency, and responds with forgiving humanity to its effect on himself and on human society: "And could I look upon her without compassion, seeing her punishment in the ruin she was, in her profound unfitness for this earth on which she was placed, in the vanity of sorrow which had become a master mania, like the vanity of penitence, the vanity of remorse, the vanity of unworthiness, and other monstrous vanities that have been curses in the world?" (xlix, 378).

In her metaphoric role, Miss Havisham joins Magwitch to replace the Gargerys as parents of the universalized projection Pip, as essential in his formation socially and psychologically as the whole human past. Corrupted to the uses of death by its complex agent Compayson, she yet retained enough affinity with life, if only through a desire for sympathy from others, to cooperate unconsciously with Magwitch's energy and Jaggers's humane reason to save Estella; and after altering Pip's course, she finally responds to him as a person like herself. Like Magwitch arbitrarily placed in Pip's way, she too deflects that way from the routine slide to the great sea. Feeding his naturally delusive mind with great expectations, they both also image archetypal conditions for his real life.

3

For Pip's love of Estella, his greatest test, pain, and joy, the mysterious, indifferent star to which he had been pointed— and in the marshes of the book's first night, the child "looked at the stars, and considered how awful it would be for a man to turn his face up to them as he froze to death, and see no help or pity in all the glittering multitude" (vii, 46)—Dickens summons an array of recollections culled and refined from his own first love. Pip's response to Estella includes the pain that caused him to abandon the autobiographical fragment; the warmth, loss, and nostalgia of the David-Dora sequence; the excitement and then amused awakening of the renewed correspondence; and the combined pity and mockery for both middle-aged survivors in Clennam and Flora. To these, Dickens adds the class inferiority he had earlier channeled into lesser projections, and accepts a new responsibility that derived from his own recent behavior: "I did not . . . invest her with any attributes save those she possessed," writes Pip. "I knew to my sorrow, often and often, if not always, that I loved her against reason, against promise, against peace, against hope, against happiness, against all discouragement that could be" (xxix, 219).

Before Ellen Ternan, Dickens had offered his chief projections fantasy figures evidently built on his sister-in-law Georgina, touched up by recollections of her dead sister Mary and his own sister Fanny as a child,[50] unexciting but endearing domestic angels from Ruth Pinch through Florence Dombey, Agnes Wickfield, Esther Summerson, Sissy Jupe, and Amy Dorrit. They are all deserving and worthy, and they all yield in *A Tale of Two Cities* to a new figure of intense feminine attraction, to Carton a woman to die for. And in *Great Expectations*, when Dickens had come to an accommodation with Ellen, he can offer her reflection Estella—the first woman in his fiction to elicit sexually impassioned writing—a sacrifice, the contrasting Biddy, a loving memorial to the old sisterly fantasies.

The spirit of changeless purity in an idyllic garden, Biddy cannot fill the dreams of the developing youth and the mature narrator looking back on him. Archetypally bringing literacy to Pip and Joe (as Georgina had taught the little Dickenses to read and write), Biddy like Georgina "came to us with . . . the whole of her worldly effects, and became a blessing to the household" (xvi, 115) from her teens. An orphan like Pip and (apparently) Estella, she too is a projected Everyman, but an alternative who undergoes the expectations in muted form— an early love for Pip—following with a slight deflection in the routine (the death of Joe's wife) the old female role that leads to Joe and the safe nest. But now, after two decades of mild fantasy, the representative lovable sister evokes only Dickens's valedictory brotherly affection. Estella was now the dream of life, the one fulfilling person or thing Dickens had written Forster he always missed.

To Estella the guides led Pip, not only her shaper Miss Havisham but also Magwitch, who gave her life, and Jaggers, who plucked her from the slime. Unlike his predecessors in Dickens's novels, Pip experienced her and kept her as a consoling memory even when he gave no thought to the loss of Magwitch's other gifts: the whole world he met in the precocious child who fascinates, snubs, and motivates him and in the scintillating beauty who fills his thoughts in the center of the novel and fits the forms of his longings. As he tells her, in a passage recalling Catherine Earnshaw's on

Heathcliff, she had become "'part of my character, part of the little good in me, part of the evil'" (xliv, 345).

Under the witch-gentlewoman's imposition of deadly ice, Estella's roots fed on other mysteries, the archetypal fires in which her mother lived and the force of unruly life in her father. The "'natural heart, even to be bruised or broken'" (xlix, 378), that Pip says Miss Havisham should have left her, asserts itself in the end. Whatever we think of the alternative endings—and since Dickens never printed the one Bulwer reasoned him out of, I see in it only a rejected draft—Dickens surely shows that if the expectations she had once embodied were chimeras, their memory was not. Whatever the ending, Pip receives an acknowledgment from this embodiment of his longings as Dickens had miraculously received in Ellen an acknowledgment from life. Even at her most mechanical, when she is most Miss Havisham's glittering ice maiden, Estella indicates her vital recognition of Pip's deserts, telling him she wishes not to "'deceive and entrap you'" as she does "'many others—all of them but you'" (xxxviii, 297). Offering him the truth about the illusion she believes herself to be, she shows that in time she can cease being that. Her maturing could only comfort the lover who remembered.

No living hope can satisfy Pip as yearning self, the dream signifying in youth our weakness and delusion and in experienced age, when it has been worn into reality and mixed with memory, our motive for living. Whether in their middle thirties at the end she is a forbidden wife or an available widow, we know her now as positive, a guarantee that Pip's greatest expectation had not been an illusion at its core. She was not the dead childlike Dora or the silly Flora Finching but youth's visions aged by the lover's own years; the same as if they had married young and matured in love. Moreover, by affecting the young Pip as the wonderful, the magical presented to him in place of the ordinary, the special quality of the self and the special rewards in store for it, and by being revealed as humanly right once he has passed his delusion into adulthood, Estella again constitutes the great expectation as prospect and as combined endearing and rueful retrospect: in short, as fulfillment.

On the issue of his own uniqueness, which Dickens had tossed back and forth in his mind from the beginning, most consciously from the first book he wrote after time to reflect, *Martin Chuzzlewit,* he was settling now, in an autumnal love, for the normal. Having raised a scandal by his domestic revolution that he now hoped would subside and permit a quiet life, Dickens wanted to see in himself the universal normal, accepting the adjustment of the secret poor dream to ordinary reality. So also is the conception of his art with which the novel seems to conclude. If we consider a recurrent image of the artist as fantasist and dreamer—an image reaching back to the mad Barnaby Rudge—we find here that Estella, the creation of the mad Miss Havisham and the poor dreaming man constructed on a base of wild life, has become a chastened, purified, grandly normal human fulfillment or helpmeet for her equal, Pip.

When Jaggers reveals Estella's birth to Pip, he enjoins continued secrecy: "'For whose sake would you reveal the secret?'" he asks (li, 392), and no one has an answer. Pip not only keeps Estella's secret safe from all but her dying father, but he also avoids telling Magwitch that he will inherit none of Magwitch's money, that Magwitch's obsession with creating an idle gentleman from the poor orphan child has joined the other apparently failed expectations. In Dickens's forties, as he more and more consciously hid a private dissatisfaction as a husband, the secrets in his novels had been humbling when exposed, or destructive: Lady Dedlock's love affair, Louisa Gradgrind's repressed emotional life, Clennam's birth and the fate of his mother. Good characters deliberately hid the truth to spare other good characters pain, as Esther chose not to expose old Turveydrop to his son and daughter-in-law, and Amy Dorrit agreed to keep Mrs. Clennam's misdeeds from her nominal son. When Dickens's own domestic unhappiness exploded, Dr. Manette's enforced public reading of his private narrative had horrible consequences in *A Tale of Two Cities.*

Unquestionably Dickens had become alert to the right of privacy as he first hid and then exposed the skeleton in his closet. On September 4, 1860 (just before *Great Expectations*), he wrote a friend that he had burnt "the accumulated letters and papers of twenty years" (*N*, III, 177). The reason he gave Macready on March 1, 1865, the "improper uses made of confidential letters in the addressing of them to a public audience that have no business with them" (*MDGH*,II,226-7), would by summer 1860 have covered the affair with Ellen Ternan. And though his rejection of Catherine for Ellen in May 1858 had occasioned great and in some respects lasting scandal, his attempts to limit it were at least partially successful—to judge by our ignorance about most of the details of his relationship to Ellen.

But its hold on his imagination and therefore its eruption into the novel is pervasive. In what its great secrets reveal about the central figure, *Great Expectations* is among other things Dickens's intensified sensitivity to the universal tie to sin, the inescapable passion that he wants us to control and civilize. Earlier, in the horror-seized minds of murderers briefly inhabited in *Sketches by Boz*, *Pickwick Papers*, and *Master Humphrey's Clock*, and more fully appropriated in Bill Sikes, John Rudge, Jonas Chuzzlewit, Rigaud of *Little Dorrit* and Mme. Defarge of *A Tale of Two Cities*, he has made us share consciousness with worse and worse outcast Cains. But here Abel too has been a violent criminal, and his child's mother, now tamed and shaped to useful work, long ago strangled a rival. On the border of civilization and the hateful marshes, Pip opens the novel in a graveyard—the body's ultimate prison, foreshadowing all the novel's metaphoric prisons—and immediately acquires guilt for stealing and for sharing a society that makes animals of men like the convict, guilt that varies and grows until Pip expiates it when the wonderful crumbles out of his expectations.

By the end, he and the other worthy figures know that like Magwitch they have paid for what they have done, even if the devil always renews himself no matter what happens to Compeyson or Orlick. Our opening couple in the mist, Pip and Magwitch, have become the beginning and mature stages of Dickens, and through his conception, of us as well: despite very different experiences, the now innocent sides of the self comforting each other in the hospital present the same record of suffering and striving out of guilt. And the final couple, trying to disperse their ignorant confusions in the December mist, know themselves as sinful but can live in hope: Everyman and Everywoman, Adam and Eve after the fall, at one with their fellows.

Approaching fifty, Dickens imagined this vision of his progress to adult Everyman as reconciling the complex elements of his moral and emotional life. Although the unfulfillable expectation and the guilt of the specially selected were his old story, now the impulse to express them was more powerful than ever. With John Dickens dead, Elizabeth Dickens helplessly senile, Catherine peeled away, and Georgina a settled spinster, Dickens imagined a need, spurred by the events of May 1858, to make amends more general and ordinary than the Christ-like Carton. Nothing in his earlier life implied a failure in humanity like his breaking up his family, and he had done nothing so offensive to conventional morality as the affair with Ellen.

In all of his occasional earlier quarrels and differences—
with his sponging relatives, exploitive publishers, intrusive
public, American pirates, snobs subverting the Royal Literary
Fund, and people who objected to one thing or another in his
writings—he could easily see himself as right. But he knew
that he was responsible for the family's division—as his
father had discreditably split the earlier family—and no
matter how fairly he felt he had treated Catherine, he could
not deny the shock or still the scandal. He hoped that by his
friends and public now, and by later generations, he would be
understood and therefore forgiven. Like *A Tale of Two Cities*,
Great Expectations reflects that hope. In *A Tale of Two Cities*,
conceiving himself in the midst of calumny as the martyred
Carton, he imagines his name vindicated and even glorified
by posterity. In *Great Expectations*, after time to reflect and
adjust, as Pip in immediate danger of being murdered by
Orlick he fears above all that his good intentions will die with
him, that all those he loves and respects will think that he has
run away, that bitter lies will falsify his memory: "The death
close before me was terrible, but far more terrible than death
was the dread of being misremembered after death. And so
quick were my thoughts that I saw myself despised by unborn
generations—Estella's children, and their children—while the
wretch's words were yet on his lips" (liii, 403-4).

To achieve reconciliation with the world and his past,
Dickens offers a sinless, changeless memorial in Pip's adult
mind for Joe and Biddy, the cheerful parents of the childhood
before the Marshalsea and Warren's Blacking whose
continuing love for him guarantees his goodness. The others,
the artificial family of later perceptions, the fluid, almost
interchangeable foster-and-surrogate relations, now ask and
receive forgiveness for all the guilts they have incurred:
Magwitch, the father and adult (sinful) self least of all, for he
has paid heavily and had been maligned and misrepresented
to begin with; Miss Havisham, the failed mother, for her

obsessive, self-centered perversion of young wards; Estella, first and last loves, for rejecting the early call to humanity; Pip, the son-lover-expecting self, for thinking (as we all do) that the world was made for him alone. All these sinners beg and receive forgiveness, on behalf of Dickens.

In Pip's growth, moreover, Dickens centered a perception of human relatedness that had stirred him earlier as arbitrary, the coming together of accidentally chosen figures in quarantine at Marseilles (*Little Dorrit*) or people swept together by social forces in the Reign of Terror. In this retrospect on his life as Everyman, he examines not only the movement up to achievement by way of observing or being tested by others, as in *David Copperfield*, but also his human ties to them, his being something to them as they are to him. Earlier, his occasional uniters and touchstones of humanity had been assertedly symbolic, often helpless—children like Oliver Twist, Little Nell, or the youthful Dombeys, unprotected older youths like Barnaby Rudge or Jo the crossing sweeper. Now, it is the central projection, the universal norm and everyman Pip who unites, requites, and is requited.

Miss Havisham needs young life to play before her, not only a toy male for her creature Estella to practice on but someone independent to keep a spark of her alive in her wasteland. Joe and Biddy separately need him until they have each other, as a person to love and to respond to them, and then need a version of him again as their child. Wemmick thanks him for the chance to exert selfless good will beyond the tight limits of his cottage, and even Jaggers needs him, to recall his own youthful poor dreams and therefore his humanity. The convict has needed him first to awaken good feelings, then to offer a better motive for living than revenge, and at last to return his grateful love. And Estella needs him to maintain an original inclination toward fire that can grow into a heart after years and suffering have worn away her ice. For all, Pip as the embodiment and memory of youth, the essence, of expecting humanity—of expecting responsiveness—has been the world's offer of a chance to be alive: as they in different ways have been for him.

Despite the autumnal context of the last scene, Dickens's imagination approaching fifty with a new love offers more cheerful prospects—expressed in Pip, youth not only recalled but again intensely imagined, again alive in the mind—than in the last several novels. The softened retrospect on his own crises—the pains of family disappointments, career frustrations, lost love, social obstacles, early and late mistakes, years of emptiness, not forgotten but blended into the universal pattern—recognizes expectation itself as normal and worthy. After the death of Carton to end its predecessor, he begins *Great Expectations* with a resurrection, the self as the little boy Carton had prophesied, and follows that self to normality and not defeat.

For that new self he conceives Estella, both the old pain and the new joy the world has provided in Ellen, arbitrary mysteries domesticated by recognized identities: Estella's sordid birth and exploited nurturing as distortions of his old fantasies about himself. Questions of Ellen's capacity to feel at so young an age, of her relations with society, and of their significance for her lover, all melt into Estella's complex figure as the requital of Dickens's expectations at fifty, and all are positively resolved at the end. Though I think his published end the right one, either end will replace emptiness with acceptance and affirm the value of the universal expectation. Even age distinctions, so important in the novels at thirty and forty, merely become signs of different degrees of experience here, where all but the few excluded devils and comic butts share the pains of delusion and prospects of warmth.

Like Dickens at this time, Pip and Estella find and earn another life as adults. Through the mediation of a trio of Dickens's older selves and guides, mythic divinities turned normally ambivalent—the life-giving, life-worn sinner Magwitch; the personified Havisham delusion, remorsefully dissolving after polishing both young surfaces against life; the arrogant celebrity Jaggers confessing a stake in ordinary decency—Pip and Estella have been brought to Dickens's condition. Their revised knowledge of good and evil means that Eden can never be theirs. As Everyman and Everywoman they leave a ruined garden hand in hand in their world of common day, but a common day warmed by growth and memory. There is not even a question whether Pip or Estella would have been better without the delusive expectations. That would mean remaining in childhood like Joe and Biddy, a condition not only impossible but—for Dickens's adult projections now and always—not desirable.

For the two, the meeting is a postscript in the novel, their union still an expectation, an undefined future; for Dickens at fifty, a heartworn hope.

VII. *Our Mutual Friend*:
Reborn with Galatea

May 1864 - November 1865

At fifty-two, Dickens was busily adding new wings to the basic structure of his old life. His dominant concern of the last few years, the revolution in his condition since he fell in love with Ellen Ternan in 1857 and aborted his marriage in May 1858, forced even greater attention to where and what he was in *Our Mutual Friend* than in earlier novels. An imagination centering in himself as father of two grown daughters (one now married) and of seven grown and growing sons whom he was helping to begin independent lives; as grateful patron to their spinster aunt, who continued to be their support and his housekeeper; as professional eminence and social conscience in the nation; and above all as Ellen's lover and guardian, projected the variety and intensity of these roles into the crowded world of his art.

At the same time that the present so much preoccupied his mind as a problem—how to be a good father to his children, a decent man to the rejected Catherine, the present Georgina, his various other dependents, and the world at large, and everything for Ellen (who did or did not love him for himself alone)—his thoughts and his imagination still wandered richly

195

among their old haunts of the past. Just as *David Copperfield*, his novel approaching forty, had reconciled him to all the rubs that had made him Charles Dickens, *Great Expectations* had smoothed them for the universal man approaching fifty, in ripe middle age. But even if it was intended as a formal retrospect, that novel had closed nothing off. To life's adventurer resolutely going on, the fading margins before and behind him always allowed new perceptions of what had been. As the present and the past changed their shapes and meanings with time, the fresh new vision in art revised the last. Though the core of all remains how Dickens and Ellen are to be to each other and the world, they have entered another stage: emancipation from the chains of delusion in Estella and Pip becomes birth into wholeness for Lizzie, Bella, Eugene, and John Harmon.

Also at the same time, Dickens continued to be his busy self in the external world, painstakingly conducting *All the Year Round*, planning more public Readings, participating in socially ameliorative organizations, maintaining a wide correspondence, and always remodeling and often entertaining at Gad's Hill. Interests relevant to the novel that he pursued in his own or others' pieces for the magazine included Children's Hospital, where Johnny Higden comes too late to survive ("Between the Cradle and the Grave," February 1, 1862), money lenders' strategies (March 11, April 8, and July 8, 1865), even dinners in Greenwich like the one Bella gives her father ("The Business of Pleasure," October 10, 1863). As if to balance *Great Expectations'* domination by the internal and universal, Dickens's social and topical concerns pervade the novel, exploiting hints and fragments of thought he had been jotting down for years to swell memory's dust heap.[51] *Our Mutual Friend* not only ranges widely through the London world but thunders at national villains, particularly Dickens's old targets the Poor Laws, Parliament, the educational system, stock speculation, the irresponsible selfishness of the rich and well-born, and the chill of genteel society. But as always the imaginative impulses that he registered on the way to the novel seem to be emanations from personal, emotional perceptions in general social settings—different reflections of his situation—rather than from current social problems.

Settling into his complex situation with new zest after the battle-worn calm of *Great Expectations*, he imagined central fragments of the coming novel's world in the resurrection of a man who plays dead, in a couple united by alienation from society, and in a human center relating two kinds of feelings and attitudes. Besides early pieces in *Household Words* touching on the grim side of the river world, an early idea in a letter to Forster conjecturally placed in 1861—during or not long after *Great Expectations*—offers a hint of John Harmon's position and two important hints for the social plot: "I think a man, young and perhaps eccentric, feigning to be dead, and *being* dead to all intents and purposes external to himself, and for years retaining the singular view of life and character so imparted, would be a good leading incident for a story," he wrote. "A poor imposter of a man marrying a woman for money; she marrying *him* for *his* money; after marriage both finding out their mistake, and entering into a league and covenant against folks in general; with whom I propose to connect some Perfectly New people. Everything new about them. If they presented a father and mother, it seemed as if THEY must be bran new, like the furniture and the carriages—shining with varnish, and just home from the manufacturers" (*N*, III, 271). On August 25, 1862, he thought of introducing arbitrary groups of people unknown to each other: "I have an idea of opening a book . . . by bringing together two strongly contrasted places and two strongly contrasted sets of people, with which and with whom the story is to rest . . . ." (*N*, III, 302).

Recreating in *Our Mutual Friend* the miraculously arbitrary change in his life, he imagines the love from three perspectives, two turning mainly on the Pygmalion-Galatea myth and the third showing the world awaiting the newly reborn lovers. No doubt in doing so he noticed himself, with amusement, playing with a favorite element in the tradition of romantic comedy, the parallel loves of a fair girl and a dark one, of a dashing lover and a sober one. Perhaps he was even consciously conflating the two popular Sheridan pieces in the repertoire, *The Rivals* (Captain Absolute-Lydia and John Harmon-Bella, Falkland-Julia and Eugene-Lizzie) and *The School for Scandal* (fashion, cynical society, even a blameless Jewish money-lender). At any rate, the conception arose for Dickens as not only the opposed societies of the opening but also, he wrote Wilkie Collins on January 24, 1864, after finishing the first two numbers, as "a combination of drollery with romance" (*N*, III, 378). Although he may not have meant to use the terms to distinguish between the two love plots, they do hint at their contrast.

Each split in two, Pip and Estella acquire independence, dignity, and an understanding of how complex a world they must act in. The men central to the main plots, John Harmon and Eugene Wrayburn, respectively project Dickens as a lover who must assure himself of his love's responsiveness and worthiness in the comic plot and as a lover facing great social obstacles in the romance one. In the young heroines, who draw Harmon from self-doubt and Wrayburn from apathy, Dickens conceives complementary visions of the woman who broke through the aloofness he said had been his lot since Maria. In both love plots, the men are reborn after near-fatal immersions in the river, and one also undergoes moral and psychological birth; and both women, like Ellen just entering adulthood, are educated in new life. The couple in the comic plot will live happily ever after, warmed by parents and surrogates and securely set in their society, the positive side of Dickens's ledger; Eugene and Lizzie know they will need to march on despite losses.

1

In the serious plot, Dickens opens with the archetypal feminine Lizzie, grown in the deadly, degrading, and mysterious river-side culture, through whom to shock the romance projection Eugene Wrayburn from his *acidie*. Eugene's listlessness and his fanciful, witty comments at the society dinner where we meet him establish that he is wasting abilities, and his nervous response to Lizzie—encountered in the arbitrary casualness of life, when he accompanies his friend Mortimer Lightwood out of that dinner on a professional errand—suggests his awareness of a new element that may change him. After Eugene's memorable vision of Lizzie weeping by the fireplace on the night the men track her father to his corpse, he turns from tentative feeling to the next stage, sympathetic action: disappearing to find an older woman to help him tell her the news. Motivated by guilt over spying on the father and fascinated with Lizzie's complexity, he develops sympathy and respect, as well as a wish to help her enter civilized life by learning to read and write.

But the very novelty and complexity of dealing with a woman from a different, debased culture leads him to endless unsettled thoughts about what to do: surely as Dickens felt when he found himself drawn to Ellen. Echoing Dickens's insistence on Ellen's purity in the "violated letter" justifying

his separation from Catherine (*N*, III, 23), Eugene tells
Mortimer that " 'There is no better girl in all this London than
Lizzie Hexam. There is no better among my people at home;
no better among your people' " (II, vi, 294). Again
presumably like the earlier Dickens in love but tied by his
marriage, he cannot answer Mortimer's " 'Then what is to
come of it? What are you doing? Where are you going?' " (p.
295) and he cannot stop. Moreover, now that Dickens has
himself seriously registered the exciting humanity of the
woman rather than intellectually conceived a symbolic one,
Eugene's superiority in the social world leads not to the easy
triumph of a Steerforth but to uncertainties, self doubts,
doubts of her. " 'If I had not been what you call removed from
you and cut off from you, would you have made this appeal to
me to leave you?' " (IV, vi, 694) he asks Lizzie when he has
followed her to her retreat. Among Dickens's earlier major
projections, Tom Pinch, John Jarndyce, and for a while Arthur
Clennam had to love without return, but only Sydney Carton
and Pip found the unacceptable love obsessive, and they too
rose from an imagination suffused with Ellen.

When Charley Hexam renounces his sister because he
assumes she will become Eugene's mistress, we realize that
Dickens has moved from the squire-milkmaid fantasy of the
adolescent projections Steerforth and Little Em'ly—
particularly fresh in his mind from his public Readings of
David Copperfield—to an adult world where social crevasses
are in fact bridged from time to time. David had to pass the
stage of wanting to be Steerforth as Dickens had passed it. But
Eugene, responding to the call of Lizzie's humanity, has not
only Mortimer (the decent, rational Traddles or Herbert
Pocket self) to answer to, but his own new, growing humanity.
As if to underline the reality of this situation in which a
complex mind has to find its way, Dickens reminds us of a
couple of artificial literary modes that will not fit. He places

Eugene like Marlow in *She Stoops to Conquer*, unable to woo an heiress his father has picked for him and instead loving a girl who won't do. But no plausible plot twist out of conventional comedy could turn Lizzie—a real lower-class love, unlike Goldsmith's masquerading Kate Hardcastle—into that heiress. Nor can this gentleman adopt Bradley Headstone's or Charley Hexam's melodramatic stereotypes to discard a soiled dove and gloat like Don Giovanni. Until his great crisis, he drifts indecisively, incapable of resolving the problem, indeed in danger of being Steerforth to her Em'ly despite their mutual respect.

But after Headstone's deadly attack, Eugene, always aware of imminent death during his conscious intervals, completes his resurrection into self-respecting responsibility, deciding and acting with Lizzie's good as his motive, as Dickens after the devastating public scandal succeeded in keeping their actual relations private. For the marriage of the lovers, which was impossible in his own life, Dickens used a device he had imagined before he met Ellen, but with the simplicity of general fantasy. "The First" story in *The Seven Poor Travellers*, the 1854 Christmas Supplement of *Household Words*, concerns a man who comes to consciousness recovering from dreadful wounds suffered at Waterloo to find he has married the angelic woman who had rejected him many years earlier as a ne'er-do-well but had now nursed him to life. He has merely been rewarded for reforming through years of loyal, self-sacrificing soldiering. Significantly, Dickens worked up this story in June 1858 as one of his public Readings, right after dissolving what he regarded as years of self-sacrifice to husbandly duties.

Awakened by his near death as well as his gratitude, his conscience, and his sensitivity to her feelings, Eugene now has intentions, plans, even a future. The vitalizing effect of love on a chief projection's wounded or indifferent spirit had been hinted in *David Copperfield* and particularly *Little Dorrit*, and affirmed through Dr. Manette and Carton in *A Tale of Two Cities* and Pip in *Great Expectations*, the novels since Ellen. But now, with their relationship established, Dickens considers her problem too in the new social situation. When Eugene exclaimed, " 'How shall I ever pay all I owe you, if I recover!' 'Don't be ashamed of me,' she replied, 'and you will have more than paid all' " (IV, xi, 753).

In Bradley Headstone, Eugene's rival—and as critics have been suggesting, his double or anti-self, the Orlick-Drummle he must purge—for the woman from the depths of the generating river, Dickens develops the horrors of those depths in all of us, in association with a social rise reflecting his own old ambivalence. Helplessly expressing the theme of pathological control and explosion, animal passion loosed and tamed, which Dickens had touched on from Bill Sikes on and tried to refine in Carker of *Dombey and Son* and Mlle. Hortense of *Bleak House* before using it significantly in Estella's parents, Headstone grounds it in the frustrations forced on him by his origin. He is not the Bounderby of *Hard Times*, a projection burlesquing a poor background to rationalize his current abuse of power, but one legitimately risen by his own painful efforts, a man who would be admired if not for the violence that rise exacted from his character.[52] "Regarding that origin of his, he was proud, moody, and sullen, desiring it to be forgotten" (II, i, 218), but too obsessed with it to allow that forgetting. Even his name suggests the ambivalence, the modern meaning of "grave marker" indicating his tie to the obscurity of death while the biblical passage in Psalms 118:22, points to divine selection out of obscurity: "The stone, which the builders refused, is become the headstone." For the confident novelist of *David Copperfield* at the peak of his world approaching forty, the will to push ahead had been shadowed with shame, the insistent sweating dampness of Uriah Heep. Now, the older man made aware of the nature of his passion affirms the struggle but repudiates its damage. Bad as I may become, his imagination says, I can surely avoid Headstone's excesses.

Headstone's controls, the rigid pattern he poured his energies into internalizing as he totally created himself against his origins, cannot bend to the different will and feelings of another human being, even a desired one. Putting forth arguments from the deep division in an author who had separated from his wife and convention, Headstone blames his beloved as " 'the ruin—the ruin—the ruin—of me' " (II, xv, 395). If he had married normally, he says, " 'and if the same spell had come upon me for my ruin, I know I should have broken that tie asunder as if it had been thread' " (p. 396). Lizzie's effect on him is not as another person, but—like that of Paris on Charles Darnay—as a lodestone: " 'You draw me to you' " (p. 396), he says, expressing Dickens's case in a love speech paralleled in his writings only by Pip's remembered feelings for Estella—in both cases supplicating pity: " 'I am under the influence of some tremendous attraction which I have resisted in vain, and which overmasters me. You could draw me to fire, you could draw me to water, you could draw me to the gallows, . . . you could draw me to any exposure and disgrace' " (p. 397). More specific to the situation than the rebellious urge Orlick, as the heedless, obsessive, selfish, even resentful side of Dickens's passion, he must be expelled, a suicide, to clear the way for solicitous love.

Now that the romance heroine, the object of that passion and that love, is not an adolescent dream or a literary convention—Little Em'ly or even Ada Clare of *Bleak House*—but a version of Dickens's living Ellen, she (like Eugene) takes on a density of life as well as personality. In

Lizzie, Dickens combines the Victorian bourgeois womanly virtues—family loyalty, industry, self-sacrifice—with the mythic feminine (which draws some of its fascination for Eugene from her distinctive milieu), lower-class social insecurity, and an independence connected with her class that helps her like Dickens "from her very babyhood promptly to do the thing that could be done" (I, vi, 71). Combining these for her context, Dickens follows the opening vision of the predatory father netting corpses in the river to feed his young on their spoils, with their boathouse home. And that home, a carefully observed London water-side hut and a nether-world, sinister echo of the Peggottys' ark, nurtures the beginning of life and feeds off its end in slime and darkness.

In such a milieu, Gaffer Hexam's daughter, like Dickens's daughters amid the ambiguities of the domestic eruption, must face "the frightful possibility that her father, being innocent, yet might come to be believed guilty" (p. 70). Distilled from Dickens's own painful experience and his professional lifetime of subjection to rumor, Lizzie's sense of that false suspicion, and of the resulting ostracism, dominates her early motivation in the novel: "she stood on the river's brink unable to see into the vast blank misery of a life suspected, and fallen away from by good and bad, but knowing that it lay there dim before her, stretching away to the great ocean Death" (p. 71). Where Ellen conceived as Estella could commit her life without a moment's concern for its value, an automaton who learns of her humanity in sorrowful time, Ellen conceived as Lizzie begins knowing well how deeply she is tied to her past.

Refusing Miss Potterson's advice to leave her father and improve herself because she fears that he would fall into moral ruin, she chooses loyalty to him and to his memory, even to the family odium, though she encourages her brother upward to respectability. Only Eugene can be sensitive to her tenuous state between worlds and can persuade her to be educated, not to reject but to rehabilitate her dead father. If she persists in illiteracy, and therefore in isolation from normal society, she wrongs him as well as herself, he says, " 'By perpetuating the consequences of his ignorant and blind obstinacy. By resolving not to set right the wrong he did you. By determining that the deprivation to which he condemned you, and which he forced upon you, shall always rest upon his head' " (II, ii, 236).

In this situation, the guilt Dickens suggests is in his capacity as Gaffer, as father to the daughters hurt by his actions. But he also registered through Eugene an awareness of Ellen's social danger from him as lover. When Mortimer explains Eugene's hint of his wish in his word *wife*, " 'You ask her to kneel at this bedside and be married to you, that your reparation may be complete' " (IV, x, 741), we are to see more than reformation, gratitude, and even love for the young woman in it. If "reparation" means both making amends and making the victim whole again, then both lawyers think Eugene owes her a moral and social debt, the reconstitution of a sound reputation and acknowledgment of having wounded it.

Eugene's argument succeeds partly because it offers her a chance honorably to appease the paternal past, partly because it indicates his respect for her feelings, and largely because she has fantasies of socially suiting him, the man with whom she has been falling in love. As Katey Dickens was to say of Ellen, she was bright, and sensibly tried " 'to educate herself, to bring her mind more on a level with his own. Who could blame her? . . . He had the world at his feet. She was a young girl of eighteen, elated and proud to be noticed by him.' "[53] Presumably also like Ellen, she keeps surprising the people Eugene introduces to her. They all look for a stereotype defined by her brutalizing milieu, as people would have looked for the theatrical in Ellen, perhaps hoping at best for a cheerful, good-natured, but hard and self-seeking type like the dancer Fanny Dorrit. To make sure that we do not mistake Lizzie for a representative good sort of river-side girl, therefore, Dickens draws us a convincing one in Pleasant Riderhood, her exact social equivalent as the daughter of Gaffer's former partner. We realize that they may both exist, but we cannot miss the immense difference.

As Lizzie expressed aspects of Ellen from Dickens's perspective as lover, she and other girls expressed aspects of his daughters from his perspective as father. The adolescent Jenny's attitude toward her father, an irresponsible drunkard whom she treats as a bad child, implies a glance at Lizzie's protectiveness toward the socially ill Gaffer, as does Bella Wilfer's teasing love of Rumty Wilfer or Pleasant Riderhood's concern for Rogue Riderhood. Dickens's relationship with his daughters, a generalized fantasy in *Dombey and Son*, had become individualized when they entered adolescence, particularly as he imagined *Hard Times* and *Little Dorrit*; now that they had stayed with him after the separation, it came with an even greater variety of admonitory and self-pleasing refinements into his imagination. One of its elements was the fear of their eventual move away and the hope that it would be, as with Lizzie, in kindness.

Though not formally our mutual friend (Harmon's designation), Lizzie exercises an attraction by virtue of the essential loving quality—as the "soul of life" among the "fictions of society" of the *Examiner* review (October 28, 1865, p. 681)—that draws and changes people. She drew the crippled, resentful Jenny Wren and the Jew Riah into warmer contact with a world otherwise inimical to both, and she offered Betty Higden a final assurance of dignity in death. At the Higden funeral, through her surprising impression on both, "she became the unconscious means of bringing [Harmon and Bella] together" (III, ix, 517). Sharing the deepest mutuality with Eugene, she also helps the process of rebirth for all the lovers by teaching Bella. Sure that women's hearts cannot " 'seek to gain anything' " (III, ix, 527) in love, she leads Bella to join her in turning their myths and fairy tales into versions of Pygmalion and Galatea in which *both* sculptor and sculpture breathe new life.

As the motherly sister Dickens so often loved to celebrate, from Rose Maylie of *Oliver Twist* through Amy Dorrit and Biddy, instinctively saving her own soul through love no matter what surrounds her, Lizzie finds—like Louisa Gradgrind and Amy Dorrit—that her warmest efforts fail with an incurably selfish brother, a brother who pulls away, who cannot be a mutual friend. Charley Hexam, named like Dickens and his oldest child, suggests the embattled rising opportunist that Dickens had feared becoming, drawn often in the novels. As Lizzie reflects the pains of self-doubts and recognitions warmed almost by a miracle (in Dickens's case of talent) in the rise from squalor, her brother, in his teens "a mixture . . . of uncompleted savagery, and uncompleted civilisation" (I, iii, 18), embodies the likelier way. Like Headstone, Charley fuels his drive with a will toward domination and resentment of those born to an easier position; but unlike him—as Dickens shows us another kind of dehumanizing in the ruthless rising self—Charley coldly resists external sympathies.

As resentment entailed in his social ambitions grows, Charley Hexam becomes worse and worse, even worse than the great rejecter Podsnap because he understands the sensibilities he is wounding. Repudiating all ties, he leaves his father without a look back—breaking up the family like Pip and Dickens (and perhaps Charley Dickens, who chose to leave Charles for Catherine), disowns Lizzie as her "low whims" in refusing Headstone threaten his interests, and then disowns Headstone for crimes that endanger a protege's reputation. Like Gaffer, Riderhood, and Headstone, he bitterly qualifies the democratic classlessness of *Great Expectations* as the small repressed voice in Dickens's old self that had urged him to abandon his dragging parents and brothers. A frozen exaggeration of the newly advanced Pip, Charley Hexam ends in isolation, the one condition above all from which everyone's mutual friend Dickens now feels liberated.

The grand isolated representative of the lower world, Rogue Riderhood, a distorted version of the father in that slime, builds as the old Fagin and Quilp projections of Dickens into the jesting devil who has committed the sins of which he accuses the guiltless self Gaffer. An ironic role-player, manipulator, and rationalizer so amusing as to lead Shaw to re-imagine him in the comic dustman Doolittle (father of another Lizzie breathed on by a genteel Pygmalion), Riderhood finds no crimes above or beneath him in his territory along the river. Unredeemable even by a near-drowning, an ally of the rot that grows where life has its source—in the vicious blood lust of Paris in the Reign of Terror where yet Carton's pure act sprang, or in the criminal underworld from which Jaggers had snatched a baby—this cynical devil in Dickens can no more be allowed to survive than the perversely proud Headstone. Like Headstone and Charley, and like the relatively guiltless Gaffer, Riderhood stands before the painfully resurrected lovers as a cautionary memory: of the predatory past, of selfishness, of slander, of malice, of resentment. As he and those others persuade us, the mythic romance affirms victory only after struggle with oneself, hope of new love only after near-despair.

2

Although the John Harmon-Bella Wilfer plot employs exotic devices, its major projection and his heroine act out their traditional fantasy in a realistic setting: its fairy tale animates a bourgeois comedy. Centered on a disguised young plutocrat in love with a vain petit-bourgeois Cinderella and testing whether she could marry him for himself, it's the sunny side of love, *She Stoops to Conquer* or *The Rivals* with a variety of favorite moral lessons. And as it registers the cheerful rise and fall of feeling to mirror the deeper movements of the other love plot, it also extends the range of the projected loving self, the variety of the beloved, the sense of delighted, precarious wonder with which Dickens conceived his situation.

A corrector of character, a seeker of truth, a versatile actor, a reflective judge of events and people, author of a vivid autobiographical narrative, "our mutual friend" connecting the groups and plots, all like Dickens, John Harmon would surely be the central projection of this novel if not for the emotional power with which Dickens's imagination endowed Lizzie as life's essential complication and goal. Scarcely more individuated than the usual jeune premier, Harmon plays these varied roles by virtue of his complex situation. Not only is he the figure trailing a distant empty life (like Clennam entering *Little Dorrit*'s world or Pip revived at the end of *Great Expectations*), arriving—from over the sea, like so many predecessors in Dickens and in other writers of his island nation, including the fiftyish author of *The Tempest* and *The Winter's Tale*—to meet an uncertain inheritance and an unknown bride, but when he first appears he has already died in police records and almost died in fact. Like the author emotionally shipwrecked when he met Ellen Ternan, Harmon awaits the new fearfully, anticipating he knows not what good. The first words he speaks in the novel, as Julius Handford, are "'I am lost!'" (I, iii, 23). But like many an earlier Dickens projection, he has great expectations; and with the self-doubting and self-destructive sides developed in others as well, he can for once exercise some control over fulfilling them.

Masquerading as Boffin's secretary, Dickens plays through Harmon with the universal fantasies of observing others' responses to one's death and of evaluating in disguise (like Sir William Thornhill in Dickens's favorite *Vicar of Wakefield*) those central in one's private hopes. Sharing a more individual fantasy with Dickens as well, " 'I cannot help it; reason has nothing to do with it; I love her against reason,' " says the otherwise placid Harmon (II, xiii, 372). Slandered with the charge of fortune hunting, he gets to make a noble speech defending and clearing himself and resigns his position, awakening his beloved's sympathy and admiration all these years after Maria's indifference. As against Estella, Bella can conquer the arbitrary, both her selfish mother's upbringing and her expectations from old Harmon's will, rather than hide behind it. In this version of Dickens's love—the requital of his newborn delight in a fresh, lively belle who loves him not for his power and fame but for the self hidden beneath that surface—they end in perfect felicity.

In the process, Harmon not only brings Bella to new life as an unselfish lover, wife, and mother, but himself undergoes transformations to confirm his resurrection. Having disappeared as John Harmon and again as Julius Handford, he lives through most of the novel as Rokesmith, giving up that name when his test of Bella has borne its happy fruit in confirming her new self as his loyal, loving wife. Tracing his own identity through the period of drugged near-death and clearing up the identity of the corpse, he lives in and out of the sinister sailor who forces Riderhood to withdraw the defamation of Lizzie's father: like Dickens clearing his good name as a husband. In all his roles Harmon reveals truths of character as well as of event, evoking the selfless goodness of the Boffins and Bella, sternly judging Riderhood and Wegg. Called the "mutual friend" of Boffin and the Wilfers, he extends the role to serve all the virtuous—thereby indulging a quality Dickens claimed for himself in the advertisement to the cheap edition of his works and in his Christmas stories. He had even given it as a name to one helpful old Frenchman, M. Mutuel, in the *All the Year Round* Christmas supplement for 1862, *Somebody's Luggage*.

Boffin the golden dustman, Dickens's other major projection in the comic plot, also comes to it from the long hiatus of routine life and adopts a misleading role for the sake of observing, testing, exculpating, and teaching Bella and anyone else who pays attention. Also as with Harmon—and metaphorically with the Dickens who has found an unsuspected new world—his life has altered and expanded through the surprising bequest from old Harmon. Going into society as two innocents,[54] he and his wife share some of Dickens's and Catherine's remembered youthful embarrassments with servants and merchants and the later petty annoyances brought about by his fame. In their mansion that was undergoing as disturbing a renovation as Tavistock House when Dickens bought it long before and his current Gad's Hill, which he was always modifying, "behold all manner of crawling, creeping, fluttering, and buzzing creatures, attracted by the gold dust of the Golden Dustman!" (I, xvii, 209). "No one knows," Dickens writes, "what a set is made at the man marked by a stroke of notoriety" (p. 210), and readers could easily make the autobiographical application.

More powerful in the plot and mood is Boffin's susceptibility, like Lizzie's and Harmon's, to the misconceptions of others. Always the same at bottom, Boffin appears to change his nature, even to act disreputably, and like Dickens, he carefully judges the responses of others. Dickens tended more and more to project the fathers (actual and surrogate) of growing children as figures like himself, with his concerns and conditions—in Micawber; in Jarndyce, Jellyby, Bagnet, Skimpole, and Captain Hawdon; in Magwitch and

Jaggers. And with Boffin—a dustman living off the shards of human experience like the novelist—Dickens suggests a projection willingly courting odium to improve a deserving young woman: Dickens in another role toward Ellen, delighting in her charm and in teaching her. A rich and successful older self, a father whose frown turned to beaming warmth, the noblest figure in the novel, Boffin sacrifices wealth for the lovers and like Prospero restores order to the universe as the curtain falls. All the envy, guilt, and scandal shadowing his arbitrary rise and shocking behavior vanish in Dickens's magical fantasy of magnanimity.

Variously reflecting Bella's course, everyone else in the comic plot tests or is tested, particularly Wegg and Venus in their subplot of grotesque farce. Deviously resourceful and willful, the wooden-legged survivor Wegg (stirring in Dickens's mind when he worked up "Mrs. Gamp" as a Reading in June, 1858, where he imagined her dead husband as a wooden-legged parasite) fails every test of honesty and good will. Greedily rationalizing his ingratitude and criminal plotting on the ground of talent, Wegg both raises the issue of the arbitrary and—by his incompetence and immorality—negates it. To catch both his pettiness and his nasty spite, Dickens imagines him on the edge of the artistic slums. First protesting that he is not really a literary artist, when he becomes used to Boffin's deference he persuades himself that he is, and wants the perquisites. Slipping into Boffin's mind, Dickens has him tell his wife that they must soothe Wegg's jealousy of Rokesmith, for as a paid reader Wegg is a literary man. " 'Lor,' cried Mrs. Boffin. 'What I say is, the world's wide enough for all of us!' 'So it is, my dear,' said Mr. Boffin, 'when not literary. But when so, not so' " (I, xv, 182).

More clearly an offshoot of Dickens as artist, Wegg's temporary ally Venus, who has also " 'climb[ed] to the top of the tree' " (I, vii, 84), makes copies of life from the bones and fragments in his chaotic shop. That shop is a parody world, idiosyncratically arranged like the world Dickens draws on, a comment on all the attempts to make meaning and use of the arbitrary in the novel. When Wegg looks back on it in the momentary glare of candles, it seems to him as if "the babies—Hindoo, African, British—the 'human warious,' the French gentleman, the green glass-eyed cats, the dogs, the ducks, and all the rest of the collection, show for an instant as if paralytically animated" (I, vii, 85).[55] Using such materials, Venus exercises important aspects of the novelist's craft, having (in Wegg's view) " 'the patience to fit together on wires the whole framework of society—I allude to the human skelinton' " (III, vi, 478). To ingratiate himself, Wegg "expatiates on Mr. Venus's patient habits and delicate manipulation; on his skill in piecing little things together; on his knowledge of various tissues and textures; on the likelihood of small indications leading him on to the discovery of great concealments" (II, vii, 303). But like other devils assigned to criticize literature and art, Wegg cannot see the great and overriding difference from the true artist and from the life-giving goddess: this Venus deals in dead surfaces and fragments. Venus himself is, however, enough of a craftsman to have the integrity Dickens usually associates with the class. Because he rejects "Weggery" (individual, rationalizing selfishness parallel to social Podsnappery), Dickens rewards him not only with the respect of the good people but with Pleasant Riderhood too. Like Harmon and Wrayburn, he must appease the beloved's sense of dignity. He will never again articulate a female skeleton, for she does " 'not wish . . . to regard myself, nor yet to be regarded, in that boney light' " (I, vii, 84).

Passing his test, Venus confirms a probity that was always there though briefly obscured, as with Boffin. But he is not born into a new life. The figure who achieves a new brilliance under testing, allowing her best nature to blossom after its constriction by artificially fostered fantasies and desires, is of course Bella Wilfer. Like Pip in the other novel that stakes so much on character change or revelation—a theme stimulating to Dickens's imagination since at least Martin Chuzzlewit and Dombey, but never so absorbing as in the last few years, when he needed to understand Ellen—she must cope with pride arbitrarily swollen by social pressures. As Lizzie develops the dignity, mystery, and passion that Pip had found in Estella, in part because her life unfolds away from the artificial social world, Bella demonstrates the charm merely ascribed to Estella, her richness of social effect. To her lover she appears in her deluded state " 'So insolent, so trivial, so capricious, so mercenary, so careless, so hard to touch, so hard to turn!' " (I, xvi, 208). But he cannot resist her beauty and buoyant, happy youthfulness, which are equally on the surface. And we others see what he hopes for and discovers by testing, the underlying goodness derived from a father who has been like Boffin a model of cheerful integrity.

Bella's relations with her father, Rumty Wilfer, show even more than Lizzie's with hers how complexly Dickens imagined the world around his concerns. One fine recent critic, Michael Slater, thinks that Bella is more likely to be based on Dickens's daughter Katey than on Ellen, in part because Bella and Rumty enact "a charmingly comic version of Katey's real-life relationship with himself."[56] On the level of conscious mental play, of Coleridgean fancy, this seems most likely. We can even add that in her lunatic self-pity Mrs. Wilfer would be a grotesque version of Dickens's perception of his wife or his mother-in-law (as Doris Alexander says); and Katey's recent marriage to a friend of Dickens's had occurred without Catherine's presence and could be imagined as evading her, as Bella's deliberately evaded Mrs. Wilfer. In Katey and himself, we can agree, Dickens could find models for manner, for superficial comic scenes and character quirks—as he claimed that only in such ways had he modeled Skimpole and Miss Mowcher on recognizable people. Podsnap his friends recognized as based on John Forster's outside, and only the outside. In the almost unconscious recreation of the world that I understand (following Coleridge) to underlie the imagination, these outsides have little share. There, Bella builds on Ellen, the child-woman Dickens delighted in having as his trusting ward through Boffin and—along with the adult side of her in Lizzie—his loving helpmeet through Harmon.

In the comic plot, the projection Harmon ends secure in the trust and love of his beautiful young wife, settled with her among nurturing friends, and wealthy. An element of the precarious—perhaps an intrusion of the tenuousness of the Dickens-Ellen liaison—does remain, for by the letter of the law their property belongs to Boffin; but Boffin has thrust it on them as theirs by a higher justice. Without wholly obliterating the chaotic past, represented in the comic plot by old Harmon's will as in the mythic by Gaffer's stubborn wishes, Dickens makes it serve a coherent prospect here. Knowing that they will live happily forever among Boffins and babies, these cheerful comic sidelights on Dickens's world leave the last of the novel for the young Wrayburns's cloudier day.

3

For the Wrayburns, more than anyone else we cheer in Dickens's fiction, English society counts: the third great element of the novel, treated with severe, ironic realism rather than symbolic richness of implication or comic excess. In *Great Expectations* and *Our Mutual Friend* far more than in earlier novels, and particularly in *Our Mutual Friend*, respectability rather than class threatens the security of the good. Although Edmund Wilson went rather far in saying that "Dickens is now *afraid* of Podsnap" because of the Ternan affair,[57] he was surely right in noticing the source of Dickens's sensitivity. Before that affair, Dickens had never distinguished the judgment of upper-bourgeois society as important to his major projections. It was the milieu for farce and melodrama in *Nicholas Nickleby* and *Bleak House* and for jokes and sneers in *Dombey and Son*, *Hard Times*, and *Little Dorrit*, not worth discussing by his young merchants and professionals. But to the socially immersed author who had left his wife and taken up with a young actress, Pip's education in society is a crux, and Eugene cannot flee with his bride to the land of the Cape wine (the no-place where Harmon had vegetated before the novel) without admitting defeat.

In a work where we are always conscious of the river flowing to the sea, we can imagine the social world with two centers, the Veneering dock of fashion floating on treacherous waters, and the rocky, slippery, fortified Podsnap island of massive conventionality to which it is tied. Both are populated arbitrarily, the dock with the currently celebrated and the island with the putatively well-connected or wealthy, and they observe each other. Slipping off the rocks—usually through debt, John Dickens's sin, or scandalous behavior—opens the way to shame and deprivation, exile to the seamy river side or struggle, obscurity, and finally loss in the turbulent sea.

In the society sequences, the Lammles—the couple Dickens early sketched to Forster as a subject—who deceive each other into marriage, play out the defeat of the financially unfit. Unlike the similarly situated Moll Flanders and her Lancashire husband, whose creator imagined social reputability as just one perch in an always precarious world, the Lammles cannot agree to scrap the marriage now and restore it if life ever lets them. Since they had bilked each other of their only goal, respectable wealth, they hate each other. Yoked with no recourse, they must endure a lifetime of mutually suspicious conspiracy against everyone else. To survive at all, they must practice what Dickens saw through much of the 1850s as his own continuous lie: "What Miss Podsnap was particularly charmed with, next to the graces of her friend [Mrs. Lammle], was the happiness of her friend's married life" (II, iv, 256).

On her way into the water, Mrs. Lammle can still manage a sip of integrity but no more. Having gambled and lost—and since *Hard Times* Dickens had been lamenting the impossibility of recouping that loss—she must eventually resign herself to swindle and scrape with her husband in England as long as they can, and after exposure to do it abroad " 'till death divorces us' " (III, xvii, 624). While on the edge she can risk her husband's brutality by surreptitiously arranging to save the Podsnap girl from them both. But after the bankruptcy that pushes them off the island she too devotes herself to predation, signaling her commitment to evil by trying to usurp Bella's place in Boffin's golden favor. If Dickens seems unfair in shoving Mrs. Lammle penniless at forty into the marriage market and then graphing her moral decay, we are to judge, as with Wegg at sixty, that her character always invited seduction.

The others connected with Mrs. Lammle in her subplot are simpler, two devils and a maligned godmother. Her husband, an incompetent shark in the social ocean, unredeemable after the marriage that was as nearly fatal as Riderhood's first immersion, exposes and temporarily disturbs his fellow shark, the money-lender and discounter Fledgeby. Declassed, the masquerader Fledgeby projects complex resentments against the island's secure inhabitants, with whom he thought his mother's birth entitled him to a place (like Gowan in *Little Dorrit*). Like Headstone excluded from his heaven, Fledgeby therefore preys on them not only for money and status but for revenge, " 'to be even with [Twemlow] for having through life gone in for a gentleman and hung on to his Family' " (III, xiii, 573).

Fledgeby's scapegoat Riah, Dickens's amends to a Jewish friend for creating Fagin, like Boffin, Hexam, and Lizzie projects Dickens as innocent victim of slander. Uneasy with the duplicity in which he finds himself, Riah has the satisfaction of motives that charitably whitewash Fledgeby's tricks: " 'I had had sickness and misfortunes, and was so poor . . . as hopelessly to owe the father principal and interest. The son inheriting, was so merciful as to forgive me both, and place me here' " (II, v, 277). While he acts Dickens as blameless blametaker, a mutual friend who suffers in a false position, the misled Jenny Wren says, echoing phrases long trained on Jews, " 'if ever my dear Lizzie is sold and betrayed, I shall know who sold and betrayed her!' " (III, xiii, 574). But when Jenny's adventures at Fledgeby's have shown her the truth—that Riah has indeed been the godmother to Lizzie she had earlier called him and not a wicked witch—she acts for the virtuous world to do him honor. Appropriately in a sequence dealing with representatives of society—as against the idiosyncratic of comedy and the universal of myth—Riah quits his position when he realizes that it encourages the misperception of all Jews and their rejection from the English community.

At the frozen center of rejecting society sits its Lord Chancellor Podsnap exuding Podsnappery, the idol of mindless convention imagined by a novelist notoriously separated from his wife and rumored to have taken a mistress. Symbolizing the social fortress around him, Podsnap is wary, defensive, an obstacle, a powerful negative influence. Whatever new appears, he condemns, choosing to order his little universe by narrow habits unrelated to human possibilities and needs. Like Venus's skeletons or Headstone's system of education, that universe is articulated but mechanical, and like the dust heaps chaotic. Podsnap is not a hypocrite. But he cannot conceive of anything outside his imprinted prejudices, blinding himself to the viciousness of the Lammle marriage until it becomes public, to the corruption of the Veneering election to Parliament, even to his own daughter's danger from any swindler who will bother with her. He cannot be taught, but he may be circumvented, propitiated, impressed by some high authority, worn down by time, and fascinated by the glitter on the dock. Though he is more an external perception than a projection, his high position, his certainty about society and morality, and his family situation make him, like Gaffer, an anti-self, a cautionary vision of what Dickens might be under the worst conditions.

Veneering, a traveling drug salesman who had swallowed up his firm, is the celebrity on the dock's momentary crest, with no past and no future, coming and going like a breath. Right after the immemorial mysteries in the first chapter of the novel—Gaffer, Lizzie, and the corpse in the river— Dickens presents in "Mr. and Mrs. Veneering, . . . bran-new people in a bran-new house in a bran-new quarter of London" (I, ii, 6), the extreme contrast, the patent "fictions of society" of the *Examiner* review. Insubstantial where the river people loom massive in their mist, the Veneerings and their guests come to us in shifting instants. Meaninglessly and irresponsibly, they exist only before the eyes of society. For all we need to know of them, Dickens directs us to their moving images in a mirror, a surface that "reflects Veneering; forty, wavy-haired, dark, tending to corpulence, sly, mysterious, filmy—a kind of sufficiently well-looking veiled-prophet, not prophesying. Reflects Mrs. Veneering; fair, aquiline-nosed and fingered, not so much light hair as she might have, gorgeous in raiment and jewels, enthusiastic, propitiatory, conscious that a corner of her husband's veil is over herself" (p. 10).

Vaguely oriental, with a camel as his crest "in gold and eke in silver," Veneering projects an old Dickens self-perception as parlor magician. Here he waves his wand like the artist creating fancies in air, making splendors appear and disappear, giving an illusion of life to the dust heap of a dinner party, to its sleepy Lady Tippins and lumpy Podsnap, its interchangeable Boots and Brewer, its bored Wrayburn and Lightwood, its always available Twemlow. Shot up to the top like a popular novelist, he lacks the artist's presumed freshness, seeming to open on new life only because he lacks connection with the old. After giving fashionable dinners— even one to celebrate the Lammle bankruptcy, a madder plausibility than Lewis Carroll's tea party—initiating the Lammle marriage, and buying a seat in Parliament, he will "make a resounding smash next week" (IV, xvii, 815), shot down without leaving a trace, to make room for another ephemerid on the wave tops.

The first guest of the Veneerings we meet, Twemlow, is also the man appealed to at the climactic middle and the last voice we hear in the novel. Though Dickens describes Twemlow as a mere bit of antique furniture at the first fashionable dinner, his symbolic effect is to offer a hope even at the end of life and beneath a surface of conventional respectability. Even from the trash of the class system, the tottering aristocrat Twemlow demonstrates integrity like Boffin from the dust heaps and Lizzie from the river-side slums, like Dickens risen out of journalism in *Oliver Twist* or

Ellen discovered amid the chaos of Dickens's forties. Despite his apparent weakness, dependency (on his vicious relative Lord Snigsworthy for an allowance; on anyone respectable who invites him out), genteel poverty, and limited intelligence, Twemlow retains the feeling heart that ached long ago for his own version of Maria (II, xvi, 409). Courageously risking his all-important social life for the desperate Mrs. Lammle as he had endangered his freedom by co-signing a note to Fledgeby, he retains integrity as well. Combining a dim sense of worth as democratic as Joe Gargery's with the birth that society professes to honor, he alone among the genteel diners preserves the ideal of community at the core of social convention.

As Dickens imagines the world of Podsnap and Veneering—Victorian bourgeois society—the canons of respectability, based on class, wealth, and appearance, sort people into arbitrary job lots, outcasts and establishment rather than community. Nearly anything provided by society, as narrowly defined by Podsnap or as wide as England's actual pattern of social organization, has been infected by the morally mixed anti-spirit, the yawn of Pope's Dullness become the belch of busy Chaos, from Poor Laws that repel Betty Higden to false rules, goals, and criteria that daunt Lizzie, almost corrupt Bella, and dehumanize Bradley Headstone and Charley Hexam. In a world dominated by Podsnap and Veneering, the institutions of community, the mechanism of mutual sympathy, have atrophied. At our first introduction to that society, Twemlow is almost driven mad wondering about a fundamental human tie; whom to call a friend of the Veneerings.

Traditional methods of organizing chaos into meaning— like Betty Higden's funeral, the weddings of the young couples, even a fair at the village where Lizzie finds work—

seem to function only when hidden from bourgeois society. Such rites are of course the meeting points of what could still be thought of as nature—the physical, moral, and psychological patterns by which God has made a unity of the world—with the desires of people to live well together over time. But the Veneerings, Lammles, Podsnaps, even the parent Wilfers, falsify the rites into incoherent dinner parties, purchased parliamentary elections, mutually deluding weddings, anniversaries without love and birthday parties without celebrants, thereby eliminating nature's share and replacing mankind's by their own self-pleasing conventions.

And where arbitrary organization turns nature into mere formalized chaos, the demands of the natural seem to justify disregarding what might once have been valuable elements in the rites. By the evil of the Lammles's reputable marriage, Dickens makes sure we see Lizzie's choices with clear eyes. She always repudiates sin, but her love is so great, and so firmly based on Eugene's merit and decent sympathy, that if she became his mistress because of insurmountable obstacles to their marriage, she would appear less sinful than in marrying Headstone against nature. Wherever we look in *Our Mutual Friend*, at whatever face of action and character, we find an infusion of vitality from Dickens's thoughts of himself and Ellen.

Despite everything, it is in this social world that the young Wrayburns must find room. No matter how much Dickens may despise the Veneerings and Podsnaps, their conventions still allow enough space on the dock for the Boffins and acknowledge a home for John Harmon and Bella Wilfer in the island fortress. There is no other civilized world for Lizzie to live in after she has moved up from the river, no better current expression of man's attempt to break the dull flow from birth through suffering to the ocean of death.

4

Dickens's great theme of the arbitrary, of the mystery of selection, insistently accompanies a sense of chaos. In this last complete novel, he again asks why, in a world governed by Providence, people appear to meet, act, and end almost at random. Early in his career, his imagination bursting with figures, actions, causes, he could merely play at meaning of character and event while he chewed on the questions directly affecting himself: why his parentage, his prospects, his rise to distinction? Though the careers of Oliver Twist, Nicholas Nickleby, and Little Nell reflected that rise, they didn't mean anything. Even *Barnaby Rudge*, drawing moral and psychological inferences from people's meeting in one large event, often conceives them from conventional models and pretends to no universal pattern of significance. But from *Martin Chuzzlewit* on, and especially after *Bleak House*, when according to Forster Dickens's mind did not so much teem with imagined life—and when his unhappiness at home deepened his brooding over the questions—he worries about finding meaning in the world around him and imagining it in his creations. Now after retracing the universal aspect of his life in *Great Expectations*, and accepting universal answers, he seems even more deeply reflective about individual ones.

The problem, as old as religious and moral inquiry—instance Job's and Aeschylus's attempts to justify God's ways with man—necessarily occurred to serious artistic imitators of life, most disturbingly in the vaguely modern years since Fielding shored up old certainties to hold off disintegration. For him, invisible order, eternally there beyond the appearance of chaos, rewards or punishes our moral choices. For his admirer Dickens, the mixture of chaos and pattern surrounding us may let us make our bits of meaning, following simple rules of honor and sympathy. Their validation lies in a traditional, unsystematic Christianity supported by the mysteries in which we live—the destined confluences of people in *Little Dorrit* and *A Tale of Two Cities*, the doubling of appearance that critics have found suggestive in his work, not only in Carton and Darnay or Harmon and Radfoot,[58] and the strange fulfillment of arbitrary plans mirrored in the John-Bella union, with which he again toyed in *Edwin Drood*—that hint an incomprehensible but benevolent plan.

In *Our Mutual Friend*, where Dickens reflects on the arbitrary with new gratitude for the grant of Ellen after recollected misery, he imagines hints and stimuli to meaning in the world and in the self. What Eugene sees when he looks through the Hexam window, Lizzie as "A deep rich piece of colour, with the brown flush of her cheek and the shining lustre of her hair, though sad and solitary, weeping by the rising and the falling of the fire" (I, xiii, 164), what the Boffins feel glimpsing Bella through the doorway nursing her baby "in a musing state of happiness" (IV, xiii, 778), is not accident, though it strikes us as arbitrary. Even irresponsible old John Harmon's attempt to shape life, like the traditional rules programmed into Gaffer Hexam, contributes to a present that seems to make some sort of moral sense.

More than any of its predecessors, the imagined world of this novel abounds in uncertain identities, unexpected and misleading behavior, treasures in dust heaps, prophetic fantasies, disappearances and reappearances, equivocal deaths and barely plausible resurrections. All of them work to stimulate the mind, which can respond either with selfish negation or with humanity. And here Dickens is romantic enough to make his criterion of meaning, of sanction by the universe, not the merely articulated but the organic. What is alive contains a principle of order, and what is dead does not:

a long leap from the Dickens of *Oliver Twist*, *Nicholas Nickleby*, and *The Old Curiosity Shop* who hallowed changeless peace as order and centered it in rural graveyards. Having imagined himself into old age as Betty Higden, Dickens gorgeously participates with her (and Tennyson's Ulysses) in fleeing the calm of routine: "'There's a deadness steals over me at times, that the kind of life favours and I don't like'" (II, xiv, 383), says the octogenarian planning to run away. The chaos of the dust heaps, as the wise dustman knows, contains only inconsequential dead things. When Lightwood proses, "'everything wears to rags,'" Boffin answers, "'there's some things that I never found among the dust'" (I, viii, 91).

From the ultimate mystery of the river world flowing with its grasping dead to the all-swallowing ocean, ultimate chaos, life also bursts upward. As the Boffins' light has been nurtured among dust heaps and Twemlow's under a "First-Gentleman-in-Europe collar and cravat" (I, ii, 10), so the corpse in the river breeds the living Harmon mystery to draw the young lawyers from a moribund Veneering dinner, and Lizzie rises from the muck to save Eugene's body and soul. In *Our Mutual Friend*, the old dream of peace somewhere out of time, moved in *Great Expectations* to an actual village smithy unavailable to urban middle-class adults, yields to the value anywhere of unselfish human intensity; and that intensity seeking and finding others finally answers the arbitrary—in defense of love for Lizzie and Bella, of social warmth for the Boffins and Riah, of self-respect in the old pauper Betty Higden and the young artists Venus, Jenny Wren, and even Sloppy.

Loving union with the arbitrarily found beloved best opposes the flow of time, Dickens feels at fifty-two, as does the ordering of the chaotic into meaning and community.

Hinting at higher meaning, a larger design, the arbitrary and mysterious stimulate the mind to new activity, arousing new responses that transform it. Even Bradley Headstone, destroyed by the arbitrary evocation of great passions, has experienced a special diversion from the drift that will never be offered to Charley Hexam. And those with the passion rightly directed can cope with the arbitrary, even—like John Harmon resurrected, Eugene meeting a call out of a society dinner and into life, or Betty Higden answering death's lure— grow through it.

To arrive at the obligation of individuals—backed by an ideal of natural community—to avoid the arbitrary under the stimulus of love, Dickens in *Our Mutual Friend* has submitted his world to the recollections, often painful, of his fifty-two years. He dredged up resentments of parental irresponsibility; affection for his older sister Fanny; fears of declassing and wasted abilities from the blacking-warehouse time; the complicated guilts and joys of rising from socially low beginnings; the pain of loving and losing Maria; years of married irritation culminating in division and scandal; a lifelong sensitivity to public adulation and calumny. He added a gathering bereavement of friends, parents, a beloved sister, brothers, a son of twenty; hopes and fears for his children; the onset of threatening illness; the cares of his country estate, city magazine, and recent and future public reading tours with their associations in his old imaginative worlds. And he infused the mixture with present thoughts of Ellen and what their tie entailed.

At fifty-two, gathering these and other elements of himself, Dickens imagines his world positively in two main impulses, a sense of rebirth and an eagerness to engage life, that unite in a striving for community. Solitary virtue had been enough in his discontented days, always with a sense of insufficiency in

Tom Pinch, David Copperfield, even Esther and Allan relegated to the far reaches of Yorkshire and Jarndyce living through vicarious families. But now, he immediately draws his two young lawyers from detached apathy into life through a power—manifested in an outlandish story and then the living complex of Lizzie—from the archetypal depths. Eugene, into whom Dickens pours himself with great complexity, suffers, as Lizzie sees in loving him, from "'his being like one cast away, for the want of something to trust in, and care for, and think well of'" (II, xi, 349): a condition Dickens projected from Tom Pinch on, with increasing pain from Louisa Gradgrind of *Hard Times* through Arthur Clennam to the partly requited, post-Ellen Sydney Carton and Pip. The other chief projection in the action, John Harmon, has abandoned a career of labors not worth specifying to know the arbitrarily bestowed Bella Wilfer and discover life's possibilities.

Offering grim, violent figures and events befitting Dickens's losses, his ominous illnesses, even the horrible railroad accident clouding the book's late stages, the world of *Our Mutual Friend* yet anticipates a fresh, new future. From Dickens's complementary perspectives as artist and aging man reliving a youthful love, each young projection, reborn himself, finds his beloved anew as Miranda and creates her as Galatea. Lizzie and Bella are not calm consolations to grow old with like Estella at the end of *Great Expectations* but complementary sides of the young beloved, full of youthful promise. Allowing for his years and family obligations in the geniality of the novel's surviving fathers—with Podsnap always a dangerous portent—Dickens projects his condition primarily through the young men in parallel stories of obsessive love: the center or culmination of his fictions since his discovery of Ellen and after the weary marriage that ends *Little Dorrit*. His world may at first appear a wasteland like the dust heaps, Venus's collection, and conventional Podsnappery, but it everywhere responds with life to the effluence of mutual feeling.

In the lightness of one heroine and the occasionally dark pain of the other, Dickens reflects the stimulation as well as the seriousness of his current world. One story, a fairy-tale comedy in which he transmutes his deficiencies as the traditional romantic lover into Rokesmith's masked celebrity and Boffin's elderly ineligibility, ends in easy happiness because Beauty discovers her true self, the old Beast assumes a rightful position as father, and once the young Frog knows he is loved he can become a Prince at leisure. Although Dickens contrives a complex plot to teach and test, he shows us that all they need for mutual endearment is to know each other.

But the other perspective on the lover and his love sees great difficulties. Eugene must move out of spiritual apathy— one self-perception of the Dickens of the 1850s—and Lizzie, the inspiring child-goddess of mournful nature, must move out of the archetypal dream into a present, adult world. Surviving internal struggles and physical dangers, they achieve a mutual confidence that assures them of the rightness of their first responses. Theirs is a movement from deep in Dickens, imaging the birth of responsive passion to accompany the intellectual sympathy of Harmon and Bella. Celebrating their creation of each other, Dickens ends this last complete novel damaged but as hopefully pugnacious as a Browning hero. Speaking for him, Eugene announces that he will not escape with his beloved to the colonies but will stay and force society—a crooked game, he knows, but the only game in town where the stake is community—to respect her. Crippled but healing with Lizzie's help, the archetypal wounded king restored to fertility by faith, Eugene says, " 'I will fight it out to the last gasp, with her and for her, here in the open field'" (IV, xvi, 813).

Imagining a secure future with Ellen, Dickens has his most timid islander uphold against Podsnappery the persistence of community within the apparent rule of chaos: "'If this gentleman's feelings of gratitude,'" the old lover Twemlow tells the rich and powerful, "'of respect, of admiration and affection, induced him . . . to marry this lady, I think he is the greater gentleman for the action, and makes her the greater lady. I beg to say that when I use the word gentleman, I use it in the sense in which the degree may be attained by any man'" (IV, xvii, 819-20). Reassured that Podsnappery—frozen thought, judgment, behavior—is as vulnerable as any other delusion, Dickens sends home Lightwood, our mutual envoy to the land of convention, gaily.

VIII. Eclectic Affinities

Tracing Dickens's parentage in these six worlds created at notable stages of life, we find signs of imaginative stimuli both from his past—crises like the blacking factory, processes with cumulative effects like his rise, and qualities in him apparently since childhood—and from the times of conception and gestation. The times and stages clearly made a difference. Individual elements built into his mind from as early as we can look—perceptions of his nature, needs, and dealings with others—advanced or receded, grew or dwindled, developed shoots and accommodated grafts, all at the service of his emotional climate when he imagined himself in a new world. Whatever the stimulus, each creation was wholly fresh. Always the reporter, for each novel he found a new set of phenomena to explain and drew them into a unique world, never recalling even his most popular favorites for continuity. Often, an external event or condition—Poor Law reform or Yorkshire schools early, the Crimean War scandals in his mid-forties, Australian emigration, Chancery, or sanitary problems as they flared into prominence—provided a heap of stuff for his shaping breath to animate. But that breath came from within, and so did the moving figures who uttered it.

1

As against more routine parentage, his age was a major consideration in the inspiring gust. When he was approaching thirty, working constantly with little chance to reflect, he provided in *Barnaby Rudge* a world opening before men as young as he, seeing in them general versions of his own chosen, rejected, or still open paths. His imagination still played with other careers, for he was struggling to support his growing family as a novelist while not yet certain of his life work. And as the past five years of novelizing and marriage had given him a basis on which to judge, he allowed his young projections precisely five years of testing before settling. In conceiving the older figures, he not only expressed his resentment toward his own father but also projected admonitory possibilities in himself in the aloof selfishness of Chester, the insensitivity of John Willet, Dennis's mad absorption in his art, and the varieties of envious rage in Rudge, Stagg, and Gashford. Both good men of fatherly age, Haredale the gloomy bachelor and Varden the artisan humoring a headstrong wife, suggest alternative fantasies of retreat and of good-natured endurance for someone—like himself—rejected by an early love.

Arrived at thirty, mentally restored by the American vacation and emotionally pricked by the accession of a Tory government, his father's irresponsible demands, and American newspaper attacks, Dickens imagined more distinct sides of himself in *Martin Chuzzlewit*'s young men. Martin begins with adolescent arrogance and frustrated genteel expectations, a less idealized Edward Chester in a denser context; Mark, as the witty, irreverent, spirited cockney, like Dickens the precocious journalist too worldly wise for normal aspirations; and Jonas as the rebellious, anti-social self, the part of Dickens (like Maypole Hugh of the previous novel) that critics trail to the blacking factory. Tom Pinch, at first a half-comic apology for the shy side of Dickens, the victim with precisely Dickens's grandparents, grows an ideal little sister patterned on Georgina Hogarth (newly in Dickens's household) and ends forever memorializing Dickens's loss of his love for Maria. The father-aged figures at the center, who reflect both Charles and John Dickens, the artist-hypocrite Pecksniff and the swindler Tigg, in different ways perform life's function of disillusioning the young Whittingtons. With old age a long way off for Dickens, only the power of one Chuzzlewit brother and the decline of the other distinguish the old at this point.

Approaching forty, Dickens surrounded his acknowledged child Copperfield with brotherly possibilities abandoned, surmounted, or happily outgrown in Steerforth and Heep, and in Traddles one creditable prospect if he had not surprised himself with talent. But he was by now looking over a life from David's older viewpoint, equally at home inhabiting the middle-aged, past and present. As the Murdstones and Micawbers damn and caress John and Elizabeth Dickens from different perspectives in the long-gone past, and the Micawbers glance at the current Charles and Catherine Dickens as well, so Spenlow and Wickfield, doting and misguiding fathers settled into professional life, are painful admonitions to Charles. After aging the senior Dombey sympathetically in the novel at thirty-five where Dickens first conveys a strong sense of voyaging on to death, he distinguishes the old in *David Copperfield* mainly by decreasing power—notable in Dr. Strong, but also in Omer the undertaker and the physician Chillip; for John Dickens, the old man he knew best and could now love without bitter qualification, was declining. Aunt Betsey, of David's grandparents' generation, continuously wields the benevolent power that Dickens ascribed to his grandmother's will in rescuing the family from the Marshalsea, but she too weakens as David achieves adulthood: an adulthood still marked by a sense of undefined insufficiency.

Settled on the self-conscious plateau of middle age at forty in *Bleak House*, Dickens projects three major stages, the young self entering life (in Esther primarily, but also in Allan, Rick, Ada, Caddy, and Guppy), the middle-aged struggling in life's labyrinth, and the old—his prospective selves holding power—pitying, exploiting, and manipulating. In the most central of each stage, Esther overcomes loss and other deficiencies to anticipate quiet, ordered felicity; Lady Dedlock, pushed from celebrity in an empty marriage, dies to join the past; and Jarndyce like Tom Pinch begins enduring in singleness David's yearning. All takes place before the eyes of the mature, omniscient self of no precise age who shares the narration with Esther, Dickens as the tribune of society taking it to task. Ruskin, Shaw, Orwell, Edmund Wilson, and others who have specially valued that role have found the middle-aged Dickens, from *Bleak House* on, their man.

Around fifty in *Great Expectations* and at home in all generations, Dickens breathes through a middle-aged autobiographer reconciled to his surrogate fathers and mothers and the woman who pained his youth. Newly focusing on that autobiographer's obligation as child to the father rather than the reverse, and emphasizing the projected parents Joe, Magwitch, Jaggers, and Miss Havisham, he implies his heavy investment in the parental role. No longer fascinated by the uniqueness of the actual self that he had drawn in *David Copperfield*, he now accepts his path in life, with losses as well as gains, as the human generic course. In

Our Mutual Friend, though the narrative follows the young to their weddings, the men act with Dickens's mature awareness of context, and the fathers (all of daughters, like Dickens at home with Mamie and Katey) are powers and sensitivities to be dealt with. Asserting strength of spirit no matter how battered the body, *Our Mutual Friend* bids us a vigorously embattled farewell as Dickens's self-recreation in fictional worlds.

Besides his age, because these pairs of novels come at sufficient intervals they show us his accumulated concerns, the working of intense perceptions drawn through his past to engage his present. In the two just before and just after thirty, powerful pressures from the well-known crises in his childhood and youth stamp his imagined worlds. The flight of Barnaby and his mother, the terror and chaos that the father's sins sowed in the youth at birth, show signs of the "Gone Astray" episode and the blacking warehouse that had already darkened Oliver's, Smike's, and Little Nell's childhoods. Like the young men in *Barnaby Rudge*, Martin and Jonas Chuzzlewit share the most enduring of Dickens's complaints from his childhood, having been abandoned or badly guarded just when direction was most needed. The last of the painfully formative episodes he was later to record, the frustrated love affair with Maria, also enters these imagined worlds, perhaps in the characters of Mrs. Varden and Dolly Varden, surely in Joe Willet's misery when Dolly's indifference leads him to take the king's shilling, very likely in Merry Pecksniff's travail and Tom Pinch's enduring solitude.

After time to reflect during Dickens's Italian sabbatical and conscious immersion in the past in *Domby and Son* and the Memoir, in *David Copperfield* he reaches through retrospection for the elements that have formed the present self. Knowing from the Memoir that the hero's one great personal initiative in the novel, the flight from Murdstone and Grinby's, explicitly recapitulates Dickens's fantasy of escaping the worst horror he remembered, and from his letters that he had relived the Maria time in David's love for Dora, we can consider the novel's evocation of Dickens's parents early and late, or of his wife early in their marriage, as at least in part deliberate. But only in part. New elements have been added, notably but not only dissatisfaction with his marriage and exposure to Mme de la Rue's mental illness. The reformed behavior of his father, like the mixture of pathos and petulance he now saw in Catherine, mingles with mysterious, unsought evocations of the past, as the response to his mother over time contributes Clara Copperfield, Clara Peggotty, Miss Murdstone, and Mrs. Micawber with and without his conscious planning. In *Bleak House*, through another retrospective autobiography and a balancing omniscient sweep over the whole society, he reports with the shock of discovery how the inexorable past intrudes into the self and the contemporary world. There, he probes to uncover the fragments and errors he had serenely avoided in *David Copperfield*, stressing what he paid and must still pay to make the future tolerable.

The novels after the retrospect of his mid-thirties also swell a theme rich with private as well as mythic associations for Dickens and his readers: social class and the pains of rising. Though he ascribed his ambitious intensity to his rejection by Maria, we can see it hinted further back, in the Memoir's recollection of how bitter was the threat of the child's wasted abilities. He knew he had been able to work with extraordinary persistence, as he advised his sons to do in their turn, but he also knew that there had been psychological

dangers and tolls along the way. Jokers, boors, and tricksters
had inhabited his fictions from Jingle of *Pickwick* and Fagin
and Sikes of *Oliver Twist* through Tigg and Jonas Chuzzlewit,
often arbitrarily. But from Heep through Headstone and
Riderhood of *Our Mutual Friend*, he makes sure that we
know the class system's share in goading his jesting devils
and rebellious brutes.

David Copperfield, after the one dreadful declassing in the
Murdstone and Grinby warehouse, swims easily in gentility;
but from their opposite ends Heep and Steerforth show the
new intensity of Dickens's feelings about class. In those
handicapped by class or showing the moral cost of
overcoming it, like Mell and Heep of *David Copperfield*,
Guppy of *Bleak House*, Bounderby of *Hard Times*, Johnny
Chivery of *Little Dorrit*, Stryver of *A Tale of Two Cities*, Pip
of *Great Expectations*, and Headstone and the young Hexams
of *Our Mutual Friend*, he knows his own case, with its
attendant victories, guilts, and fantasies of corruption and
defeat. His hatred of the irresponsible, arbitrary nature of the
class system permeates the novels, as does his respect for
status derived from achievement. When he wrote to
Catherine on December 3, 1853, urging her to apologize to
Mme. de la Rue for jealous behavior, he reminded her that
marriage to him had "given you station better than rank, and
surrounded you with many enviable things."[59]

In the newborn worlds as Dickens approached fifty, he
examined social movement with sympathy for its cost in Pip,
Bradley Headstone, and particularly Lizzie Hexam, perhaps
because he was sharing a new social vulnerability with Ellen.
But now the decent opinion of one's decent neighbors, not
one's position on a scale, is all that matters. Only such bad
people as Bentley Drummle, Headstone, Charley Hexam, and

Podsnap find moral significance in the class system; the good
ones like Pip, Herbert Pocket, Bella, the Boffins, Wrayburn,
Lightwood, Twemlow, and Harmon learn to disregard or
conquer class and help others do the same. Instead, *Great
Expectations* and *Our Mutual Friend* take their terrors from
Dickens's new prickliness about reputation, his own and
Ellen's, his daughters', and Georgina's. Pip's snobbery
toward Joe after his rise in class is bad, arousing guilt for
which he must privately atone. But owing that rise to a
criminal is shameful, publicly damaging; like Estella's birth,
a social rather than moral deficiency. The first must be negated
(by the loss of Magwitch's money), and the second kept
secret. Dickens no longer cares about low origins or high
ones. But he does want a quiet life on the social island.

In his last two completed novels on both sides of fifty, the
critical events of his past life, as he embroidered them in
recurrent remembrance, modified by what had happened to
their participants over time—his father's reform and death,
his mother's decline into senility, and the stunning
reintroduction of Maria through her letters in 1855—enrich
and color but do not determine his shaping of other families
and other loves under the pressure of his intense current
experiences. The death of his sister-in-law Mary at
seventeen; the long and nurturing presence in the family of
her sister Georgina; the growth to personality of his children;
the developing sense of his wife's insufficiency, indeed of the
whole twenty-two years of cohabitation as a waste of his
spirit; the wild public separation from her; and finally the
deep involvement with Ellen, all registered their power and
haunted his imagination till the end. By fifty, earlier
expectations and their consequences had become merged in
Pip's universally symbolic experience, and everyone's
prospects were settled on the great, new, redemptive and
most precarious expectation: Ellen.

2

As the last two novels again emphasize, the powerful, driving, uniting element in Dickens's imagining his novels is the pressure of intense current experience, the urgency of understanding himself and his world now. The affair itself was the culmination of Dickens's yearning for requital in a woman, which after the Maria failure he sought in marriage to Catherine. But he had long since found the marriage an incurable irritation—and therefore also an emotional and imaginative stimulus. Although critics differ on his retrospective claim that incompatibility appeared in the first years, we can find a hint of dissonance even in Nicholas Nickleby's greater pleasure in courtship than in marriage (chap. xlix), when Dickens was only twenty-seven, and it swelled into occasional annoyance at thirty and resentment at forty. In the novels, the wife appears early with conventionally comic attributes in Mrs. Kenwigs of *Nicholas Nickleby* or Mrs. Quilp in *The Old Curiosity Shop*, where in one case a harried and in the other a malicious version of Dickens found her a mild nuisance, as Mrs. Varden is a great one in *Barnaby Rudge*.

After Catherine's jealous reaction to his mesmerizing Mme. de la Rue, he imagined his first seriously resentful wife in Edith Dombey. In *David Copperfield*, the next novel, he presented so many case studies of dubious marriages that the institution itself appears arbitrary and irresponsible. Beginning with *Bleak House*, his plots hinge on past mistakes often recorded, like the marriages they at times affect, in documents that are or should be circumvented; *Hard Times* highlights perverse, corrupting mismatches and specifically attacks England's marriage laws; and *Little Dorrit*, the novel before the explosion, opens with a villain who justifies having murdered his wife, has a hero almost destroyed by his father's marriage, pauses to record a couple of bad marriages (the Gowans and Sparklers) and a planned absurd one (Mr. Dorrit and Mrs. General), and dwindles into a wedding we may settle for calling not unremarkably uncheerful.

From the point of view of his literary creations, the increasing disappointment with his marriage and with Catherine heightened Dickens's career-long wish to understand and accommodate that grand extreme of the arbitrary, the difference of sex. Before Ellen, he often created emotionally effective female figures, but there was little distinctively feminine about them aside from their situations. Suffering first the uncertainty of birth and then bastardy, old fantasies about himself, even Esther Summerson, Dickens's most intimately inhabited woman character before he met Ellen, reminds us that Little Nell wandering on London streets, the Marchioness rising from abuse and illegitimacy, and Florence Dombey alienated in her home and lost as a child in London project Dickens's old fantasies as vividly, and in the same way, as his boys and young men do.

Beginning with Florence and Edith Dombey—when at thirty-five Dickens was swimming in memories—he tried more distinctly to conceive our own day's favorite subject of chitchat, the female psyche. But even Florence, who suffers her father's rejection because she is not a boy, remains a deeply studied abandoned child rather than a distinctly female one. And his early attempts at impassioned women, Edith Dombey and Rosa Dartle, now seem merely literary, stereotypes from melodrama and romance; Louisa Gradgrind's more affecting moment of passion is a dead faint. In *Little Dorrit*, the novel before his domestic revolution, his continued mental play with the issue led to a catalogue of complex women in the modes of Chaucer or Browning: Amy Dorrit, Fanny Dorrit, Mrs. Clennam, Miss

Wade, Tattycoram, Pet Meagles, Flora, and Affery, including as well comic types like Mrs. Merdle and Mrs. General. While writing that novel, however, on January 21, 1858, he implicitly confessed dissatisfaction with his attempts in a letter to the unknown but, he said, certainly female author of the *Scenes from Clerical Life*: "If ['those moving fictions'] originated with no woman, I believe that no man ever before had the art of making himself, mentally, so like a woman, since the world began." [60]

For the first time since his adolescent passion for Maria deeply involved with a woman, recognizing her as his equal in their undefinable situation, he was finally able in the last two completed novels to create female figures affecting his projected male selves with complex otherness. Estella, Lizzie, and Bella themselves carry sufficient charges of Dickens to be alive on their own; but they also live with special effect for the men. After the social if not legal dissolution of his tired marriage, his new fascination with Ellen and with their situation—complicated by her contemporaries his daughters and the continued amiable presence of Georgina—helped him to his richest conception of the lover's sense of his beloved. In Estella as symbol of the whole world's meaning for Pip, and in the deep and sunny heroines of *Our Mutual Friend*, he could fashion Ellen Ternan into versions of the whole, arbitrary, destined other self he had earned. These are still not full-scale portraits of full-scale women, not Clarissa Harlowe or Isabel Archer, but they are not child-women or sister-lovers either.

Though less dramatically demonstrable, his imaginatively varied use over time of the old story of his family suggests the same process. Changing his perspective, he consciously and unconsciously recreated old states and events in response to new experience—his father's and brothers' inconsiderate demands on him when he was thirty, that father's reformed behavior in the mid-1840s, his mother's increasing helplessness in the 1850s that almost atoned for what she had done when he was twelve, or his own concerns as a father of children with desires and capacities he had not foreseen. Summoning the past and speculating on the future, he imagined family members in the novels all at once from the viewpoint of the child, the youth on the way to adulthood, the father, the potential grandfather. The past remains, particularly the early attitude of the child discovering separateness, its resentment as well as yearning, which always appears with special vividness somewhere. But it is in the service of the present condition and its best development: what direction to choose at thirty, how to foil loneliness at forty, how to live well with his new love at fifty.

As the tensions of sex, family, heredity, class, and environment continue to stir the self imagining the world, Dickens comes more and more with time, as I have suggested, to seek a place for the perplexing arbitrary that underlies them all. The most fundamental element in fiction, thrust on Dickens first by the fortunes of his family and then by his years as a reporter, the arbitrary was a challenge particularly to his sort of realist. At first he was largely content to register it in its marvelous variety, in "Sketches" requiring a mere morsel of prosing or no explanation at all. From the start of his fiction, he almost haphazardly married the arbitrary of event, the reporter's discoveries in horrible slum life or Yorkshire schools, with the novelist's reveries exploiting the facets of his own temperament and past—in Oliver Twist's birth, flight, and eventual accession to gentility, in Bill Sikes's raging hatred complicated by society's irresponsibility, in the cunning self-aggrandizement of Fagin, in the apotheosis of the prostitute Nancy, in Nicholas Nickleby's rescuing Smike or wrecking Dotheboys

Hall. As late as *Barnaby Rudge*, the young and even the father-aged men are largely representative samples, like the young men in the *Sketches* or *Pickwick Papers*, colored with the private qualities and feelings of the young Dickens, and brought together in a national eruption decorated with gothic stage effects.

But in *Martin Chuzzlewit*, also following a group of young men and of fathers (now surrogates), he combined the reportorial concern for the eccentric and the personal sense of alternative possibility with a new idea of coherence. Having imagined life as a series of oddities, beginning with the oddity of his own childhood awakening to a family of diverse others, and having observed himself moving out of a series of unexpected turns and finding unexpected abilities and startling successes, he began in *Martin Chuzzlewit* at thirty to explore the possibility that the arbitrary actually meant something, not merely the surprises of Smollett or the omens and ruddigore of Scott. Using the American vacation as an opportunity to reflect, he had discovered what Fielding found out for *Tom Jones* after glorious discreteness of effect in his earlier novels and what Jane Austen brought forth with casual ease after years of polishing: relationship, unity. Now the significant figures act out universal experience in private terms. As against the relations between Sir John Chester and his sons, for example, those between the old Chuzzlewits and their wards Martin and Jonas, individual and distinctly detailed as they are, mean something in terms of the rest of the novel's world and of ours. The American Eden, the Anglo-Bengalee swindle, even Pecksniff and Pecksniffery, all arbitrarily sought and met, serve significant purposes in the lives of his projections.

Deliberately courting great changes in his art and his course of life in his thirties, he seems to have grown both more introspective and ever more fascinated by the problems of relating human life to chance. Although like any narrator imagining a moral world he had always made reaction to the arbitrary a test of character, he now searched deeper and saw in it an offer of choices. His projections could affirm or reject guilt, define intentions, arrive at fulfillment or frustration, embrace or escape (through alternative selves, sometimes arbitrary look-alikes) children, wife, routine work, and the drift to death, and find or bypass intensity, new connections, resurrection. With the arbitrary he comes to identify not only the stimulus to striving, the opportunity, and the inevitable mixed victory and defeat—the great expectations and their consequences—but the external itself, the block or boon in the way that calls forth our quality in the human adventure.

Now in the fiction from his mid-thirties on, he found sources of created worlds in fantasies of old possibilities. After directly in the Memoir and figuratively in *A Christmas Carol*, *The Haunted Man*, and *Dombey and Son* evoking the arbitrary events that fed his present consciousness, he makes clear that his legitimate child David had responded to them with characteristic and determining choices, often unawares. Indeed, the events themselves, beginning with the accident of birth, have an appropriateness, a connected meaning in the formation of the fictional autobiographer. They had to lead to the respected novelist enjoying and lamenting the (confessed) fantasy of winning Maria as Dora and (not confessed) revenge on both her and Catherine in Dora's death and replacement by a sisterly ideal. In *Bleak House*, he indulged another alternative fantasy to the actual affair with Maria in the past, through Captain Hawdon and the girl who became Lady Dedlock. The effects now played out are melodramatic and self-pitying for the lovers—a wasted life for the Hawdon self, bitter regrets for the rejecting beloved—and yet a consoling achievement in the self's resurrection as Esther: all given meaning in the larger world through interlocking, detailed accidents and choices.

When his new love for Ellen Ternan fell upon his imagination, he brought to Carton's devotion to Lucie Manette, Pip's yearning for Estella, and the various obsessions and allowances of *Our Mutual Friend* a mind prepared by these old fantasies of Maria; fantasies that had been renewed and modified by the special ironies of the arbitrary—Maria's letters and her reappearance as fat and dull—and his play with the reversal in Flora Finching's pursuit of Arthur Clennam. Not only memory, but even more the mind's elaboration of memory helped form his current stance, emotional and imaginative, to make meaning of the arbitrary and interrupt the drift. After his own renewal at forty-five through the miraculous gift of Ellen, Dickens offers rebirth through mysteriously managed arbitrary love as the best response to both the questionable shaping by human forces—the Frankenstein Havisham and Magwitch in one view, the dead fathers and living social judges in the other—and the inescapable flow.

Particularly in imagining the world of his last two novels before and after fifty, Dickens found the new passion a rebirth that could unite almost the extreme of eccentricity with a sense of universal meaning, the most distinctive with the most representative. The revolutions in Dickens's private and visible life led him in *Great Expectations* to see his personal course of life as a progress among arbitrary surprises, selves, and stages that yet parallels everyone's way. Through this successful symbolic world, more evidently than in *David Copperfield*, the self moves from the childhood idyll of the Gargery forge to the Satis world of adolescence to the young adult's shared chambers and finally to the routine years of the merchant, rejecting and accepting forms of father and mother, suffering intense hope of union and meaning, listening to the call of the past and its mythic reverberations in the present and to come, acting to restore what can be restored. For the central projection of *Great Expectations*, Estella images both the old pain and the new joy given by the universe, the great arbitrary mystery of love compounded of her sordid birth and distorting nurture (exaggerations of his own, and therefore of everyman's) with her refinement as his star, rising from slime to mix inspiration with a whole palette of passions.

Insisting that human warmth and memories of meaning can halt the flow to death, *Our Mutual Friend* reaffirms the normal, the universal, in uniting Eugene, long mired in genteel adolescence but reborn in his late twenties, with the sordidly born Lizzie and the adversity-tempered Harmon with the subdued Bella—a happy fantasy for an aging lover also masquerading as a fatherly Golden Dustman. As alternative marriages were objects of unhappy study in Dickens's early forties, when he was brooding over the pain of his own, so in his last created world what look like misalliances become miraculous triumphs of respectability, full shares in the human lot. By dissolving his own conventional marriage, he had opened his way to the traditional pattern, the societal norm: mutual, equal love. In his fiction also, his distant and special projections win to normality, through social accidents of every sort and despite the continuous seduction of dying.

Experience both of the world and of his art—of focusing the elements in his imagination—came with time, contributing materials and techniques to those elements. If we want to judge their relative strength and effect, we can begin with the concurrent outside world, which certainly entered his art through social issues, for example, from the

Poor Laws that oppressed Oliver Twist in 1837 to the Poor
Laws Betty Higden feared thirty years later. Moreover, we
must register the daily odds and ends of news or
observation—the famous signpost to Blunderstone that found
a birthplace for David, the view from Gad's Hill suggesting
Pip's—as well as people to turn into characters, some making
private or public jokes about Leigh Hunt, Katey Dickens,
John Forster, Georgina Hogarth, and above all Dickens
himself.[61] His imagination also seems to have been touched
definably by intense current commitments, like his activities
in Urania Cottage, his campaign to improve the Royal
Literary Fund, and his public readings when he created his
last two novels.

Next in ascending order of significance would be
conscious reflections on current private matters, as he
speculated on Georgina's future by way of Esther
Summerson or Amy Dorrit or played with relations between
himself and his daughter Katey in the Bella-Rumty Wilfer
scenes. The new interest in medical care from his study of
mesmerism, his painful fistula, or even his tending a seasick
wife probably prepared for the nurses and doctors of *Martin
Chuzzlewit*, as the deaths in *Bleak House* that amused Ruskin
by their quantity reflected the devastation around Dickens
when he conceived that novel. In *Bleak House*, domestic
concerns surely blended his son Charley's vacillation about a
career into Rick's instability, as the effects of a son's leaving
the family (like Charley Dickens to join Catherine, and his
younger brothers to enter careers) provide some of Joe's and
Biddy's feelings in *Great Expectations* and Gaffer's and
Lizzie's in *Our Mutual Friend*.

But such deliberately shaped elements, from without or
within, from the present or recollected, seem to modify the
grander ones only superficially. Pecksniff's manner and

appearance may have been based on a contemporary
journalist, and his political relevance on Peel, but more
fundamentally as a source of the world's illusion and as a
figure at the center of a world he embodies Charles Dickens's
response to John Dickens and warning to himself at thirty.
Harold Skimpole and Esther Summerson are more
admonition and recollection than the people living in 1852
named Leigh Hunt, Esther Elton, and Georgina Hogarth.
However much Bella Wilfer echoes Katey Dickens in her
dealings with her father, in Dickens's vision of life, she is the
dazzling gift of Ellen.

Even the past, a powerful force turned on attitude and
feeling, whether operating unconsciously before Dickens's
mid-thirties or more or less consciously after, contributes
what we may call the vehicle of feelings rather than the tenor.
The intensity with which past episodes lived in his mind (and
formed the substance of his dreams) thrust out great sensuous
details in response to a sufficient stimulus, but that stimulus
was in the present. These recollections, bringing the past
event to his artistic ear as harmonics for the current emotion,
imaginatively capitalizing on what was just felt or felt long
ago and mulled over, can recreate in David a rich context of
varied family relationships, in Esther a center for dealing
with responsibilities and crises, in Pip or Eugene the yearning
of uncertain love. But if the blacking factory provides old
fantasies of flight and the Maria affair old sensations of
puppy love for David, they are all in the service of creating
the David of now to reflect the emotional Dickens world of
now.

In these novels, I have argued, a greater influence on
Dickens's imagination is the pressure of his current emotional
concerns, operating to color the creation of his characters and
the relationships among them. At thirty, the family attitudes

and youthful tensions were dominant, modified in *Barnaby Rudge* by the exhaustion of constant labor and in *Martin Chuzzlewit* by the ambition to scold the hypocritical world as well as to account for Whittingtonian disappointments. Around forty, he was consciously occupied with understanding who he was in what world, summoning all recollections and associations to explain himself, indulging his sense of dissonance with his wife and weighing achievement and erosion midway in life. At fifty, his imagination was steeped in his newfound life with Ellen and his thoughts were occupied with how to sustain it.

Cooperating with the emotional concerns at the time of artistic conception were his characteristic mental attitudes of the sort I have inferred from his letters. Some of them may be arguable: what strikes me as an unusual sensitivity to opposition or an unusual sense of play may seem ordinary to someone else. I believe, for an example of what is arguable, that the kinds of selves projected to cope with preoccupations of the three periods—his predatory father at thirty, his drooping marriage at forty, his love for Ellen at fifty—relate to, and illuminate, the conflict between rebellious and orderly strains that critics have noted in him. In all these situations, the rebellious figures—all the revolutionaries in *Barnaby Rudge*, doppelgangers like Jonas Chuzzlewit, Heep, Steerforth, Mlle. Hortense, Orlick, Headstone, and the rest—may earn some sympathy because the authorities have been deficient.

It seems to me, as it has not to some others, that Dickens unequivocally condemns the rebels who commit crimes. At each stage, his conception includes an awareness of oppositions within himself, of guilty feeling represented by the negative figures, and of countering rightness in the morally affirming Tom Pinch and the two Martins prevailing over Jonas and Pecksniff. The kinds of virtuous authority and excessive rebellion change as he understands the world more, but the moral base stays pretty much the same from Gabriel Varden to Boffin. Good fathers should be obeyed, good marriages maintained, good social patterns respected. At these times and in these situations, Dickens has been victimized by bad ones, been forced to rebel, and has incurred guilt, which in art he can expel through the Heeps and Orlicks.

But Dickens's most fertile quality as an imaginer of projected selves is, I think, not disputable: a continuous curiosity and wonder about himself always tinctured with pitiless self-observation. Most successful creators of fictional narrative have the self-consciousness; enduringly memorable ones, the objective appraisal as well. For Dickens, the fantasy-spinning memory always feeds on that appraisal, which is signaled most obviously by projected doubles like Jonas-Tom, David-Uriah, and Eugene-Bradley, and pervades distinctive figures of all ages and sexes, helping him to imagine who this special being is and what the world means in touching him. Even where Dickens affirms the common lot as the right one for his projection, that comes at the cost of efforts to moderate distinction or achievement; on their way to a medical practice in darkest Yorkshire, as Esther triumphs over personal catastrophe and her lover over shipwreck. And conversely those shown to be special, arbitrarily privileged in talent or position, are pushed toward the norm, even the successful novelist Copperfield, the fashionable dazzler Lady Dedlock, and Jaggers the terror of the Old Bailey. Mocking pretensions to specialness like the eighteenth-century writers he had loved in youth, the creators of Gulliver, Joseph Andrews, and the Vicar of Wakefield, unlike them he registers great respect for the capacity and dedication of the ordinary.

For the roots of a quality as deep-seated as Dickens's suspicion of privilege, his ironic revulsion against the period's Don Giovannis, Childe Harolds, Fausts, Ahabs, Heathcliffs, Teufelsdrecks, and Rastignacs, we might ransack the variety of sources affecting his life that I have noticed here and there. But none is decisive. What is clear is that he saw the possibilities of extraordinary, mischievous selfishness in himself, in the jesters and magicians from Jingle to Riderhood and Veneering—all of them relics of cockney pleasure in up-ending the bourgeoisie—as well as in the arrogantly powerful from Ralph Nickleby through Steerforth and Tulkinghorn to Podsnap and old John Harmon, and rejected them. Sharing a world tiring of the Napoleonic with their contemporary Raskolnikov, figures like Clennam, Pip, even Eugene and David are on trajectories past Ahab and Faust toward Bloom and Herzog.

Here, as earlier, I have wished to open avenues of criticism toward the novels, toward the art rather than the artist. I have been seeking not the impenetrable mystery of his inner self but affinities among that self, its expression in art, and ourselves. Most evidently in the most admired works, the novels are worlds made coherent by a principle of imaginative connectedness, not compendia of mixed projections. When they work best, *all* is interconnected: the projections, their expectations, those who frustrate and those who fulfill, and the scene where they act. In one of the best, for example, elaborating his domestic condition before his mind—like the castle in the air he loved as an image of fantasy—through Esther, Lady Dedlock, Jarndyce, Snagsby, and all the others struggling with Chancery and all it represented, he gave it a fullness of feeling by the ways the figures reflected and modified each other. All in themselves arbitrary, accidental, they all take on meaning and larger, mythic significance in relation to each other. They all center,

252DICKENS IMAGINING HIMSELF

DICKENS IMAGINING HIMSELF

moreover, on Dickens's reveries about his current situation: thereby sharing the novel's principle of connectedness, its very life.

In seeking the nature, degree, and variety of projection as it contributes to the informing unity of these reveries, and in trying to determine their tendency—defining who and where Dickens is in a metaphor with room for us as well—lies the justification for this essay. If we can arrive at those reveries, our understanding of the work is refreshed and extended. Richly unfolding his condition in his created world, Dickens also unfolds ours to us. Whether his essential self had more facets than other people's is a psychological Chancery I beg leave to sidle by. But his ways of seeing them in complex new worlds at different times in his life, and his ability to revive numbers of them with fullness and intensity for the special world of each novel, offer us a cornucopia of Dickenses. By recreating a dazzling variety of fresh selves in coherent, packed worlds rich enough for us to join him in, Dickens achieved his famous universality: his consanguinity, through his imagined offspring, with us.

Notes

1. Of the various editions of Dickens's letters, the Pilgrim Edition is the most complete and accurate so far as it goes: with Volume VI, through 1852. Those collections to which I most frequently refer are cited in the text by code letters, as follows:

P   *The Letters of Charles Dickens.* The Pilgrim Edition. Ed. Madeline House, Graham Storey, *et al.* Oxford: Clarendon Press, 1965—.

N   Charles Dickens, *Letters.* The Nonesuch Dickens. Ed. Walter Dexter. Bloomsbury: The Nonesuch Press, 1938, 3 Vols.

MDGH Charles Dickens, *Letters.* Edited by His Sister-in-Law and His Eldest Daughter (*i.e.,* Georgina Hogarth and Mary Dickens). London: Chapman and Hall, 1880. 2d. ed., 3 Vols.

The most authoritative edition of Dickens's novels is the Clarendon (Oxford: Clarendon Press), so far as it goes. I have used the Clarendon edition as follows: *David Copperfield,* ed. Nina Burgis, 1981.

Dombey and Son, ed. Alan Horsman, 1974.

Martin, Chuzzlewit, ed. Margaret Cardwell, 1982.

For *American Notes, Barnabv Rudge, Bleak House, Great Expectations, Our Mutual Friend,* and *A Tale of Two Cities,* I cite the Oxford Illustrated Dickens (London: Oxford University Press, 1948-1958). All citations of the novels and *American Notes* are by chapter as well as page (for *Our Mutual Friend,* book, chapter, and page) for the convenience of readers with other editions.

2. George Orwell, "Charles Dickens," rpt. George H. Ford and Lauriat Lane, Jr., eds., *The Dickens Critics* (Ithaca: Cornell University Press, 1961), p. 171.

3. Alexander Welsh, *From Copyright to Copperfield: The Identity of Dickens* (Cambridge: Harvard University Press, 1987), pp. 28, 45.

4. "A Fly-Leaf in a Life," in *All the Year Round,* May 22, 1869, p. 589. Hereafter cited as *AYR.*

5. Mamie Dickens, *My Father as I Recall Him* (New York: E. P. Dutton, n.d.), pp. 48-49.

6. John Forster, *The Life of Charles Dickens,* ed. J.W.T. Ley (London: Cecil Palmer, 1928), p. 25. Hereafter cited as Forster.

7. For Katey's comment, see Gladys Storey, *Dickens and Daughter,* 1939 (rpt. New York: Haskell House, 1971), p. 109. For the recent estimates, see Fred Kaplan, *Dickens: A Biography* (N.Y.: Morrow, 1988), pp. 38-43, and Michael Allen, *Charles Dickens' Childhood* (N.Y.: St. Martin's, 1988), p. 103.

8. See "New Year's Day," in *Household Words,* January 1, 1859, vol. XIX, p. 98. Hereafter cited as *HW.*

9. See M. Golden, "Dickens, Oliver, and Boz," *Dickens Quarterly,* IV (1987), 75.

10. Fred Kaplan, *Dickens: A Biography* (New York: Morrow, 1988), pp. 309-10, has noted some of these projected qualities and situations.

11. For the stormy context in 1841, see John Butt and Kathleen Tillotson, *Dickens at Work* (London: Methuen, 1957), p. 82.

12. Reprinted in *Collected Papers.* The Nonesuch Dickens (Bloomsbury: Nonesuch Press, 1937), I, 127-42.

13. Michael Siater, *Dickens and Women* (Stanford: Stanford University Press, 1983) p. 235.

14. The *Monthly Magazine*'s series on "Freemasonic Revelations" in early 1840, particularly Chapter III (March 1840), "The Entered Apprentice's Lecture," pp. 293-300, would have been a useful manual for Dickens here.

15. On the disturbing effect of rumors of his being confined in an asylum, see, e.g., to Forster, September 1840 *(P*, II, 126).

16. Stephen Marcus entitles the appropriate chapter of *Dickens from Pickwick to Dombey* (New York: Basic Books, 1965), "*Barnaby Rudge*: Sons and Fathers."

17. In Philip Collins, ed., *Dickens: Interviews and Recollections* (Totowa, N.J.: Barnes and Noble, 1981), I, 34.

18. James Fenimore Cooper, *Gleanings in Europe: England* (1837), ed. Donald A. Ringe, Kenneth W. Staggs, James P. Elliott, R. D. Madison (Albany, N.Y.: SUNY Press, 1982), pp. 276-7.

19. Reprinted in Butt & Tillotson, *Dickens at Work*, p. 89.

20. John D. Sherwood, in *Dickens: Interviews and Recollections*, ed. Philip Collins, p. 45.

21. Jonathan Swift, *Correspondence*, ed. Harold Williams (Oxford: Clarendon Press, 1963), III, 329.

22. Michael Slater, *Dickens and Women*, p. 239.

23. On burning the papers, see *N*, III, 177; on Dickens's reticence, see e.g., a passage from a letter by Dickens's daughter Katey to Bernard Shaw in *P* I, xiv, n. i; his son Henry in *Memories of My Father* (Great Britain: Duffield, 1929), speaks of "a strange reticence on his part," p. 19.

24. In *Dickens and Education* (London: Macmillan, 1964), Philip Collins says that Dickens was not much concerned for elite schools or even ordinary ones, but for "the more striking establishments for

256   *DICKENS IMAGINING HIMSELF*

the maimed, idiot, delinquent, or the desperately poor," identifying
with them, pp. 4-5.

25. Angus Wilson, *The World of Charles Dickens* (London:
Secker & Warburg, 1970), plausibly speculates on likely family
talk about the grandparents when Dickens was a child, p. 21.

26. Philip Collins, ed., *Dickens. The Critical Heritage* (N.Y.:
Barnes & Noble, 1971), *passim*, esp. p. 13.

27. Fred Kaplan, *Dickens: A Biography*, p. 189.

28. *Mr. & Mrs. Charles Dickens. His Letters to Her*, ed. Walter
Dexter (London: Constable, 1935), p. 228.

29. *Dickens's Working Notes for His Novels*, ed. Harry Stone
(Chicago: University of Chicago Press, 1987), pp. 151, 153, 165.

30. *From Copyright to Copperfield*, p. 123.

31. In Collins, ed., *Dickens: Interviews and Recollections*, I, 17.

32. *Dickens's Working Notes*, pp. xix, 165.

33. Or Drouet, a schoolmaster in Tooting who had just been
acquitted on a technicality of criminal neglect in the spread of
deadly infection among his charges, in a case Dickens followed in
the *Examiners* of January 20 and 27, March 3, and April 21, 1849.

34. See Doris Alexander, *Creating Characters with Charles
Dickens* (University Park; Pennsylvania State University Press,
1991), p. 134. Ms. Alexander also makes a good case for basing
Uriah Heep's appearance and manner on Hans Christian Andersen,
pp. 78-81.

35. Dickens's Preface to the first book publication, rpt. the
Penguin Classics ed. of *Bleak House* (1986), p. 43.

36. *The Speeches of Charles Dickens*, ed. K. J. Fielding (Oxford:
Clarendon Press, 1960), p. 129.

37. Doris Alexander, *Creating Characters with Dickens*,
pp. 70-75.

38. *Dickens and the Trials of Imagination* (Cambridge: Harvard University Press, 1974), p. 191.

39. *Letters from Charles Dickens to Angela Burdett-Coutts 1841-1865,* ed. Edgar Johnson (London: Jonathan Cape, 1953), p. 254.

40. See Harry Stone, ed., *Charles Dickens' Uncollected Writings from Household Words* (Bloomington: University of Indiana Press, 1968), I, 84.

41. In Collins, ed. *Dickens: Interviews and Recollections,* II, 283.

42. Butt & Tillotson, *Dickens at Work,* p. 27.

43. Fred Kaplan, *Dickens: A Biography,* p. 294.

44. *Letters . . . to . . . Coutts,* p. 239.

45. Published 1851, just before *Bleak House,* and anticipating two of its notable situations. In *HSG,* chap. vi, "'Cousin,' said Phoebe, 'did you speak to me just now?' 'No, child,' replied Hepzibah." It was Clifford, Hepzibah's brother, just as Ada mistakes Lady Dedlock's voice for Esther's in *BH,* chap. xviii. Chap. xviii of *HSG* is a kind of reverie about, and at times to, Judge Pyncheon dead alone in his house, forecasting the scene of Tulkinghorn's death.

46. For the canceled American tour, see Ada Nisbet, *Dickens and Ellen Ternan* (Berkeley & Los Angeles: University of California Press, 1952), p. 55; for the lease, Fred Kaplan, *Dickens: A Biography,* p. 409

47. Charles Dickens, *Pictures from Italy,* ed. David Paroissien (New York: Coward, McCann & Geoghegan, 1974), p. 65.

48. See Charles Dickens, *The Public Readings,* ed. Philip Collins (Oxford: Clarendon Press, 1975), p. 21.

49. Among her suggested sources in the writings of others, two would certainly have been known to Dickens: "The Dirty Old Man," a verse tale in *HW* of January 8, 1853, about a man who forty years earlier had prepared a grand luncheon for his beloved and friends, and left it to rot in a locked room at news of her sudden

death; and Wilkie Collins's *Woman in White,* which Dickens had just serialized in *AYR.* Jerome Meckier, *Hidden Rivalries in Victorian Fiction* (Lexington: University of Kentucky Press, 1987), ch. 5, informatively discusses Dickens's interaction with Wilkie Collins in *Great Expectations.*

50. See Harry Stone, "The Love Pattern in Dickens's Novels," in Robert B. Partlow, Jr., ed., *Dickens the Craftsman: Strategies of Presentation* (Carbondale: University of Southern Illinois Press, 1970), pp. 1-19, and Michael Slater, *Dickens ard Women,* p. 25.

51. See *Charles Dickens' Book of Memoranda,* ed. Fred Kaplan (New York: New York Public Library, 1981), *passim.*

52. Philip Collins, *Dickens and Education* (London: Macmillan, 1964), p. 159, observes of the trained teacher of the 1850s and 1860s, that "Usually he had risen, like Headstone and Hexam, from a humble origin; his success in doing so might be regarded as admirable, and his decent salary a well-earned reward for hard work. At least as often, however, it touched off lower-class prejudice against the man who deserts his kind, and middle-class prejudices against the *parvenu."*

53. Gladys Storey, *Dickens and Daughter,* pp. 93-94.

54. "Mr. Chops the Dwarf," a Reading prepared in 1861 from "Going into Society," a Dickens contribution to the *HW* Christmas Supplement of 1858, forms a context for the Boffin experience. Its hero had frequently told the narrator, "'Toby, my ambition is, to go into Society,'" and after winning the lottery he goes, to be disappointed.

55. On February 25, beginning the novel, Dickens wrote Forster of being taken by his illustrator Marcus Stone to a shop in St. Giles where he found the "extraordinary trade" that became Venus's (*N,* III, 380).

56. Slater, *Dickens and Women,* p. 197.

57. E. Wilson, *The Wound and the Bow,* p. 78.

58. Besides the novels, Dickens showed his interest in doubles by publishing "Striking Likenesses" in *AYR,* September 28, 1865, and "Martin Guerre," June 29, 1867.

59. *Mr. and Mrs. Charles Dickens,* ed. Walter Dexter, p. 228.

60. *The George Eliot Letters,* ed. Gordon S. Haight (New Haven: Yale University Press, 1954), II, 424, 428.

61. In her most valuable *Creating Characters with Dickens,* Doris Alexander convincingly argues for a number of specific sources of this sort, often ably relating them to the large concerns of the novels.

Index

A

Ainsworth, William Harrison, 22, 28
Albert, Prince, 7, 42
Alexander, Doris, 111, n. 34, 117, 130, 148, 214, 247, n. 61
Allen, Michael, 12, n. 7
All the Year Round, 5, n. 4, 14, 56, 94, 164, 168, 177, 182, 196, 211, 224
Andersen, Hans Christian, 111, n. 34
Arnold, Matthew, Marguerite poems, 1
Austen, Jane, 84-85, 243; *Emma*, 3; *Northanger Abbey*, 25; *Pride and Prejudice*, 4

B

Balzac, Honore de, 4, 83, 109, 251; *Les Illusions Perdues*, 170
Barrow, Charles (CD's grandfather), 69
Bathsheba, 104-5, 115
Beadnell, Maria, 13-14, 18, 24, 42, 56, 62, 70, 101, 113, 120, 132, 135, 137, 138, 142, 165, 167, 198, 210, 221, 226, 232, 236, 238, 239, 240, 244, 248
Beard, Thomas, 127
Becket, Samuel, 168
Behnes, William, 8
Bellow, Saul, *Adventures of Augie March*, 3; *Henderson the Rain King*, 123; *Herzog*, 251
Bentley, Richard, 15, 47, 104
Bentley' Miscellany 21, 55

"Between the Cradle and the Grave," 196
Boswell, James, 6
Brandywine Emmet Association, 74
Bridgman, Laura, 27, 36
Bronte, Charlotte, *Jane Eyre*, 3, 130
Bronte, Emily, *Wuthering Heights*, 185-6, 251
Browning, Robert, 107, 240; "Childe Roland To the Dark Tower Came," 161; "The Bishop Orders His Tomb," 92; "My Last Duchess," 75
"The Business of Pleasure," 196
Bulwer Lytton, Edward George, 21, 147
Burgis, Nina, 1, n. 1
Burnett, Henry, 35
Butt, John, 22, n. 11, 52, n. 19, 145-6
Byron, George Gordon Noel,Lord, 80, 103, 106, 180; "Childe Harold's Pilgrimage," 38, 251

C

Carlyle, Thomas, 22, 45, 77, 158; *Heroes and Hero Worship,* 84; *Sartor Resartus*, 251
Cardwell, Margaret, 1, n. 1
Carroll, Lewis, *Alice's Adventures in Wonderland*, 220
Cervantes, Miguel de, *Don Quixote*, 25
Charlton, Elizabeth, 111
Chaucer, Geoffrey, 240
Chesterfield, Lord, 45, 137
Chisholm, Caroline, 142

Chorley, Henry, 146
Christian, Eleanor E., 35
Coleridge, Samuel Taylor, 214-5
Collins, Philip, 35, n. 17, 54, n. 20, 100, n. 31, 143, n. 41, 202, n. 52
Collins, Wilkie, 166, 198; *Woman in White*, 181, n. 49.
Conway, General, 39, 46
Cooper, James Fenimore, 43, 46, 55
Coutts, Angela Burdett, 62, 91, 122, 131, 134, 149, 156, 181
The Critic, 90
Cruikshank, George, 127
Crusoe, Robinson, 3, 140

D

Daily News, 92
Dante Alighieri, *The Divine Comedy*, 13, 62, 68, 101, 123, 151, 152
David, King, 104-5
Defoe, Daniel, *Moll Flanders*, 3, 216
De la Rue, Augusta, 90-91, 100, 151, 236, 237, 239
Denman, Thomas, Lord, 128
Dexter, Walter, 1, n. l, 91, 237, n. 59
Dickens, Alfred (CD' s brother), 68
Dickens, Catherine (CD's wife), 6, 7, 8, 10, 12, 25, 42, 60, 61, 62, 76, 85, 90-91, 99-100, 101, 108, 117, 118, 119, 120, 126, 135, 142-3, 158, 166, 179, 189, 190, 195, 200, 207, 214, 216, 218, 233, 236, 237, 239, 240, 244, 247
Dickens, Charles, WORKS.
American Notes, 1, n. l, 19, 40, 54, 55, 56, 67, 73; *Barnaby Rudge*, 1, n. l, 6, 17, 18, 21-52, 54, 58, 64, 81, 82, 105, 232, 223, 235, 239, 243, 249; *The Battle of Life*, 90, 107; *Bleak House*, 1, n. l, 3, 14, 18, 43, 64, 91, 118, 125-62, 163, 164, 173, 174, 177, 180, 202, 203, 216, 223, 234, 236, 237, 239, 244, 247; "Chambers," 14; "A Child's Story, "94; *A Child's History of England*, 156; *The*

Chimes, 63, 78, 90; *A Christmas Carol*, 7, 9, 68, 78, 84, 90, 177, 244; "A Christmas Tree," 94
The Cricket on the Hearth, 118; *David Copperfield*, 1 & n. l, 10, 13, 14, 18, 87-124, 125, 126, 138, 140, 143, 146, 148, 163, 172, 190, 196, 200, 202, 233-4, 235-6, 237, 239, 245; "A December Vision," 128; "Demoralisation and Total Abstinence," 127; *Dombey and Son*, 1, n,l, 8, 40, 56, 67, 87, 91-92, 113, 114, 134, 144, 155, 161, 202, 206, 216, 235, 244; "The Fine Old English Gentleman. New Version," 23; "The First," 201; "A Fly-Leaf in a Life," 5; "Frauds on the Fairies," 152; *The Frozen Deep* (with Wilkie Collins), 166; "The Ghost in Master B's Room," 94, 168; "Going into Society," 211, n. 54; "Gone Astray," 14, 139, 235; *Great Expectations*, 1, n. l, 13, 14, 18, 56, 70, 128, 157, 163-93, 196, 197, 202, 208, 209, 215, 223, 225, 227, 234, 237, 238, 245, 246, 247; *Hard Times*, 18, 20, 126, 138, 152, 163j 164, 180, 202, 206, 216, 217, 227, 237, 239; The Haunted Man, 87, 105, 113, 120, 244; "Health By Act of Parliament," 127; "The Last Words of the Old Year," 128; *Little Dorrit*, 43, 126, 130, 163, 164, 165, 172, 180, 181, 188, 191, 202, 206, 209, 216, 218, 224, 227, 237, 239-40; *Martin Chuzzlewit*, 1, n. l, 7, 18, 53-85, 88, 89, 90, 91, 115, 138, 152, 187, 223, 232, 243, 247, 249; "The Martyrs of Chancery," 128; "The Martyrs of Chancery. Second Article," 128; *Master Humphrey's Clock*, 17, 21, 24, 52, 188; Memoir, 11, 26, 67, 72, 87, 88, 93, 94, 99, 117, 120, 125, 235-6, 244; *Memoirs of Joseph Grimaldi* (ed), 21, 175; "Mrs. Gamp,"

212; "Mr. Chops the Dwarf," 211, n. 54; "The Mortals in the House," 182; *The Mystery of Edwin Drood*, 224; "New Year's Day," 14, 57, 177; *Nicholas Nickleby*, 6, 8, 15, 21, 46, 49, 53, 79, 81, 100, 152, 216, 225,239; *Old Curiosity Shop*, 4, 16-17, 21, 36, 40, 43, 45-46, 47-48, 49, 60, 79, 138, 152, 225, 239; *Oliver Twist*, 4, 15, 17, 21, 41, 46, 47, 49, 60, 68, 79, 81, 101, 138, 207, 220, 225, 237; *Our Mutual Friend*, 1, n. 1, 4, 13, 14, 18, 41, 64, 68, 137, 138, 167, 195-229, 235, 237, 238, 241, 245, 246, 247; *Pickwick Papers*, 4, 16, 21, 39, 51, 53, 58, 63, 67, 90, 152, 188, 237, 243; *Pictures from Italy*, 92, 167-8; "Preliminary Word" to *Household Wor ̔ ɔ*, 121-2; Report of a Committee "Appointed to Inquire of the Persons Variously Engaged in the University of Oxford," 79; *Sketches by Boz*, 3, 21, 39, 55, 66, 94, 134, 137, 167, 188, 243; *Sketches of Young Gentlemen*, 15, 103; "Subjects for Painters. (After Peter Pindar)," 77; *A Tale of Two Cities*, 1, n. l, 96-97, 101, 126, 130, 137, 138, 163, 164, 172, 180, 185, 188, 190, 202, 224, 237; "Uncommercial Traveller," 177; "What Christmas is, as We Grow Older," 99; "Where We Stopped Growing," 139, 152; "Whole Hogs," 127; "A Young Man from the Country," 56
Dickens, Charles Culliford Boz, Jr, ("Charley," CD's son), 10, 13, 134-5, 207, 247
Dickens, Dora (CD's daughter), 126, 165, 179
Dickens, Elizabeth Ball (CD's grandmother), 70, 234
Dickens, Elizabeth Barrow (CD's mother), 12, 18, 41, 72, 111, 141, 166, 182, 189, 233, 236, 238, 242
Dickens, Fanny (CD' s sister), 14, 35, 97, 101, 184, 226
Dickens, Frederick (CD' s brother), 26
Dickens, Henry Fielding (CD's son), 11, 63, n. 23
Dickens, John (CD's father), 11, 12, 32, 33, 37, 38, 47, 51, 66, 68, 69, 83, 111, 116, 126, 148, 165, 173, 178-9, 189, 190, 216, 232, 233, 236, 238, 241-2, 248, 249
Dickens, Kate Macready ("Katey," CD's daughter), 12, 63, n. 23, 175, 176, 205, 214, 235, 238, 241, 247, 248
Dickens, Mary ("Mamie," CD's daughter), 1, n. 1, 5, 176, 235, 238, 241
Dickens, William (CD's grandfather), 29
"The Dirty Old Man," 181, n. 49
Disraeli, Benjamin, 37; *Coningsby*, 150
D'Orsay, Alfred, Count, 126, 147
Dostoievski, Fyodor, 5; *Crime and Punishment*, 34-35, 251
Drouet, a schoolmaster, 110, n. 33
Dryden, John, *Absalom and Achitophel*, 2; *MacFlecknoe*, 153

E

Egg, Augustus, 149
Eliot, George, 109; *Scenes from Clerical Life*, 241
Eliot, T.S., "The Love Song of J. Alfred Prufrock", 129
Elton, Esther, 130, 148, 248
Elton, William, 130
The Examiner, 22, 23, 34, 54, 67, 77-78, 79, 92, 109, 110, n. 33, 113, 122, 127, 128, 181, 206, 219

F

Faulkner, William, 46; T*he Sound and the Fury*, 140
Felton, Cornelius C., 7
Fielding, Henry, 84, 223; *Joseph Andrews*, 98, 250; *Jonathan Wild*, 54; *Tom Jones*, 25, 83,

243
Fielding, K.J., 127, n. 36
Figaro in London, 42
Ford, George H., 3, n. 2
Forster, John, 6, 9, 11, 12, 13, 31,
    39, 77, 92, 101, 116, 117, 123-4,
    134, 165, 166, 178, 185, 197-8,
    213, n. 55, 215, 216, 247

G

Galatea, 198, 207, 227
George III, King, 33, 44
George IV, King, 33
Gilbert, W.S., *Iolanthe*, 85
Goethe, Johann, *Faust*, 37, 44, 123,
    251
Golden, M., 15, n. 9
Goldsmith, Oliver, *She Stoops to
    Conquer*, 201, 209; *The Vicar of
    Wakefield*, 105, 114, 210, 250
Gordon, Colonel, 39
The Gordon Riots, 22, 30, 43, 44,
    47, 50, 51, 54, 80
Greenwood, Grace, 143
Guild of Literature and Art, 163

H

Hall, Basil, 55
Hall, Samuel Carter, 77
The Haunted House, 182
Hawthorne, Nathaniel, 158; *House
    of Seven Gables*, 155, n. 45
Hemingway, Ernest, *The Sun Also
    Rises*, 3
Hogarth, Georgina, 1, n. l, 18, 100,
    101-2, 121, 149, 160, 166, 180,
    184, 185, 195, 233, 238, 241,
    247, 248
Hogarth, Georgina Thomson (CD's
    mother-in-law), 166, 214
Hogarth, Helen, 166
Hogarth, Mary, 41, 51, 72, 83, 99-
    100, 101-2, 113, 149, 184, 238
Horsman, Alan, 1, n. l
House, Madeline, 1, n. l
Household Words, 14, 57, 94, 99,
    109, 121-2, 127, 128, 139, 146,
    147, 152, 156, 158, 164, 177,
    181, n. 49, 197, 201, 211, n. 54

Howe, Samuel Gridley, 27
Hunt, Leigh, 147, 150, 247, 248

I

Ibsen, Henryk, *Peer Gynt*, 58,131

J

James, G.P.R., 10
James, Henry, *Portrait of a Lady*,
    241
Jeffrey, Francis, Lord, 147
Johnson, Samuel, *Rasselas*, 61, 121
Joyce, James, *Ulysses*, 3, 251

K

Kafka, Franz, *The Castle*, 4
Kaplan, Fred, 12, n. 7, 18, n. 10, 90,
    148, n. 43, 166, n. 46, 196, n. 51
Kent, Duchess of, 42

L

Lamert, James, 11, 169
Lane, Lauriat, Jr., 3, n. 2
Landor, Walter Savage, 147, 150
Lewis, Monk, 24
Ley, J.W.T., 11, n. 6
Longfellow, H.W., 65
L'Ouverture, Toussaint, 22
Lucretius, *Of the Nature of Things*,
    168

M

Macready, William Charles, 7-8,
    147, 188
Macready, Mrs., 7, 126
Marcus, Stephen, 32
"Martin Guerre," 224, n. 58
Martineau, Harriet, 22
Meckier, Jerome, 181, n. 49
Matthew, St., 7
Melville, Herman, *Moby Dick*, 44,
    123, 155, 161, 251
Metropolitan Sanitary Association,
    127
Miller, Arthur, *Death of a
    Salesman*, 71
Milton, John, 158; *Lycidas*, 52;
    Paradise Lost, 44
The Mirror, 78, 79, 90, 128

Mitton, Thomas, 65, 68
The Monthly Magazine, 28, n. 14, 78
Morpeth, Lord, 91
Mozart, W. A ., *Don Giovanni*, 98, 105, 201, 251

N

Nisbet, Ada, 166, n. 46

O

O 'Connell, Daniel, 22, 74
O'Connor, Fergus, 22
Orwell, George, 3, 124, 164

P

Paroissien, David, 168, n. 47
Partlow, Robert B., Jr., 184, n. 50
Peel, Robert, 77-78, 248
Perkins Institution for the Blind, 27
Pope, Alexander, 80; *The Dunciad*, 221; *An Essay on Man*, 28
Proust, Marcel, 89
Punch, 77
Pygmalion, 19 8, 20 7

Q

The Quarterly Review, 40

R

Richardson, Samuel, *Clarissa*, 121, 241
Royal Literary Fund, 137, 156, 190
Ruskin, John, 20, 164, 234, 247

S

Scott, Walter, 21, 23, 38, 39, 40, 46, 106, 243
The Seven Poor Travellers, 201
Shakespeare, 165; *Hamlet*, 182; Sonnets, l; *The Taming of the Shrew*, 63; *The Tempest*, 209, 212, 227; *Twelfth Night*, 28; *A Winter's Tale*, 209
Shaw, George Bernard, 20, 63, n. 23, 112, 124, 164, 234; *Pygmalion*, 208
Shelley, Mary, *Frankenstein*, 3, 24, 245

Shelley, Percy Bysshe, 84; "Hymn to Intellectual Beauty," 161
Sheridan, Richard Brinsley, *The Rivals*, 198, 209; *The School for Scandal*, 77, 198
Sherwood, John D., 54, n. 20
Slater, Michael, 24, 62, n. 22, 96, 184, n. 50, 214
Smith, Sydney, 147
Smollett, Tobias, 243; *Peregrine Pickle*, 3
Somebody's Luggage, 211
Stanfield, Clarkson, 8-9
Sterne, Laurence, *Tristram Shandy*, 1, 3
Stevenson, R.L., *Dr. Jekyll and Mr. Hyde*, 3
Stewart, Garret, 132
Stone, Harry, 94, n. 29, 110, 142, n. 40, 184, n. 50
Stone, Marcus, 213, n. 55
Storey, Gladys, 12, n. 7, 205, n. 53
Storey, Graham, 1, n. l
"Striking Likenesses, " 224, n. 58
Swift, Jonathan, 57; *Gulliver's Travels*, 3-4, 250

T

Talfourd, Thomas Noon, 147
Tennyson, Alfred, 85; *In Memoriam*, 98, 145
Ternan, Ellen, 25, 165-229, 238, 240-41, 245, 248, 249
Thackeray, W.M., *Vanity Fair*, 130
Thoreau, H. D ., 1 55
Tillotson, Kathleen, 22, n. 11, 52, n. 19, 145-6
Tom Tiddler's Ground, 182
Trollope, Frances, 55
Twain, Mark, *Huckleberry Finn*, 3

U

Urania Cottage, 91, 98, 109, 114, 122, 126, 163, 247
Uriah the Hittite, 10 4- 5

V

Valentine and Orson, 37-38
Victoria, Queen, 7, 9, 42, 44
Voltaire, *Candide*, 83

W

Warren's Blacking, 11, 16-17, 24, 43, 58, 59, 60, 66, 71, 95, 96, 111, 117, 134, 143, 169, 182, 183, 190, 226, 231, 235
Watson, Richard, 126
Wellington, Duke of, 15
Wellington House Academy, 14, 110
Welsh, Alexander, 4, 96
Whittington, Dick, 3, 56, 58, 60, 61, 63, 70, 83, 84, 105, 134, 140, 158, 162, 233, 249

Williams, Harold, 57, n. 21
Wilson, Angus, 69, n. 25
Wilson, Edmund, 27, 33, 36, 216, 234
Wordsworth, William, 17, 48, 83, 84; *The Prelude*, 88; *Tintern Abbey*, 50

Y

Yeats, W.B., "The Wild Swans at Coole," 157